FLIGHT *of* REMEMBRANCE

A World War II Memoir of Love and Survival

D1367188

Marina Dutzmann Kirsch

Dear Rebecca,
Like the Dutzmann family, may
you also be blessed to fulfill
your dreams!
Regards,
Marina Dutzmann Kirsch

KIRSCHSTONE BOOKS™
Kensington, New Hampshire

Kirsch, Marina Dutzmann.
    Flight of remembrance : a World War II memoir of love
and survival / Marina Dutzmann Kirsch.
        p. cm.
        Includes bibliographical references.
        LCCN 2011910888
        ISBN-13: 978-0-9835653-4-5
        ISBN-10: 0-9835653-4-1

    1. Dutzmann, Rolf, 1919- 2. Dutzmann, Lilo, 1921-
3. World War, 1939-1945--Germany--Biography. 4. World
War, 1939-1945--Women--Germany--Biography. 5. Latvia--
History--1918-1940.   I. Title.

D811.5.K57 2011   940.53'092'2
                           QBI11-600142

Unless otherwise indicated, all photos are part of the Dutzmann
family collection.

Although the author and editors have made every effort to
ensure the accuracy of all of the information in this book
including historical facts, no responsibility will be assumed
for errors, inaccuracies, omissions or inconsistencies.

For more information, please visit
www.kirschstonebooks.com
or email the author at
mkirsch@kirschstonebooks.com

Rolf and Lilo Dutzmann, postwar Germany, 1949

Flight of Remembrance is dedicated to the people of Wakarusa, Indiana, a small town with a big heart, and to my parents, Rolf and Lilo, two otherwise ordinary people whose unfailing devotion to God, family and each other makes them a shining example to all who know them. These characteristics form the golden thread that runs throughout their wartime and postwar experiences even up to the present time, weaving events of their lives in extraordinary ways to create a rich tapestry of love, hope and optimism amidst adversity. But this book is also dedicated to the millions of people who did not survive to share their stories of the twentieth century's most gruesome and devastating war.

Contents

Acknowledgments..ix

Foreword: In War's Vortex xii

Preface..xvi

Prologue: Farewell to the Old World xxi

Map: Northern Europe, December 1939 xxv

PART I IMAGINATION (Rolf's Story)

Chapter 1: Storm Clouds Gather.......................................3

Chapter 2: Taking Flight from Latvia............................14

Chapter 3: An Invitation from the SS............................19

Chapter 4: Harsh Awakening in Poland........................24

Chapter 5: Early Years on the Baltic Sea........................27

Chapter 6: A Boy with Vision 32

Chapter 7: Developing a Technical Calling 38

Chapter 8: The 1936 Olympics.....................................41

Chapter 9: The Final Years in Latvia.............................46

Chapter 10: Delaying the Draft..............................51

Chapter 11: May I Have This Dance?..............................59

PART II FAITH (Lilo's Story)

Chapter 12: A Girl Who Dreams..............................79

Chapter 13: Learning to Walk 85

Chapter 14: School Days End 91

Chapter 15: On Wings of Song 98

Chapter 16: When Sirens Sound..............................103

Chapter 17: The Crossing Letters 107

Chapter 18: The Zoppot Idyll 112

Part III SURVIVAL

Chapter 19: Drafted into the Luftwaffe..............................123

Chapter 20: A Second Serving of Käsetorte..............................130

Chapter 21: Terror in the Night..............................135

Chapter 22: The Bombing of Peenemünde 143

Chapter 23: Berlin Amidst the Ashes 149

Chapter 24: The War Effort Falters 156

Chapter 25: The Family Home in Ruins 159

Chapter 26: Escape to Havelberg 164

Chapter 27: Perfecting Hitler's Secret Weapon 168

Chapter 28: Something Borrowed, Something Blue 174

Chapter 29: Flower Petals Along Their Path 179

PART IV DESPERATION

Chapter 30: The Allies Advance 193

Chapter 31: The Russians are Coming 201

Chapter 32: Crossing the Harz Mountains 208

Chapter 33: Dispatch to the Front 212

Chapter 34: POW in the Freezing Mud 219

Chapter 35: Escape from the Soviet Zone 228

Chapter 36: A Startling Revelation...............................233

Chapter 37: The First Woman I See 236

Chapter 38: En Route to Bingen..................................241

PART V HOPE

Chapter 39: Postwar Privation and Pleasure 249

Chapter 40: The Harshest Winter..................................254

Chapter 41: On the List for America............................262

Chapter 42: I Look to the Hills 267

Chapter 43: Last-Minute Surprises 275

Epilogue: From Dream to Reality..................................281

Endnotes...290

Appendix 1: A Word about Sources and Dialogue 294

Appendix 2: A Word about Ernst Dutzmann............299

Appendix 3: The Mittelbau-Dora
Concentration Camp Memorial............320

Bibliography 323

Index 325

Acknowledgments

The Dutzmann family will be forever indebted to the people of Wakarusa, Indiana, especially Jesse and Amanda Longfield, Roy and Grace Summers, and Edward and Liz Nusbaum who bore the risk of sponsoring members of our family to immigrate to the US. Along with the Bittingers, Rogers, Lechlitners, Weldys, Browns, Yoders and others, they also spared no expense or effort to make us feel welcome. Their kindness was of a magnitude that can never be adequately repaid. In retrospect, we realize that we were fortunate to be "adopted" by a group of Americans as helpful and altruistic as any to be found on the North American continent. We are also grateful to C. G. Conn, Ltd. (cgconn.com), an industry leader then and now in the manufacture of musical instruments, for offering Rolf and Ernst their first employment in the USA.

There are numerous people who assisted with this book. I thank Dr. Angelo Codevilla, veteran author (claremont.org/scholars/id.25/scholar.asp), Professor Emeritus of International Relations at Boston University, and former senior member of the Senate Select Committee on Intelligence, for the insightful and heartwarming foreword he supplied to introduce and accompany my family's story, including glimpses into his own postwar experiences in Italy.

Sound advice that I received from Sam Baily, Rutgers University history Professor Emeritus, regarding sections of the narrative, as well as clarification of sources in the appendix and bibliography, was tremendously helpful and has served to make the book more informative to readers.

Additional feedback and recommendations for the technical sections of the manuscript about the V-2 rocket and Appendix II about Ernst Dutzmann, as well as corrections to the December 1939 map of northern Europe, were graciously supplied by Dr. Michael J. Neufeld of the National Air and Space Museum of the Smithsonian (gosmithsonian.com/ museums/ national-air-and-space-museum).

Dr. Jens-Christian Wagner, director of the Mittelbau-Dora Concentration Camp Memorial in Germany (dora.de), provided transcripts of my grandfather, Ernst Dutzmann's, statements after the war, as well as websites and general information that helped me to piece together the scenes dealing with my grandfather's technical work during the war and supplemental information about him to include in Appendix II. He also read all of the technical sections of the manuscript to ensure accuracy and provided an informative tour of the Mittelbau-Dora Concentration Camp Memorial site when my husband and I visited in September of 2011. It is heartening that the memorial presents its grim subject matter in such a thorough and thoughtful manner, with the deepest respect and recognition rendered to the thousands of concentration camp inmates who suffered and died at that location during World War II.

Three German relatives, Marta Siemes, Ilse Dietel and Dr. Guido Dietel, searched through their family photo archives to come up with additional wartime photographs. Theirs is also the family that so generously took in my mother, my aunt and both grandmothers during the early postwar time in Krefeld, Germany when housing was so scarce.

During the final months before publication, I received much-appreciated suggestions from Janet Szarmach, director of the Kensington, New Hampshire Public Library (kensingtonpubliclibrary.org).

My heartfelt thanks to all of the aforementioned for their valuable assistance.

My central support and primary cheering section throughout the process of researching, writing and editing this book have been my parents, Rolf and Lilo, and my older brother, Ingo, Senior Pastor at the First Lutheran Church of Boston (flc-boston.org). They verified a myriad of facts, proofread countless versions of the manuscript, prevented a multitude of mistakes and regularly offered priceless encouragement in order to support my vision for this book. A close friend, Helen Kredo, also devoted considerable time to reading versions of the manuscript and offering suggestions. I deeply appreciate their love, consideration and efforts.

In the final phase of the writing odyssey, I was fortunate enough to work with three outstanding editors, all three of whom are knowledgeable about World War II material—Paul Schneider (www.schneiderbooks.com) and Maggy and Alan Graham (wordsandpicturespress.com). Paul's insightful comments on the first chapter led to a rewrite of the entire book to make it more consistent, descriptive and compelling. Maggy has been my sounding board and guiding light for the entire finished manuscript, helping to mold it into the best work possible and dispensing many valuable suggestions along the way. She has an impressive ability to ferret out small errors and inconsistencies without ever losing sight of the big picture and the central themes of a story. Towards the end of the editing process, her husband, Alan Graham, offered his services to read the manuscript with an eye to restructuring some of the content. The result was a narrative that flows more smoothly with a more consistent point of view. I am very grateful to all three editors for their friendly professionalism, enthusiasm and attention to detail.

Websites for Wakarusa, Indiana:

amishcountry.org/explore-the-area/cities-and-towns/wakarusa

wakarusa.org

wakarusachamber.com

In War's Vortex

By Dr. Angelo M. Codevilla

ost of the millions of people caught up in wars direct their energies to surviving them with their persons, families, morals and hopes for the future as intact as possible. When forces bent on war press any country's inhabitants into service, they narrow the options for survival, demand the utmost of labor in exchange for the meagerest sustenance, and subject all to circumstances and arbitrary decisions, each of which can make the difference between life and death. At the war's end, survivors unlucky enough to be on the losing side must try to keep body, soul, family and hopes alive through even greater privation imposed by victorious forces over which they have even less control.

Americans, having been blessed with peace at home for a century and a half, have no direct knowledge of such things. That is why Americans should read *Flight of Remembrance*, the story of the Dutzmann family's odyssey from 1920s Latvia through the Germany of World War II, ending in immigration to America's Promised Land.

All families, all circumstances, are special. The Dutzmanns are unusual in that all of them lived through the war. Their technical expertise gave them access to military specialties that reduced their exposure to death, shielded their lack of enthusiasm for the Nazi cause, enabled them to earn enough not to starve, and eventually improved their eligibility for immigration to the United States. Nevertheless, their experience is in many ways familiar to all Europeans who struggled through war and occupation.

The Dutzmann family's story grips me: as a student of war, as someone whose childhood memories are of privation in war-torn Italy, and as a family man grateful for never having had to conjure up morsels of food and lumps of coal day after day, and for never having had to stand in front of officials who held my family's life in their hands. The author of this story, Marina Dutzmann Kirsch, born days before the family came to America, organized her parents' and grandparents' remembrances into snapshots of her father's and mother's families at different stages of their lives. Most chapters, while recounting deeply personal concerns with life and love, achievement and disappointment, are set in the context of major international events. The point could not be clearer: as the war ground on, ordinary people tried not to be ground to dust.

The Dutzmanns, like many if not most Europeans, were of mixed nationality: legally citizens of Latvia, ethnically German, but formerly subjects of Imperial Russia, in whose army Ernst Dutzmann, the author's grandfather, had served as an officer during World War I. The Stalin-Hitler pact that started World War II turned Latvia over to Stalin, forcing the family to choose between immediate execution or exile to Siberia on the one hand or repatriation and service to Germany on the other.

How much loyalty do you owe to a government you dislike and to a war that has already deprived you of your home? Ernst Dutzmann reminded his family that it had some moral obligation to Germany, a country that had rescued them from the fate that Stalin reserved for ethnic Germans and outspoken anti-communists in the Baltic States, and the only country that welcomed the family to pursue life within its borders. The German war machine continued to stand between them and the Soviets. Besides, it would be senseless suicide for ordinary people to flout or sabotage the regime. Yet to live was to work, and to work was to help a regime not of the family's choice. Ernst, employed as a top-notch engineer, performed as such. Rolf's upbringing and schooling had prepared him to follow in his father's professional footsteps. He was drafted. Ethics and practical necessity merged to steer him into decisions where he could do the best for himself while fulfilling his duties and doing the least harm. At the time, father and son could have done much better for themselves and their family by joining the Nazi party and the SS. But neither did that. Their wartime story was of hunkering down and hoping that the peril would pass them by.

As the storm rages, people think above all of their loved ones. Does he love me? Does she love me? Rolf asked himself whether Mother and Father would approve of his choice of a marriage partner and whether lifetime commitments even make sense at a time when all lives hang by the slenderest of threads. Lilo, on the other hand, had her own reasons to be wary of the relationship. Would they finally decide to marry? Would Rolf be able to obtain wedding leave during some of the darkest times of the war? Would the couple find a clergyman willing to straddle the line between Catholic and Protestant? Where and how would enough food be obtained for the celebration amidst severe wartime rationing? If they did finally marry, would they survive to make a life together or would they become just two more casualties of Nazi Germany's devastating Total War policy?

Most surprising to readers who have never had to struggle through war's grip is how peripheral the huge events of the epoch are to those who endure them, and how central, how memorable, are such personal concerns as maintaining one's honor, developing one's career, making a good marriage, and keeping the family together with as much contact as possible with its past, as well as meeting the daily challenges of survival. For many civilians in wartime, a cup of real, instead of ersatz, coffee or a handful of vegetables from a local farm, along with acts of kindness exhibited by friends and total strangers alike, provide vivid and lasting memories, while accounts of the major turning points of war, the battles and the casualties, are destined to remain once removed from consciousness.

As World War II's storm passed, it left millions of Central Europeans destitute, separated from their families, and subject to competing jurisdictions. For these millions, the paramount preoccupation was to get away from the

Soviet troops and thereafter to reconnect with their families while saving such material means of survival as they could. The Dutzmann and Wassull families were no exception to this, experiencing upheaval after upheaval and chaos upon chaos in the quest not only to survive, but to piece together what remained of lives harshly compromised by the dire circumstances of wartime.

Americans—and Europeans younger than fifty-five or so—can hardly imagine what America meant to the generation of Europeans who lived through World War II. My earliest, most pleasant memories in postwar Italy were of receiving care packages from America and chocolate from American soldiers. America was the place whence all good things flowed, a place that had to be inhabited by people far more powerful and far more beneficent than any human beings that ever walked the soil of the Old World. Children dreamed of America. Adults yearned to go there. We really did not understand America. But all sensed that it was different, and better. The care packages themselves were wonders, filled with life-giving fats and proteins, with canned meats measured in pounds rather than scant grams. And the Americans were just giving these things away, even to former enemies. Why the Americans were more generous and more trusting as well as richer, none of us knew. But many of us were so struck by the idea of America that we wanted to become Americans. Some of us were actually blessed with the chance so to transform ourselves.

The Dutzmanns' flight of remembrance ends with their flight to America. This reader, who celebrates the anniversary of his own 1955 arrival in New York Harbor past the Statue of Liberty more fervently than a birthday and whose first contacts with American society still fill him with wonder, recommends that the author someday explore further her family's remembrances to encompass the contrast between their former lives as Europeans and their new ones as Americans.

Dr. Angelo M. Codevilla
Professor Emeritus, Boston University
Author of *War: Ends And Means*
Plymouth, California

Preface

I grew up in a German immigrant family during the expansive 1950s in the American near-West. The first language my brothers and I learned was not English, but German—the predominant language spoken at home in those early years. By the time I reached school age, however, the English language was rapidly gaining linguistic dominion over our household.

In order to preserve our German language skills, my parents chose to amuse and inspire us with tales from German storybooks, with our favorite being *Der Struwwelpeter*, loosely translated as *Shock-Headed Peter*, an endearing and cleverly illustrated, sometimes funny, occasionally frightening, children's book of cautionary tales. Written by Dr. Heinrich Hoffman, a nineteenth century German physician and psychiatrist (1809-1894), it is a classic that has been around to entertain and instruct generations of children ever since the mid-1800s, including both my parents' and grandparents' generations. It contains stories about the tragedies that might befall children who play with matches, refuse to eat their dinner, don't watch where they are going, or suck their thumbs. As I got older, it dawned on me that many of the stories have a depth of meaning hidden from the very young by charmingly simple words and pretty pictures. Underneath the frequently humorous surface details, they actually address some of the larger issues in life, such as bigotry and racism, cruelty towards people and animals, disregard for authority, and the realization that consequences continually spring from all of our actions. Having played a part in my parents' formative years as well as my own, *Der Struwwelpeter* provides a colorful common thread weaving through the *Flight of Remembrance* narrative. It is a familiar icon to many people of German descent but also a poignant reminder to readers everywhere that even in the midst of the utmost turmoil, people struggle to maintain their daily life and a sense of normalcy: to eat, to breathe, to seek warmth, comfort and shelter, and to read stories to their children.

As an adult, I continue to be intrigued and entertained by a good story. I absorbed bits and pieces of my parents' and grandparents' wartime experiences throughout my growing up years. But it was not until the fall of 1994, when I finished reading the 230-page family history painstakingly written by my parents over the course of many years, that I finally gained an overview of the expansive saga spanning the years from World War I through post-World War II. I was stunned by the emotional sweep, the high drama and suspense, and the profoundly human elements, as well as the astonishing, synchronistic chain of events, that make their narrative so compelling and so memorable. Almost a decade later, in November of 2003, I was moved anew by their story when a New Hampshire newspaper, *The Concord Sunday Monitor*, printed a lengthy front-page article "For German soldier, a long, strange road to freedom," complete with sepia-tone World War II era photographs. Again in 2004, *The Laconia Citizen* ran a story on the front page of the "Living" section entitled "Love conquers all: German couple celebrates 60th wedding anniversary." In the spring of 2009, the *Citizen* ran yet another story in honor of my father's approaching 90th birthday. Over time, I became convinced that this story should be offered to a much wider readership.

At a time when eyewitnesses to World War II are dying out and the world is still struggling to come to grips with the reality of that most devastating of all armed conflicts, *Flight of Remembrance* provides a glimpse into the lives of ordinary people who were positioned on "the other side." Swept along on a tide of dire necessity and circumstance, Rolf, a young man with a passion for aeronautical engineering is forced to relocate from his Latvian homeland to Nazi Germany. There, in the pursuit of his career, he is drafted into the military and becomes embroiled in a war that threatens to bring about his demise. But it is also a story of the seen and unseen forces that coalesce to keep him, his family and the love of his life, Lilo, alive as they experience relentless, cataclysmic events beyond imagining for anyone who has not experienced the ravages of war waged on home soil.

Whereas *Flight of Remembrance* chronicles a young man's passion for his calling and his pursuit of a technical career against daunting wartime odds, it is first and foremost a tender and enduring love story that plays out against a panorama of worldwide chaos and destruction. What became crystal clear to me as I researched historical material for this book *is* the truly worldwide scope of suffering in World War II, with almost every nation across the globe tragically affected. I also found that the atrocities and genocide perpetrated under the Stalin regime were equally or more horrifying and brutally destructive than those masterminded by the Nazi regime in Germany. Countries such as the Baltic States, Poland and other eastern European nations that were precariously situated between the two dictatorships suffered devastating consequences. In the case of the area of Europe now known as Poland, repeated takeovers accompanied by executions, deportations and massive human and material losses occurred during both World Wars.

Through my work on this book to retell my parents' wartime experiences, I feel that I have lived and breathed the most agonizing chapter in twentieth century history, thereby experiencing indirectly a world shattered by conflict, but I have also had the delightful privilege of coming to know my parents in a totally new and different way—as the two young people they were before I was born. They were two people in love, but fatefully positioned in Nazi Germany, at the epicenter of a worldwide conflagration that ruthlessly incinerated the hopes, the dreams and the lives of tens of millions of people.

Although reports of World War II death rates vary widely, the death toll is generally estimated at between fifty and seventy-seven million, with the total military dead approximated at twenty-five million including four to five million prisoners of war. The Allied forces suffered over eighteen million losses, largely due to the vast number of Soviet casualties, and the Axis forces six million. Roughly three and a quarter million of those military losses were German.

Far more staggering than the estimate of military casualties during World War II, however, is the civilian death toll of forty to fifty-two million people worldwide. As many as twenty million people perished from war-related disease and famine. Almost nine million were Holocaust victims, among them six million Jews. Civilian deaths in Germany numbered upwards of two-and-a-half million, with an estimated 543 thousand of those resulting from air raids on German cities.

Flight of Remembrance portrays a group of strong, resilient German women, but they could have been women from any other time and any other place in the world who survived a major war. Lilo, Gertrud, Maria and Ruth share the everyday hardships and emotions common to women everywhere during such harrowing times as they deal with the catastrophic circumstances that crash in on them not just once, but over and over again like deadly breakers on a hostile shore. Fears for personal survival and the survival of loved ones, interminable times of waiting for news and receiving none, the loss of home and possessions due to bombings and forced relocations, the ever-present physical trials and setbacks—these and other experiences were common themes in their daily lives.

But the distinguishing feature of this group of women, lending a sense of light and hope to the story, is the combination of their eternal optimism, faith in God, and fearless, instinctive ingenuity in the face of adversity. These traits enabled them to display extraordinary courage and determination, to take risks and make decisions that, under ordinary circumstances, would have been the prerogative of the men of their era. They also maintained a perennial attitude of hope that flew in the face of dire outer conditions and rejoiced in the small pleasures of life wherever they could still be found during wartime. The overall resourcefulness and fortitude displayed by the women in the family created a chain of mutual assistance that helped to ensure the survival of all whom they loved and far surpassed what they would have been inspired to do under peacetime conditions.

Selfless acts of kindness from others and the assistance of total strangers proved pivotal to my family's survival as well, suggesting that, side by side with the baser aspects of human nature that were exhibited to such an appalling degree during World War II, there also existed a nobler urge that surfaced at times—an underlying sense of connectedness and mutual responsibility that prompted the human family to act from kind-hearted, altruistic motives.

It is unlikely that a mere instinct for survival would have resulted in the kind of positive outcome that my family experienced at a time when millions of their generation perished. Technical skills undoubtedly helped them to survive, but throughout the war and postwar years, they also displayed a resilient sense of inner purpose along with an unwavering conviction that a better future awaited them. From being airborne in a glider over the fields of Latvia to the development and use of his skills in the US many years later, my father, Rolf, never lost sight of his dream. Perhaps it was farsighted attitudes such as these that enabled members of my family not only to embrace opportunities that would ensure survival, but also to remain solidly focused on future prosperity and happiness amidst tragic and turbulent times. Whatever the reasons, they blazed a determined path of survival through a daunting wilderness of death and destruction, emerging out of the rubble to embrace a bold new vision of their destiny.

The Berlin Wall fell on November 9, 1989, exactly twenty-two years prior to the day I wrote this paragraph. That day marked a literal and symbolic reunification of what was ripped asunder during World War II, bringing with it a much-needed healing. The enormous trauma of World War II combat, programmed mass genocide under both the Nazi and Soviet regimes, communities being torn asunder, homes destroyed, families irrevocably separated, the land ravaged, lives cut short: all created a tremendous *Weltschmerz* (universal pain and suffering). Images of that time captured in film, photos, print and memory will continue to rise as ghastly specters to haunt the human family for all generations to come. It is my hope, without in any way diminishing the stories of those who perished unjustly, that *Flight of Remembrance* will provide an uplifting reminder that out of somber darkness, new life can arise like a radiant dawn. May humanity now rise to usher in a future of peace and freedom, in which kindness is extended to all beings and all people are empowered to realize their most cherished dreams.

Marina Dutzmann Kirsch
Kensington, NH
December, 2011

Farewell to the Old World

On a cold, blustery, late December day in 1951, a tall man clutching a felt fedora held a little boy firmly by the hand as they crossed the windy tarmac to board a waiting Swissair flight. The hem of his long, double-breasted topcoat flapped insistently with each step. Just ahead of them, a woman of medium height with soft, gentle features and blonde hair neatly upswept beneath a felt hat, carried an infant bundled up like a cocoon against the chill morning air.

"Will we be going very high in the air above those clouds, Papa?" Ingo asked as he skipped alongside his father.

"Ja, Ingolein, we will be going very high," his father replied somewhat distractedly while scanning the overcast sky and distant horizon.

"How high, Papa?"

After thinking a moment, he replied, "Oh, I would say fifteen thousand feet or so." Then, noticing his son's puzzled look, he added, "It would take many Empire State Buildings one on top of the other to get as high in the sky as we will be going."

There was silence as the little boy digested this bit of information, obviously impressed. Ever since his parents, Rolf and Lilo, had told him that they would soon be leaving their homeland and going far, far away across the ocean, the little boy had been bursting with curiosity about the place called America. And of all the wonders that he had been told about the new land, the Empire State Building had always struck his young imagination as the most magnificent and magical of all.

"That is very, very high, Papa! And what will keep us from falling out of the sky?"

At this, Lilo turned in amusement, her expression soft and gentle. "Don't start your papa on that, Ingo. You will get a very long, confusing answer that you won't be able to understand because you are too young."

Ingo was carrying a little red suitcase in one hand, and under his other arm, a picture book. As Rolf helped him up the metal steps to the plane, Ingo hugged the book more tightly to his side. Rolf smiled. The book had been Ingo's favorite for most of his four years. The little metal suitcase, however, was brand new— an early Christmas gift received from his grandmother just a couple of weeks previously. Ingo looked up at his father, ready to launch another question, when a sudden strong gust of wind stole the words from his mouth. Rolf turned his intense gaze to Lilo, ahead of them on the steps, who somehow managed to hold onto her hat while cradling their infant daughter more tightly in the other arm.

Once safely settled on board, Ingo held up the treasured book to Rolf insistently. On the cover was an amusing, colorful figure with unkempt hair and outrageously long fingernails with the title *Der Struwwelpeter* arched above it in bright red, antique script. All of Ingo's favorite stories were in that book, accompanied by colorful illustrations: the story of *Struwwelpeter* (*Shock-Headed Peter*), who refused to cut his hair and nails, as well as stories about what happens to little boys who suck their thumbs, who refuse to eat their dinner and who are cruel to people and animals. Rolf noticed that Ingo quickly turned past the story that never failed to make him cry, the one about Paulinchen, a little girl who insisted on playing with matches and came to a dreadful end. It was no day for sad stories.

"Please, Papa, read me this story, the one about the little rabbit in the leafy nest and the man with the gun!" he pleaded as he wriggled back into his seat to get more comfortable.

Rolf, having settled his wife and daughter, smiled tenderly at his son and began to read about a hunter who goes out to shoot a rabbit, but the rabbit outwits the hunter by stealing his gun while he is taking a nap under a tree. The rabbit then turns the gun on the hunter, but only manages instead to shoot a coffee cup out of the hand of the hunter's wife, who is leaning out of the window of their house. This causes hot coffee to spill and burn the nose of the rabbit's child, a little bunny who is sitting in the grass below the window.

Lilo attempted to rock her daughter to sleep by humming softly to her. But the baby was wide awake, her pensive, blue-eyed gaze widening as if captivated by the sound of her father's voice, or perhaps mesmerized by the clouds outside the window that swept with relentless urgency across her field of vision.

Not until adulthood did I finally understand the lesson of that story—that the results of our actions continue to reverberate into our future whether we realize the connection or not, that for every action there is a reaction and a consequence for good or for ill. But on that day in December of 1951, I was too young to understand the stories in my brother's book, much less to realize the impact that this solitary plane flight would have on my family's future—a future very different from the past we were leaving behind. This flight to the New World was the culmination of a long sequence of flights—from my father's first flight in Latvia on a glider marked with the historic cross of the Latvian National Guard, to flights of technical genius, flights of imagination, and flights of the human spirit that made possible courageous leaps of faith into dim uncertainty. Even more poignant were the flights of raw desperation, sheer necessity and stark survival that tore like mortar shells through the years before I was born. The vast conflict gripping the world ripped away at the very fabric of my family's existence, threatening to immolate with merciless finality all living generations, along with those yet unborn, in a brutal, yet spell-binding incendiary display.

Flight of Remembrance Locations and Journeys Map

(Showing northern Europe with December 1939 borders)

The Dutzmann family's escape from Latvia to Germany by ship in December 1939, arriving in Seebad Bansin, then Posen and Litzmannstadt in German-occupied Poland, then in Berlin, Wiegandsthal and Benneckenstein in Germany proper. Rolf and Ernst were moved to additional locations on this map during their military service.

Lilo and Gertrud's journey first from Berlin to Havelberg to escape the bombing in March 1944, and then 100 miles on foot from Havelberg to Benneckenstein to flee the advancing Soviet troops in May 1945

Rolf's 160-mile journey on foot from the front near the Rhine River to Benneckenstein in April 1945

Gertrud's three round-trip solo journeys by train, on foot and hitchhiking into the Soviet Zone between 1945 and 1947

Map of Dutzmann and Wassull Journeys

Part I

IMAGINATION

(Rolf's Story)

"The future belongs to those who believe in the beauty of their dreams."

— Eleanor Roosevelt

Chapter 1

Storm Clouds Gather

The details and circumstances of the morning when the phone call came were not so different from most other mornings. Like a footprint left in the sand of one of Rolf's favorite Baltic beaches, a footprint destined to be washed away by a merciless surf, the phone call came and went. He had no way of knowing that in its wake, all that had become comfortably familiar in his life would be swept away wholesale in the storm surge of subsequent events. Had that phone call never come, life as he knew it might have continued for a time, but before long, the disaster and loss that was soon to descend on Latvia would have overtaken his family as well.

"Rolf, you must come home right away!" his father insisted emphatically over the wire.

It was October 21, 1939, when Rolf received the call in the hallway of the boarding house in Riga where he was renting a room in order to pursue his aeronautical engineering studies at the University of Latvia. He had been filled with excitement upon arriving in the city that was both the capital of Latvia and a key seaport—a city situated on the Daugava River just nine miles from the Gulf of Riga where the river spilled into the vast, blue expanse of the Baltic Sea.

"Why such a hurry?" he asked, fighting back a sense of rising alarm.

His query only received the cryptic reply, "We will tell you when you get here. Just come home as quickly as you can!"

There was no mistaking the urgency of the message, and not just from the tone of his father's voice. Of all the people in the world, his father, Ernst, understood better than anyone how much Rolf's aeronautical engineering studies meant to him. It often seemed to Rolf that all of his twenty years up to that time had been a preparation for what he considered to be his calling. Now that he had finally begun his technical training, the abrupt summons home was all the more troubling, since an interruption to his studies, begun only two months prior, could prove to be a serious setback. He surmised that there must be very bad news indeed.

It was with great trepidation that Rolf hurriedly packed a bag with a few clothes and necessities, including class textbooks and notes. He left the boarding house, walking briskly to the Riga train station, which at midday was nearly empty. From the platform, he soon saw the train approaching, steam pouring out of its smokestack, bringing with it the familiar smell of coal smoke, a smell that he had always associated with pleasant memories of vacation, travel and adventure. Although he was unaware that in the next seven years such trips would no longer be so pleasant, he *did* sense, as he settled into his seat on the half-empty train, that this journey was somehow different, that he was leaving carefree times behind.

Even as the locomotive pulled out of the station, gaining speed towards Liepaja, 120 miles westward on the Baltic coast, Rolf's thoughts were just as rapidly overtaken by a sense of dark foreboding. After crossing the Daugava River, long celebrated by poets as "The River of Destiny," and once beyond the city limits, the passing scenery opened up to flat countryside with woods, meadows and farmland stretching into the distance, only occasionally interrupted by smaller cities and towns.

The first foreshadowing of things to come appeared during that train ride. On sidetracks, about fifty miles outside Liepaja, waiting to continue westward, long, sinister transports carrying an odd assortment of old tanks, horse-drawn wagons and other outdated military vehicles and equipment stood lined up and ready, like macabre, silent sentinels awaiting orders to a new post. Jerked out of his reverie, Rolf stared with alarm at the railroad cars, marked with a symbol that was by that time all too familiar to most people living in the Baltic States. On the side of the motley cars, in bold, red paint, was the dreaded Soviet hammer and sickle.

Even though Rolf was well aware of recent events in Europe, there was a missing piece of the puzzle, to which he and most people not associated with the Latvian military were not yet privy. He was aware from radio reports that two months prior, Germany and the Soviet Union had signed a secret pact, but he did not know that it entailed a plan to partition Poland and to bring the Baltic States of Lithuania, Estonia and Latvia under Soviet domination. The German-Soviet Non-Aggression Treaty, also known as the Molotov-Ribbentrop Pact, established Nazi Germany and the Soviet Union as secret partners in crime.[1] The pact unleashed a flood of miseries, secretly sanctioning Hitler's invasion of Poland on September 1, 1939, and the official outbreak of World War II while the Soviet giant stood passively and enigmatically on the sidelines. Or so it seemed at first.

The ominous transports only served to confirm Rolf's worst suspicions, for in his heart he already feared that the summons from his father must be connected with the Soviet threat that had been hanging like a storm cloud over Latvia, Estonia and Lithuania ever since the Russian Revolution toppled the Czarist Regime in 1917. That was two years before Rolf was born, but he knew from the history books in school and from dinner table conversations growing up that Latvia had been part of the vast Russian Empire until the beginning of World War I when Germany defeated the Russian armies there and gained control. In 1918, after World War I ended, the country nominally gained its independence, but for two more years Germany and the new Soviet government each made numerous attempts to reestablish a foothold in Latvia. It was only with the help of Great Britain and France that the Latvian people were finally victorious. In 1920, peace was established and an independent, democratic Latvia emerged out of the chaos.

During the tumultuous years of World War I, Rolf's father Ernst, a Latvian of German descent, had served as a Czarist Russian officer and was taken prisoner of war by Germany. He continued working in Germany upon release from the prisoner-of-war camp at the war's end. Shortly thereafter, he met and married Maria. It was there in 1919, among his mother's people, in the part of Germany west of the Rhine River called the Rhineland, that Rolf was born. German-born Maria would have much preferred to stay in her native land indefinitely, but in September of 1921, with peace seemingly restored in Latvia, Ernst insisted that the family return to his Baltic homeland.

Unfortunately, in the aftermath of war, relations between native Latvians and those of German descent chilled to the point of open hostility. If the truth be told, they were never particularly amicable. Native Latvians made up about seventy percent of the population, with the remaining thirty percent split between Baltic Germans and Latvian Jews. The Baltic Germans were historically landowners and professionals, the Jews were mostly merchants, and the native Latvians, by and large, worked as farmers and laborers. Much farther back in feudal times, many of the native Latvians had labored as serfs on the great estates of Baltic Germans, so there was a long trail of animosity.

Yet Ernst had been optimistic that the hostilities would blow over, as they often had in the past. Once Rolf and his sister Ruth, who was born in Latvia in 1923, were old enough to understand, Ernst merely cautioned them to speak only Latvian in public. Never mind that their mother, Maria, had been born in the Rhineland and had never learned Latvian. And never mind that the toddler, Rolf, with his very light blonde hair and blue eyes, was impossible to pass off as a native Latvian. But Ernst had been partly right: after the First World War ended, things in Latvia did settle down to a stable, if occasionally tense, coexistence between the various national and ethnic groups.

After switching trains, Rolf reflected on his life in Latvia as the train raced along the tracks to Kara Osta, the suburb north of Liepaja where his parents lived. Despite memories of a few difficult times during his formative years, Rolf had always considered the little nation by the Baltic Sea to be his home. He did not think it likely that the ancient tension with the native Latvians was the reason for his father's sudden call. Rolf was aware that just a couple of months earlier, the Latvian military had abruptly ordered a partial mobilization of its forces for purposes of national defense, fearing that the Soviets might take advantage of Europe's preoccupation with the war and attempt to reestablish a foothold in the area. And during the previous month, there had been rumors that the military base in their home city of Kara Osta, along with many other bases in Latvia, would soon be taken over by the Soviets and leased to them for ten years. What that really meant had been unclear, but his father's cryptic summons now suggested that things had taken a turn for the worse; the presence of Soviet transports outside of Liepaja confirmed it.

By late afternoon, Rolf arrived at the family home, a five-room apartment in a sturdy, imposing, two-story granite building that had formerly provided quarters for Czarist Russian officers and their families, and which now was the official housing for Latvian military families. This had been the Dutzmann family's comfortable haven for over seventeen years, but on the day of Rolf's return, the once orderly and peaceful home was a beehive of frenzied activity. Most of the rooms in the apartment, freshly painted and redecorated just a few months earlier, were in wild disarray with boxes and wooden crates strewn everywhere and a multitude of packing projects underway.

Ruth, Rolf's sixteen-year-old sister and only sibling, was carefully packing the family's china, crystal and glassware in the dining room. Aunt Paula, one of his father's sisters, was also present to help. She was the aunt that Rolf had come to know best over the years because of all the time she had spent helping him to master the Latvian language which had caused him such affliction during his early school years.

His father was not present, but his mother, Maria, a woman in her early fifties, with features too sharp and angular to be beautiful in the classical sense, but a smile that had the ability to light up her face, stopped what she was doing to give him a hug and to inquire whether he was hungry or thirsty. Rolf noticed immediately that her usual impeccable sense of style and grooming had been abandoned. She had taken little care in her appearance that day and there was a strained look about her eyes as she smiled up at him, taking his face between her hands and pushing the wavy blonde hair back from his forehead.

"We're moving?" Rolf asked anxiously, his striking blue eyes wandering around the untidy quarters.

"Yes, the Russians are coming and all Latvian military personnel must be out of the area by November tenth," replied Maria.

"So that includes Father?"

"Yes, that includes your father. His plant is being moved to Salaspils, southeast of Riga. I will let him tell you the rest when he returns home."

She set Rolf to work packing his own possessions, and then turned her attention once more to overseeing the packing of the family's collections of books, china, crystal, silverware, linens and other valued items. The rest of his questions would have to wait.

When his father came home that night, Rolf was still awake. He knew right away that Ernst was home because he could hear his voice in the front hallway and, even at that late hour, the sound of laughter from Maria as he regaled her with some humorous anecdote. His father's perennial sense of humor had always been one of his most admirable qualities. A man of medium height with a strong build and a dark-haired, distinctly Slavic appearance, Ernst had piercing eyes that, like the nearby Baltic Sea, could rapidly change from sky-blue to storm-gray. Although commanding full respect at the artillery laboratory where, as a captain in the Latvian Army, he supervised a munitions shop, he maintained a relaxed attitude at home with his wife and children, having long since relinquished the role of household disciplinarian to Maria.

Rolf intercepted his father in the hallway, his sister, Ruth, following close behind. Ernst's face lit up as soon as he saw his children, especially Rolf, whose presence had been sorely missed since he moved away to Riga. Ernst's pride in his son would have been evident even to the most casual observer as they exchanged a characteristic, hearty embrace.

When Rolf launched into a barrage of questions, Ernst explained that he was personally responsible for organizing and supervising the packing and transport of all of the equipment from the artillery laboratory, leaving only the empty shells of buildings behind for the Soviet takeover. He would be unavailable, therefore, to assist with the dismantling of the household.

"We have other decisions to make, however," he continued, addressing the entire family.

Signaling Maria, Rolf and Ruth to follow him into the sitting room, he laid out the basic facts of the family's situation. The picture that he painted of their future in Latvia under a Soviet regime was alarming. They would not be welcome under the new regime. All of their lives, but especially his own, would be in danger. Even if their lives should be spared, there would be few if any opportunities to make a living. Finally, Ernst closed by saying that life under Soviet domination would be oppressive and uncertain at best, and that many of the personal and collective freedoms that they had enjoyed in the previous two decades of Latvian autonomy could be expected to disappear virtually overnight.

"Our only recourse," he concluded, "is to leave Latvia."

Rolf quickly grasped the seriousness of their situation. What took longer to sink in was the absence of agreeable alternatives. Turning the family's dilemma over and over in his mind, no other viable solution presented itself—the comfortable life to which they had become accustomed was over. However, with so much to be accomplished, he found little time to dwell on those thoughts. They merely formed a persistent backdrop to the round of daily activities during those transitional months—a backdrop of fear and uncertainty tempered by an involuntary touch of excitement and curiosity about the new life awaiting them, either of which could set his heart racing wildly.

Under the able direction of Maria, the packing project was rapidly accomplished with most of their possessions carefully wrapped and placed into wooden crates to be transported via rail to Riga. However, there was also much that needed to be left behind and they faced many difficult decisions in the days ahead.

A few days later, Ernst called an extended family conference at Rolf's grandmother's home in Liepaja—a two-story wooden house with two apartments on the first floor that were usually rented out to tenants and a large, comfortable living space on the second floor that was occupied by Rolf's grandmother and two of his aunts. The gardens behind the house, generously planted with berry bushes and apple trees, and a nursery with a greenhouse next door, still verdant in the month of October, made the home almost seem to be out in the country, situated though it was in a row of similar houses on a residential street.

When they arrived, the table was already set. An aromatic, lattice-top *Apfelkuchen* (apple cake) sparkling with sugar and cinnamon crystals and a platter piled high with Rolf's favorite cinnamon pastries were already set out on the coffee table in the large dining room. By that time, Rolf's grandfather was no longer living, but present were his paternal grandmother, Julia; two of his father's sisters, Paula and Ada; and his father's younger brother, Alfons. Emily, a third sister of Ernst's, lived on a farm a considerable distance away and was unable to be present. An atmosphere of heightened tension and expectancy held sway over the gathering. Even Aunt Paula, in spite of her assistance in packing, had not yet been fully apprised of the family's plans, which Ernst, Maria, Rolf and Ruth had established just three days prior. Rolf noted that his father waited until after they had enjoyed the cake and coffee to make the announcement that he knew could only come as a bitter blow to the extended family.

"As all of you know," Ernst began, speaking in German so that all including his wife Maria would understand, "the Soviets will very soon be occupying the local military base and we are moving to Riga where I will continue my employment for a time. The fact is that Latvia has had to decide between waging a hopeless, bloody resistance to the overwhelming military might of Soviet Russia or giving its consent for a takeover. For better or for worse, Latvia has chosen the latter."

He paused for a moment.

"What you do not yet know is that we have decided as a family to accept the offer of repatriation extended by the German regime."

There was a collective, audible gasp of shock at this news. It was seventeen years prior that Ernst had returned to Latvia from Germany after World War I, bringing with him his two-year-old son and his German bride, Maria, a woman more than eight years his senior. Ernst, the oldest of five siblings, had been welcomed back into his family with great relief and celebration. The shock and consternation on their faces now at this unpleasant news, revealed the anguish they felt at the prospect of losing him yet again.

Rolf noticed his grandmother and Uncle Alfons glancing furtively over at Maria. Their distrust and lack of acceptance of this German woman born in the Rhineland, who had neither learned the Latvian language nor made much attempt to assimilate into their culture or to make herself liked, had never before been so painfully evident.

"Is there no other alternative, Ernst?" asked Rolf's grandmother.

Ernst continued, "The Soviets are notorious for breaking their agreements and I am sure the ten-year lease of our military bases to them will be no exception. Mark my words, once the Soviets arrive here, they will topple the government and Latvia will become a Communist territory in no time at all. It is easy to guess what our fate would be if we were to stay. I have many overt and covert enemies at the artillery laboratory, mostly native Latvians with Communist leanings and an axe to grind against Baltic Germans like us. For two decades they have witnessed my outspoken criticism against Soviet policies and Communism in general."

"If we stay, Father would most likely be executed immediately or sent to Siberia," Rolf interjected. "Either way, we would be unlikely to ever see him again."

After a pause, Ernst continued, "Maria, Rolf, and Ruth would also face increased danger on my account, and I consider their survival to be my chief responsibility. After discussing this as a family," directing a pointed look at his mother and Alfons, "Even with the uncertainties surrounding a return to Germany during wartime, we all consider the repatriation offer to be the lesser of two evils."

This pronouncement was followed by a stunned silence, finally broken by Aunt Paula.

"And what about your engineering studies, Rolf? With Germany already at war, will you be allowed to continue them?"

"Unfortunately, I may not know until we arrive there. Father has said that it is unlikely we will even be told of our resettlement location until after we embark," stated Rolf with a tone of barely disguised unease.

"Well, even though I am as shocked as everyone else, I think you cannot be too careful with so much at stake. And therefore, I must say I find myself in full agreement with your decision, Ernst," responded Paula.

Paula was the second oldest only to his father and Rolf had always considered her a force to be reckoned with—a woman equal in intelligence, drive and energy to any man, a woman who refused to be intimidated or "kept in her place." He especially appreciated her keen intelligence and common-sense approach at a time like this.

"You cannot afford to risk staying here," she continued. "We know the Russians' reputation for dealing harshly with anyone who is not in alignment with their propaganda. They would most certainly kill you, and maybe Maria, Rolf and Ruth too. Perhaps we all would be in greater danger if you chose to stay."

At this, her sister, Ada, nodded in wordless agreement.

There was a short silence after which Alfons stood up and, switching to the native Latvian tongue, stated in a carefully controlled tone, "Have any of you considered that what you are contemplating will make you traitors to your homeland? You will be abandoning Latvia to her fate along with all of us, your own family. Not only that, but the country that you are defecting to is one that has been an enemy of Latvia for centuries!" He rose from his chair, his voice also rising as he became increasingly distraught. "You will be traitors! Does that matter to you at all?"

"That will be enough, Alfons!" The matriarch of the family stared him down and turned to Ernst. "You must do what you think is best to save yourself and your family. But just remember that your home will always be here in Latvia."

She turned to look at Alfons, as if challenging him to respond, which he did.

"Latvia will never accept you back again," spoken in a tone as cold as Baltic ice. He turned on his heel indignantly, heading for the door, but then swung back to face them for one last rebuke: "And I for one, hope never to see any of you again!"

His departure was followed by an awkward silence in which his words hung suspended like a lifeless victim in the hangman's noose. Rolf was stunned.

Eventually Ernst commented quietly to his mother and sisters, "It is just as well that he has left. I want you to know that not a word of our intentions should leak out to anyone else. I will continue my work at the artillery laboratory after the move to Salaspils without telling anyone of our plans to repatriate. My enemies among the ranks would think nothing of turning us in."

"Where will you live, Ernst?" asked Paula.

"We will find temporary housing. Suspicions may be aroused by the fact that we will not be looking for permanent housing in the area and that our shipments of furniture and other personal possessions will not be arriving. An unexpected delay in our departure could be disastrous."

The rift with Uncle Alfons continued to haunt Rolf's thoughts in the following weeks, a time of great activity, but also of anxious anticipation of a new and uncertain phase in his life to commence. He did not know at the time of his uncle's outburst that Alfons would indeed never see any of them again, but then he was also totally unaware of the impending cataclysm that, in the span of only a few short years, would not only bring sweeping changes to his own life, but would fundamentally change the face of Europe forever.

Chapter 2

Taking Flight from Latvia

ecember 6, 1939, the eve of the Soviet takeover of Latvia, was marked by feverish wharfside activity in the port city of Riga, fueled by fear that had assumed monstrous proportions due to the stories of atrocities committed by the Soviets in other areas they had already occupied. After a few anxious months of keeping up a pretense of permanent resettlement in Salaspils, Rolf, along with his family and two thousand other "enemies" of the Soviet regime, were preparing to board a large passenger ship, the *Oceana*, for repatriation to Germany. The twenty-thousand-ton ship, used in peacetime as a cruise ship for vacationers, had been abruptly pressed into service for the less light-hearted pursuit of transporting people at risk out of the foundering Baltic States. Like Rolf and his family, most of the people boarding the ship were Baltic Germans, people of German descent living in Latvia. Many of these families had called Latvia home for centuries, some as far back as the late twelfth century, when the German Teutonic Order came to the area and founded the city of Riga.

Rolf and his father were carrying the small amount of luggage that the family was allowed to take on board with them. In addition to a suitcase and one smaller bag, Rolf carried a small stack of magazines: *Modern Mechanics*, *Model Airplane News* and some German technical periodicals. Occasionally, he put the suitcase and bag down and rested the magazines on them, leafing through the topmost issue.

Suddenly a man standing near them addressed Ernst. "I think I know you. Aren't you the inventor of the automatic assembly machine from the artillery laboratory?"

Rolf saw his father stiffen in alarm. They had taken great precautions in the previous six weeks to tell no one other than immediate family members of their plans to leave Latvia.

The man continued, "I was a co-worker of the three men who were blown to bits there in '31 before that new German press and your invention improved safety conditions."

Sensing the man's friendly intentions, Ernst relaxed and smiled. "I am surprised that anyone would remember that."

"I remember because my family was also fortunate enough to obtain one of your custom-built radios. Sixteen years old now, but still working. That's how we keep up with all the news."

"Just don't believe everything you hear," replied Ernst with a smile as the line began to move. He turned to board the ship with Maria and Ruth.

The man shifted his attention to Rolf, who was gathering up his stack of magazines. "Are you his son?"

At Rolf's affirmative nod, he inquired, "How are you measuring up against your father's reputation as engineer and inventor?"

"I've been building my first plane, a single-seater with a Walter four-cycle, air-cooled engine, and I have started my studies to be an aeronautical engineer. It's what I want more than anything," replied Rolf proudly, and then added, his face reddening a bit, "I have a girlfriend too—Anna. And we like to dance."

"Leaving a lot behind then, aren't you, young man?" the man replied, with the hint of a smile.

"I hope to continue my education once we arrive in Germany," Rolf answered, picking up his suitcase and magazines and preparing to follow his father. And then with a laugh, "As for girls, I've heard it said that they exist there too!"

Rolf's feelings inside, however, did not match the happy and confident exterior. It was with a sinking heart that he realized his university studies would be disrupted, perhaps without the possibility of resumption at their destination. He remembered the sad misgivings with which he and his sister Ruth had participated in taking apart, stick by stick, the only home they had ever known, and then moving to the spartan, temporary quarters at Salaspils. From nearby Riga, their belongings were scheduled to go by ship to Germany where they would sit in storage until the family managed to establish a new residence, either in Germany proper or in the Warthegau, the westernmost zone of what was by now occupied Poland.

Whereas Rolf had been born in Germany twenty years earlier, he was too young when the family left to have any memories of it, and the thought of moving back there did not hold any attraction for him. He realized that for Ruth, born and raised in Latvia, it was an even more wrenching farewell because Latvia was the only home she had ever known. Their grandmother, uncles, aunts and friends—people with whom they had spent many happy times—were all staying behind. Ruth's high school education was being interrupted and would have to be resumed in a strange country, and Rolf would have to apply to continue his university studies in new and alien surroundings if he qualified to continue them at all. He realized that if he were to be turned down, the result would be swift induction into the German military, a prospect that filled him with morbid dread. In addition, Rolf had been forced to leave behind all of the prize-winning airplane models, so lovingly and painstakingly assembled from the time he was ten years old, to say nothing of the handcrafted kayak and the full-sized plane that he had worked on with so much effort and pride. All remained in storage at his grandmother's home in Liepaja.

As the ship pulled away from the pier, the family stood on the top deck amidst other people who were waving goodbye to family members and friends. Would they ever see any of their relatives again, Rolf wondered? Would those remaining behind be all right once the Soviets took over? It was just as well that he did not know the answers to those questions, for Latvia was perched on the brink of many tumultuous years. There was some hope of reconnecting with his mother's relatives in the Rhineland—if Germany proper was, in fact, to be their destination, but even Ernst was still not privy to that.

Rolf had felt all along that his mother might be secretly glad that they were returning to her homeland, but on board the *Oceana*, her expression was unreadable. The relatives they were leaving behind in Latvia had not usually been kind to this German woman who remained an aloof outsider to their language and customs. What new trials, he wondered, would they all face in the months and years ahead? Would they be accepted where they were going?

As the ship left the harbor, Ernst mused to his son with a tone of regret, echoing Rolf's own wistful mood, "I will never live in my homeland again. It is certain that once the Soviets have a foothold here, they will take over completely." Then, continuing after an introspective pause, "I have no great desire to return to Germany, a country that will never seem like home to me. But, better to swim in a barrel of water than a barrel of mud."

Ernst lapsed into silence again as they watched the city of Riga becoming smaller and smaller on the horizon. Such personal disclosures were uncommon from his father, a man who had experienced massive changes in his life with fortitude and good humor. Rolf reflected only briefly on the meaning of his father's comment, then was lost in thought over the whirlwind of events that had forced them to flee their home. Now finding himself adrift toward an uncertain future in a land not only unknown to him but also one that was at war, he was unable to suppress a shiver. A shiver of anticipation or of dread? He was not sure. For the first time in his life, he felt that the future was slipping out of his control. A tide of vulnerability washed over him, creating an uncomfortable knot in the pit of his stomach.

Eventually Ernst continued with a sigh of resignation, "Sad, that we are not headed for America, the place of my dreams. As a young boy I would sit for hours on the hillside of my parents' farm, gazing at a sliver of the Baltic Sea glistening like a string of jewels in the distance and imagining myself the captain of a ship bound for America. In my early twenties, I wanted to make good on that dream, but no sponsor was to be found. All my life I have entertained the same dream—to be on a ship bound for America."

The shoreline disappeared from view altogether, swallowed up as much by bands of cold fog as by the distance they had traveled. Rolf and his family, as well as two thousand fellow passengers, were now officially without a home and without a country, completely at the whim and mercy of Hitler and the Nazi regime.

Chapter 3

An Invitation from the SS

B y noon of the second day on board the *Oceana*, the suspense finally lifted along with the fog when the Dutzmann family received word that their destination would be Swinemünde, a German port city on the Baltic coast (modern day Swinoujscie, Poland). Rolf was glad that they were heading for Germany proper rather than occupied Poland, an area already subjected to great wartime hardship and peril. At Swinemünde, Nazi Party officials greeted the passengers amidst the clamor of a marching band and anti-aircraft practice over the harbor. A train was standing by to take the passengers to their assigned temporary quarters.

The Dutzmann family's destination was announced as Seebad Bansin, a small, elegant resort town about twenty kilometers west of Swinemünde, where they were greeted by their hosts, the von Wedels, a friendly, elderly widow with two grown daughters. All three were favorably impressed by Ernst's former Latvian officer status. Their own family boasted a long line of Prussian officers, and the widow's son, a captain in the German army, was recuperating in a military hospital from wounds sustained during the invasion of Poland.

The von Wedel home was a large, luxurious three-story mansion on a corner lot filled with elegant antique furniture and surrounded by trees and gardens that were no doubt lovely in the spring and summer months. The Dutzmann family was allotted two generously sized rooms with a balcony overlooking the tree-lined street. During the summer season, most of the rooms were rented out to vacationers who flocked to the area to enjoy the sea air and the pristine, sandy beaches; but in the month of December, all of the guest rooms were vacant and the Dutzmanns' arrival was a welcome diversion for the von Wedels and their neighbors.

Since no ration cards had yet been issued to Rolf and his family, they were allowed to take their meals three times daily at local restaurants. Rationing in Germany had been introduced in September of 1939, just after the war began. By this time, sugar, meat, butter, margarine and oils, tobacco, and most baked goods were being rationed. Other food items that had to be shipped from overseas eventually became completely unavailable, most notably coffee, which was replaced by roasted grain substitutes known as "ersatz" coffee. Bananas, citrus fruit and chocolate also disappeared from the average diet, but potatoes, vegetables and locally grown fruit remained readily available for those who could afford to pay for them. Though there were few luxuries permitted, food allotments were still adequate for most people. Since some bakeries were allowed to produce unrationed baked goods in addition to rationed ones, Rolf and his family were able to purchase additional bread, rolls and pastries from a local bakery with pocket money supplied by the German government.

Rolf enjoyed the beautiful seaside location and spent his time reading on the balcony and going for long walks on the beach and in the surrounding woods, sometimes alone and sometimes accompanied by Ruth or his parents. So far, repatriation was suiting all of them very well.

It was during the Dutzmanns' time in Seebad Bansin that they heard a radio broadcast reporting that the Soviet Union had been expelled from the League of Nations. Ernst, ever vocal on Soviet topics, stated that the hidden imperialist designs of that murderous regime were finally becoming apparent, first with the brutal occupation of eastern Poland in September and more recently, with the totally unprovoked invasion of Finland that had outraged the world and led directly to the expulsion from the League. Rolf wondered with an inner shiver about Latvia. Would the tiny Baltic state sitting defenseless on the doorstep of the Soviet Union be the next victim of Stalin's brutal campaign for world conquest? Surely Nazi Germany posed a lesser evil.

Three days later, the Dutzmanns were called to the local Sicherheitsdienst (Security Enforcement Office) for an interview. After a long, appraising look at Rolf, taking in his tall, strong physique, blonde hair and blue eyes, the official behind the desk handed him a special, sealed envelope with instructions to deliver it to the local SS office at the family's final destination.

Upon returning to their rooms at the von Wedels', Rolf left the envelope unopened on a table for three days, deliberating what to do. He had strong suspicions about the contents of the envelope and the consequences of doing as he was told. On the third day, he ripped it open. The envelope contained a letter recommending the bearer for preferential consideration for the SS. Rolf tore it up and promptly disposed of it.

"Something told me I should open that letter. I absolutely refuse to be an SS man!" he exclaimed to his mother and sister.

Ernst, upon hearing of Rolf's reaction, agreed that he should not consider joining the SS. He had already looked into the alternatives for Rolf. Membership in a Nazi organization, but not the Nazi Party or the SS, was a prerequisite for admission to a German university. Ernst recommended the NSFK, or National-sozialistisches Fliegerkorps (National Socialist Flying Corps), one of the least fanatical branches of the National Socialist Party and one that would prevent Rolf from being drafted into any branch of the military other than the Luftwaffe (German Air Force). By joining the NSFK, he might manage not only to delay active military service, but also to improve his chances for survival in the event that he were to be drafted since, in view of his aeronautical engineering education, he would be much less likely to be sent to the front. Moreover, he would be in a better position to advance his technical skills.

"Do I have any other choice?" asked Rolf with a resigned tone.

"No! These are not times where you can afford to be indecisive! The aeronautical career you have chosen depends completely on serving your country, whatever and wherever that country is. Keep that clearly in mind at all times, along with the passion for learning that you already possess. Make the right decisions and you will be successful. Make the wrong decisions and you will be either killed or imprisoned as a political enemy. Do you want to continue your aeronautical education? Advance your career? Get married, have a family?"

Ernst was talking loudly, even stridently in Rolf's face. "Do you want to survive? Then be willing to excel in your chosen field, but also to harness your career ambitions to a sense of duty! It is a task that is not always comfortable!"

In the ensuing silence, Rolf pondered his father's words. Ernst's entire engineering career had been dependent on military service in the countries he served, first Czarist Russia, then Latvia, perhaps eventually in Germany too. While Rolf admired his father's practicality and his determination to survive under less-than-optimal conditions, he, unlike his father, had no desire at all to be in the military. He especially did not want to serve in the military of a country that was not his homeland, that he felt no loyalty toward and that was already embroiled in a brutal war. Rolf had also attained enough self-knowledge to realize that, whereas he was strong and athletic, excelling in basketball and swimming, his primary capabilities were technical rather than physical. But he was not free to choose his ideal future. Without some involvement in a German political organization, he realized he would not be allowed to continue his studies at all and would most likely be drafted immediately and sent to the front. Already it seemed that his career was being forced into a political and military mold contrary to his personal inclination. He felt deeply distressed by the lack of viable alternatives, and even more by the need to make a decision quickly lest the decision be made for him by the Nazi regime, with potentially catastrophic consequences for his future and perhaps his very survival.

What finally swayed Rolf was his passion for aeronautical engineering and his hopes for a productive future in a technical field. His desire to make it through the war alive was a powerful motivation as well. He finally agreed that Ernst's suggestion to join the NSFK might be his best and perhaps only option. It might provide him with an opportunity to receive pilot training in addition to delaying the dreaded assignment to the front. He secretly comforted himself, however, with the fervent hope that the war might be long over by the time he finished his university education. Within ten days, he received his physical and was admitted as an official member of the NSFK. Although Rolf was apprehensive about the torn-up SS letter for many months after this, no repercussions ever resulted from that action.

The von Wedels' wounded son, Peter, was finally sent home for recuperation at Christmastime. He related in gruesome detail his personal experience of the harsh conditions on the Polish front in winter, how he had been shot through the chest while standing in the turret hatch of his tank and the difficult, painful and frightfully cold transport to a military hospital, where he subsequently lost a lung due to his injuries. Despite these disconcerting insights into the stark reality of front-line duty, the Dutzmanns spent an enjoyable holiday with the von Wedel family, the privations of wartime as yet still comfortably distant.

Rolf, Ruth and Ernst engaged in a cross-country ski tour the following week in the woods near Seebad Bansin, and encountered a mysterious, partially completed concrete structure in the woods not far from the shores of the Baltic Sea, triggering animated speculation between Rolf and Ruth. Rolf was immediately aware from Ernst's silence and intense interest, that it might be more significant than it appeared.

He foiled his sister's further questions by throwing a snowball at her and retorting playfully, "It's a surveillance tower, Ruth, and they will be watching you day and night!"

A noisy, heated snowball fight ensued with Ruth finally running in full retreat to the concrete structure for cover. She occasionally emerged from behind it to throw a snowball at Rolf and usually missed, but Rolf hit his target more often than not. While they were laughing and having fun, Rolf could not help but notice that his father was quietly conducting a thorough inspection of the structure. However, not even Ernst had any inkling yet that his own technical career would soon become embroiled with the purpose of that mysterious and sinister tower.

Chapter 4

Harsh Awakening in Poland

*I*n early March, notification arrived via mail that the Dutzmann family would be transported by train to the city of Posen in the Warthegau, a part of Poland that had been incorporated directly into Nazi Germany during the previous year, and one of the four newly formed administrative regions into which the German portion of defeated Poland was divided. But Rolf and his family were still in the dark as to where or how soon final resettlement would take place. En route, they witnessed extensive war damage for the first time. Blown-up bridges had been hastily replaced by temporary, makeshift structures, and there were many bombed-out factories and other completely or partially destroyed buildings. As had been his habit for many years, Rolf recorded much of what he saw and experienced during their travels in his daily journal.

As if the destruction were not enough to make them all feel anxious about what lay ahead, Rolf and his family soon found themselves quartered in a camp where conditions were dismal, the men sleeping on straw in frigid army barracks and the women on bunk beds in separate but equally cold and uninviting quarters. During the day there was little to occupy their time other than reading, but the cold, uncomfortable conditions in the barracks rendered even that pastime less than pleasurable.

Meals were not much better.

Upon sampling the tasteless, watery soup that was served the first evening, Ernst, with his unique, dry sense of humor, remarked under his breath, "Auch dass Pech noch!" loosely translated as, "And this misfortune too (in addition to all the rest)!"

Nevertheless, he delivered that remark with a smile, which caused Rolf and Ruth to burst forth in peals of laughter despite the bleak surroundings. Even on Maria's face, a hint of a smile surfaced. After their luxurious stay at the von Wedels', the new accommodations seemed cheerless indeed, and any opportunity for humor was a welcome one.

Meanwhile, Rolf began his inquiries into opportunities to continue his college education. He had an advantage over many other applicants since he had already commenced his studies at the University of Latvia. To his vast joy and relief, he was promptly chosen to go through the application process, but he quickly found out that this did not necessarily ensure his acceptance. Rolf was ordered to appear for registration in Posen, but—like any applicant—he could still be arbitrarily placed at any university throughout Germany.

As he approached the registration desk, the seated official did not even deign to look up at him as he barked the order, "Papiere bitte!" ("Papers please!")

Rolf knew exactly what was being asked and handed the official an envelope.

After opening the envelope and glancing at the top document, the man remarked loudly with a snort of undisguised disdain, "University of Latvia! As an upstanding person of German descent, what were you doing at a non-German university? Or perhaps you are not an upstanding German at all, but only pose as one?"

This elicited unfriendly laughter and additional sarcasm from others standing nearby as the official looked up at Rolf with a hostile, unblinking stare.

"Let's see about that, shall we! Vielleicht sind Sie Jude?" ("Perhaps you are Jewish?") he remarked as he looked down at the next sheet of paper that proved not only Rolf's Aryan status with no Jewish blood, but also the fact that he was born in Germany proper.

The intimidation tactics and hostility left Rolf feeling both angry and vulnerable, but in the end it was his German origins and his membership in the NSFK that came to his aid.

"You are lucky that you were born here. But for that and your NSFK membership, we would never admit the likes of you, and we may still not!" the official hissed. "You are free to go. You will receive notification via mail." A curt dismissal with a wave of the hand followed.

To one who had experienced bigotry over his German ancestry while growing up in Latvia, the irony was not lost on Rolf that he should now be experiencing discrimination on account of his Latvian upbringing in German-occupied Poland.

Chapter 5

Early Years on the Baltic Sea

Walking home from school, Rolf was taunted mercilessly by the boys in the schoolyard as he crossed their path.

"Girly hair, girly hair, funny, funny girly hair!"

It was only his third week at Cakstes Pamatskola, the local elementary school named after the first president of Latvia, and already he wished he had never come. He felt acutely how much he was disliked for his poor command of the Latvian language and for the pale blonde hair that, on his mother's insistence, was worn long in a pageboy style, while all of the other boys wore theirs clipped very short. But his German ancestry posed the greatest barrier to making friends at school.

"They might resent you for being a Baltic German," his father had cautioned him before his first day at school.

"But I am not German. I am Latvian!"

"Not to them. They will always see you as German because you were born in Germany to a German mother. But this too shall pass. Just ignore them if they tease you, apply yourself to your schoolwork and be proud of both your Latvian and German heritage."

Rolf was not the only member of his family to feel unaccepted in Latvia. From his earliest years, most of the songs his mother sang to him were mournful ones that made him want to cry. He disliked those songs, but came to realize as he got older that they were expressive of the loneliness she felt as a foreigner, surrounded by people who did not like, understand or accept her. The songs provided a way of communicating the heart-wrenching inner sadness that she felt to her children, the only people other than her husband with whom she felt a bond in those alien surroundings. There was one song in particular that she sang to him quite often when he was very young and that continued to haunt him throughout his life, a moving lament that had been popular with soldiers fighting in the trenches during World War I:

Morgenrot, Morgenrot,
Leuchtest mir zum frühen Tod?
Bald wird die Trompete blasen,
Dann muß ich mein Leben lassen,
Ich und mancher Kamerad!

Sunrise, Sunrise,
Do you light my premature demise?
Soon the Trumpet will sound,
and I will lose my life,
I and many a comrade!

Rolf learned the fundamentals of reading, writing and arithmetic at home from his German-speaking mother and therefore skipped kindergarten. By the time he reached the first grade, however, he suffered from a lack of proficiency in the Latvian language and he also had difficulty with arithmetic. To his great distress, the scholastic challenges, coupled with his German background and odd hair style, marked him as different in very obvious and negative ways from other boys in the school, who regularly made him the object of mistreatment and ridicule. Even the teachers frequently singled him out unfairly due to his German ancestry. His proficiency in the German language only served to further stoke the embers of hostility towards him. The subjects Rolf most enjoyed were the natural sciences, but even better were summer vacations since they provided a much-appreciated respite from the petty animosity that he faced throughout the school year.

From a young age, Rolf had been fascinated by his father's inventions. Ernst spent much of his spare time during Rolf's formative years designing and building things. Among his many projects in the 1930s was an aircraft-propeller-driven speedboat. It was a disappointment, however, since the only available engine was a twenty-horsepower motorcycle engine lacking sufficient power to bring the boat up to adequate speed. Rolf learned early to expect that some projects or inventions would fail, but that with patience and persistence, the efforts might still pay off in time.

The payoff in this case was the family's motorboat. In the summer of Rolf's eighth year, he accompanied Ernst to the yacht club where the family had obtained a membership. His father had searched far and wide for a yacht club with openings for new members, but most clubs in Latvia posted no vacancies that summer. Eventually, through the owners of a local clothing store where Maria often shopped, Ernst obtained an invitation to a predominantly Jewish yacht club. Such mixed company was frowned upon by native Latvians in the area who, if not openly anti-Semitic, still considered it highly inappropriate for Jews and Christians to mingle socially. For Ernst, however, never a slave to convention, it posed no problem. He accepted the offer with enthusiasm.

Ernst proudly unveiled the boat to Rolf. The hull was built by a professional shipbuilder, but Ernst had finished everything else himself, including the interior and exterior of the cabin and the installation of a twenty-five horsepower, two-cylinder gasoline engine acquired from Germany. The boat was twenty-five feet long, large enough to accommodate the entire family on day trips and even for an occasional overnight excursion. The wood of the hull gleamed with multiple coats of carefully applied paint and varnish. Moving around to the port side, Rolf smiled to see that his father had christened the boat *Ruth* in shiny brass letters standing out against the white finish of the hull.

"Today we are going to launch her for the first time," Ernst remarked.

Shortly after the boat was pulled to the ramp and lowered in, Rolf was dismayed to see it filling with water. Ernst assured him that this was only temporary while the wood was swelling, thereby sealing up all of the gaps in the planking. Once the planks were sealed, they pumped out the water and the boat was ready for tours on the lake.

After that first launch, the family regularly enjoyed boat trips on the Lake of Liepaja, a shallow, glacier-carved lake located east of the city of Liepaja and joined to the Baltic Sea at the northern end by a channel. Almost every weekend, the family motored to a resort location at the southern end of the lake, and occasionally—when the River Bartava swelled from heavy rains—they were able to venture south almost to the Lithuanian border. For such longer trips, they packed plenty of food, water and blankets and spent idyllic nights sleeping on the boat either under the stars or in the cabin. Ernst's lifelong interest in astronomy provided hours of fascinated stargazing for Rolf and Ruth, who lay looking up at the sky with a sense of wonder at the majesty of nature while he pointed out planets and constellations.

During the next eight summers, the *Ruth* provided much enjoyment, relaxation and adventure for the entire family. Early exposure to boating and the great outdoors encouraged Rolf's love of swimming and sailing. In fact, Rolf came to delight in anything to do with water—being in it, on it or near it. They often invited friends out on the boat with them, usually motoring to one of their favorite picnic spots on the shores of the lake or on the Bartava River, and after a refreshing swim, spreading out a blanket and enjoying Maria's delicious cuisine-in-a-basket while relaxing in the summer sun.

For Rolf and Ruth, growing up during the small window of peace and stability in Latvia between the two World Wars, it seemed that those sunny, idyllic days would go on forever. There was no reason to think otherwise—no sense of impending chaos lurking beneath the placid surface of their familiar and comfortable lives. Of course, they were young and knew little of the convulsive changes rocking the political scene in Germany and the Soviet Union, much less the resulting upheavals that would be in store for Latvia. Already in 1920, when Rolf was only one year old and Ruth not yet born, Adolf Hitler had outlined the radical political platform of the National Socialist German Workers' Party and shortly thereafter, the Nazi Party was born. In 1925, his book, *Mein*

Kampf, was published—a book that spelled out many of the devastating ramifications that the Nazi regime would eventually bring to pass across Europe. As for the Soviet Union, when Joseph Stalin came to power after the death of Vladimir Lenin in 1924, he gradually assumed the role of unchallenged dictator and expanded the reign of crime and terror that he had already begun as a member of the Bolshevik party. But Rolf and Ruth never read *Mein Kampf* and, as children, only occasionally heard negative remarks about Soviet policies from their father. They did not realize that their tiny homeland lay sandwiched between two of the most brutal, bloodthirsty and heartless despots of all time, who would bring nothing but misery, tyranny and death to countless people caught helplessly in their path.

There were signs, however, that the ravages of World War I were still being felt in Latvia and that life was not as easy for everyone. For years, Rolf, Ruth, and all of their classmates, as well as thousands of children across Germany and Austria, were fed daily by a Quaker relief agency called the American Friends Service Committee. Each morning, volunteers ladled out a steaming bowl of porridge topped with fruit preserves for each child at their school. To ensure that no child who needed it went without, they did not discriminate—every child received food, even those like Rolf and Ruth who were not malnourished. Other than a vague awareness, however, that some children in their school did not have enough to eat, life in those early years seemed nothing other than safe and predictable to Rolf and Ruth, and the warm summer breezes wafting across the Lake of Liepaja did not yet betray any hint of the turmoil and tragedy to come.

A major disappointment for Rolf came in 1935, when Ernst decided to sell the family boat to an acquaintance. It was just as well, because after the outbreak of World War II, the *Ruth* was commandeered by the German occupation forces and used for patrols until she was accidentally run onto the rocks and destroyed during a storm, a fitting metaphor for the fearful conflict descending on Europe that would shipwreck the hopes and threaten the survival of millions of people including Rolf and his family.

Chapter 6

A Boy with Vision

With a look of intense concentration on his face, ten-year-old Rolf leaned squinting over the kitchen table. The challenge before him was to attach a thin strip of plywood to a partially constructed object composed of many intricately cut wooden pieces. The table was covered with sheets of newspaper to protect the surface from the glue and paints that he was using to finish his project.

"This piece needs to be attached just so," he thought to himself.

He bit his lower lip and held his breath as, slowly and carefully, he lowered it into place, then patiently held it waiting for the glue to set.

His project was beginning to come together. Next to it on the table was a diagram he referred to often. It was from a German newspaper called *Die Grüne Post* (*The Green Post*), with the heading "Glider-Trainer" at the top in large block letters. Spread out in haphazard fashion near the article were additional thin pieces of pre-cut wood, the remaining parts for the glider that he was constructing. He had already worked on it for days, and was completely engrossed in his project.

Rolf often found himself in another world, a world that had fascinated him for most of his young life. His imagination had been captured at an early age by articles in *Model Airplane News* chronicling the exploits of aviation pioneers who risked their lives in daring test flights of gliders and powered flying machines. He obtained the American magazine regularly from a friend whose mother had emigrated from Latvia to the USA. While he was not yet fluent in speaking English, he was able to read and understand many of the articles by frequently consulting an English-Latvian dictionary.

Over the years, he eagerly absorbed the exploits of the world's aeronautical pioneers, among them Otto Lilienthal, who flew more than two thousand successful flights suspended from his devices until he was killed in a tragic crash in 1896; Samuel Langley, the American astronomer, who first added an engine to a glider and called it an aerodrome; and finally, the Wright brothers who had managed the first successful flight of the Kitty Hawk in 1903. From that point on, engineers in America and Europe surpassed the early technology of the Wright Brothers' efforts with dizzying speed, and to Rolf's amazement and delight, in 1927, Charles Lindbergh stunned the world by flying across the Atlantic from New York to Paris relying only on a magnetic compass, his airspeed indicator, and sheer instinct.[2]

But there were contemporary heroes closer to home who fired Rolf's imagination as well, such as Oberleutnant (Lieutenant) Ernst Udet, the second-highest-scoring German ace of World War I, turned stunt pilot. It was with fascinated delight that Rolf read of Udet's daring ability to fly so low that he could pick up a napkin from the ground with a hook attached to the wing tip of his plane. Aeronautics was a rich and colorful field of endeavor that fueled Rolf's most cherished dream—to be able to fly someday himself.

Vaguely, Rolf registered that he was being summoned out of his reverie.

"Rolf, Rolf, why don't you answer me?" called his mother with an irritated tone. "It is time for dinner and you need to clear off the table!"

When he delayed a few more minutes in order to finish cutting pieces of paper that needed to be glued to the wings, she objected more insistently, "And I mean now! Your father will be home soon!"

Rolf hurried to collect all of the remaining pieces and all of his tools, placing them on a spare chair in the corner of the room. Then he proudly and carefully transported his fragile model over to the sideboard in the dining room where it would be displayed in style for his father to see when he arrived home. He suddenly realized that he was famished and that the aromas wafting his way from the immense, Russian-style *Kachelofen* (tile stove) where his mother was cooking were those of the hearty goulash with a traditional, rich, onion gravy that was a family favorite. As usual, this would be accompanied by boiled potatoes and carrots fresh-picked from their garden in back of the apartment building.

In their younger years, Rolf and Ruth had shared a room, but by 1929, Ruth occupied what was formerly the nursery, while a partition on one side of the oversized kitchen created a room for Rolf. His room also included a bathtub and wood-fired water heater, both added in recent years by Ernst, since the apartment's bathroom contained only a washbasin and toilet.

Rolf and Ruth were put to work setting the table. Ruth had already been in school for two years. Her hair was darker and her appearance more Slavic than Rolf's, and she had not encountered any of the animosity that had tormented Rolf during his first several years at school. She had even managed to acquire a loyal circle of friends.

Later that evening, by the light of an electric lamp suspended over the table, Rolf finished his glider by gluing the precut paper decals to the wings and laboriously adding details to the wings and body with colored paints and a small brush, making sure to regularly consult the plans.

At the other end of the table, his father was working on a custom-built radio for a customer—a lucrative pastime that had for years augmented the meager compensation obtained through his work at the artillery laboratory. He worked many evenings and weekends to fill orders for new receivers as well as an increasing number of radio repair requests that flowed in from well-to-do customers. No radios were commercially available in Latvia in the 1920s, so there was a steady demand for custom-built units, though only the well-off could afford them. Thanks to Ernst's skills, the Dutzmann family had owned a radio for as long as Rolf could remember. They also had a camera, which enabled them to capture many important events in photographs.

Ernst looked up just in time to see Rolf holding the finished model glider aloft, his young face registering triumph and satisfaction.

Rolf woke up very early the next morning with a sense of great anticipation. It was on this day that he would test his new glider! The day dawned crisp and clear for midsummer, and since it was a Saturday, Ernst was not expected at work. Breakfast consisted of oatmeal and a thick slice of the hearty, home-baked, whole wheat bread that was one of Maria's specialties, lavishly topped with butter and homemade red currant jam.

Afterwards, Ernst, Rolf and the one friend that Rolf had managed to make at school, Paul Liepins, headed off on foot from their apartment building in the government enclave of Kara Osta with Rolf proudly carrying his model. Ruth also insisted on going along, curious as to how Rolf's first plane would perform. After a fifteen-minute walk, they arrived at a wide-open, treeless area of glacier-formed, inland dunes at a place called Skoda—the perfect setting for a boy's delightful first experiment with the principles of flight.

The launch system consisted of a rubber band attached to two hundred feet of string with a metal ring at one end. Upon arriving at the dunes, Ernst instructed the boys to attach the ring to the glider. While Rolf held the glider, Paul stretched the rubber band as far as it would go.

"Ready? One, two, three, GO!"

Rolf let go of the glider which catapulted into graceful flight. Finally the ring dropped from the bottom and it continued in lofty free-flight with Rolf and Paul running along below in excited pursuit, Ernst and Ruth following at a more leisurely pace. After less than a minute aloft, the glider drifted to a soft landing in the dune grasses ahead and Rolf proudly retrieved his prize project. It was the first of his many successful model-building projects and test flights.

At age twelve, with his interest in technical subjects already well established, Rolf was allowed to visit the artillery laboratory with Ernst. It was his first real exposure to military surroundings and protocol and his first insight into his father's work.

They left home early, walking briskly past the gardens maintained by the residents of their apartment building and through the surrounding dense pine forest. After a fifteen-minute walk, they arrived in a clearing well hidden in the middle of yet another dense pine forest. Ahead was a large complex of buildings surrounded by a high fence bristling with barbed wire and guarded by armed soldiers at the gate. Ernst, who was in uniform, was immediately admitted, but he had to sign Rolf in as a visitor. As they entered the complex, Ernst pointed out the underground munitions magazines.

Ten years had passed since Ernst, as a second lieutenant in the Latvian Army, was hired to supervise a shop in the army munitions laboratory. He had become well known, though not universally liked. The advent of the Great Depression had wrought massive changes in Europe and around the world. Among other things, the German democratic government had unraveled, setting the stage for Hitler's rise to power. And in the Baltic States as well as in Germany, Communism had gained momentum, causing Ernst to fall into disfavor with many of the native Latvian workers due to his anti-Communist views. He warned Rolf not to talk politics while on the premises.

Originally, work at the artillery laboratory consisted of reconditioning old ammunition, mainly artillery shells. But later the plant started manufacturing new ammunition. Both were extremely hazardous jobs, since they involved handling explosives, and few safety measures were in place to protect the workers. In 1930, three men were killed while boiling old shells in a kettle to melt out the charge. When one of them poked around in the kettle against orders, a deadly explosion was triggered.

Deeply disturbed by that incident and also relishing a technical challenge, Ernst distinguished himself by designing an automatic assembly machine to fill percussion primer casings with powder and seal them shut remotely. Whereas the boiling of old ammunition still continued, Ernst's invention ensured that workers no longer needed to be in close proximity to explosives during other dangerous production procedures. As a result, safety conditions in the plant improved vastly and there were no further tragic incidents.

Ernst pointed out to Rolf the isolated area where the most dangerous activities took place. He showed him the workings of the automatic assembly machine, then they walked out to the firing range where the muzzle velocity of various munitions was determined. Finally they visited Ernst's personal office area and workspace, the birthplace of many useful inventions and devices.

"I am working on a new fuse for artillery shells," Rolf's father told him. "Soon it will be in production. Next will be an improved device to measure initial shell velocity."

Rolf beamed with pride for his father. He could see himself performing work for Latvia someday, but he hoped it would be in aeronautical engineering rather than munitions. Beneath the seemingly placid surface in Latvia, however, there was already rampant unrest and discontent in political and military circles that would lead to adverse changes in years to come and a return to authoritarian rule. By 1935, it would no longer be the same Latvia that Rolf had known during his formative years and by the end of the decade, no longer a place where he would want to spend his future.

Chapter 7

Developing a Technical Calling

Along with regular prayers before meals and at bedtime, church attendance was one thing that Maria insisted on for her children's religious upbringing. Most Sundays, Rolf and Ruth dressed up in their best clothes and walked to a nearby, ornate, Russian-style cathedral for services.

Maria would have preferred a Catholic church, but since there were none anywhere in the immediate vicinity of Kara Osta, she settled for the best alternative—a former Russian Orthodox cathedral that had been converted to a Lutheran church in 1926. A large, impressive structure adorned with numerous onion domes and lined inside and out with intricate mosaics, it stood vacant and neglected for many years, the victim not only of time's passage, but also of local children throwing rocks against the sides in a generally vain attempt to dislodge pieces of gold. During the renovation, the original Russian Orthodox cross was replaced by a Western-style cross and Lutheran services soon began to be held there for local Latvian servicemen and their families.

Since Maria did not understand Latvian, and Ernst's inclination was to attend only at Christmastime and Easter, Rolf and Ruth were usually sent to church by themselves. Attendance in winter was understandably sparse: the church contained no pews and no heat. In the winter months, as they stood in the balcony, shivering despite their heavy coats, hats and scarves, Rolf was always relieved that the service only lasted half an hour.

Occasionally they were sent via horse-drawn carriage to the nearest Catholic church, located in Liepaja. Afterwards they always took the subway home. To augment those Sunday rituals, Rolf and Ruth were also sent for confirmation classes to the Catholic church, where they were eventually confirmed. That mixed-denominational religious upbringing encouraged an open-minded outlook in Rolf when it came to spiritual matters.

After suffering from anti-German prejudice during his first few years in school, Rolf found that a few things did eventually begin to change for the better. Most significantly, he managed to make a few new friends, several of whom shared his interest in building model airplanes.

Rolf's first year in high school, however, was a disaster due to his ongoing problems with Latvian grammar and his inability to grasp the principles of algebra, a continuation of his difficulties with math in general. He was forced to repeat that grade, which helped him ultimately, since he managed to improve his comprehension and to earn much better grades. Aunt Paula, who taught at a school across town, often came to help him with his Latvian grammar. She was kind but firm in her encouragement, and Rolf appreciated the tutoring even though he never fully came to like the subject.

The following year, given a choice between a science and math curriculum requiring only one language or a curriculum concentrating on an assortment of languages, he gladly chose science and math and left the despised Latvian grammar behind. His decision was reinforced by his model-building skills and by the ninety-percent aptitude for technical subjects that he had displayed in the final year of elementary school. He elected English for his language requirement, since he had been reading American technical magazines for many years and was already convinced that the future of aeronautical engineering would be in America.

At age sixteen, Rolf realized that the only thing missing for him and the other young men who enjoyed building model planes was a meeting place—a clubhouse, a shop and a haven—where they could work undisturbed on their projects. Since Kara Osta was a Latvian government enclave housing army, navy and air force units and also providing quarters for officers and their families, it occurred to Rolf to inquire about obtaining a workspace for his group. He approached the commanding officer of the seaplane squadron, who was immediately captivated by Rolf's vision and enthusiasm and allowed the young men to occupy a small building under his jurisdiction. It was completely, spectacularly vacant except for dust, cobwebs and a few old tables, but Rolf was elated. A week later, he and his friends arrived to start setting up shop and were surprised and gratified to find that the space had been cleaned, renovated, and supplied with chairs and additional tables for their use.

The young men began to meet regularly. In 1936, they joined the Latvian Model Airplane Club, which enabled them to enter both local and national competitions. Rolf built twelve or more models, winning all local contests that he entered. His Sopwith fighter model, carefully built from plans published in *Model Airplane News*, was too heavy to fly—balsa wood was not available in Latvia, so he had to construct it with thin pieces of plywood. But he was pleased with it anyway and displayed it proudly.

One day in May 1934, on the way to school, Rolf saw military guards posted on the bridge over the canal at Kara Osta and at the local post office. The seeds of change sown in Latvia a few years earlier had brought the first of a far-reaching series of upheavals. The president of Latvia, Karlis Ulmanis, had effected a coup d'état, abruptly dissolving the parliament and sending all known Communists and Communist sympathizers to makeshift concentration camps. Most of those prisoners were released within a year, but others remained incarcerated until the Soviet takeover in 1939, at which time the tables were turned and the former Latvian president, along with other anti-Communists, was deported to the Soviet Union where he perished several years later.[3] By the mid-1930s, the stage was already set for an end to safe, predictable times and for Rolf's own precipitous departure from Latvia.

Chapter 8

The 1936 Olympics

olf dribbled a basketball across a field in Kara Osta, a task made difficult by mud puddles, uneven ground and alternating stoney and grassy areas. Constantly altering his dribbling technique to accommodate the changes in terrain, he dodged the players from the opposing team while making his way toward the basket at the other end of the primitive outdoor court. Just as he was about to pass the ball to a teammate, a slippery patch of mud caused him to lurch sideways and go down. Spattered with mud from head to foot, he jumped back up, laughing, but also thought ruefully of the work his mother would need to put in at the washboard to clean his muddy clothes. But the game had to go on. His team gained the lead and eked out a narrow victory.

The ten young men, five on each team, were enthusiastically devoted to the sport called basketball that, while relatively new in Latvia, was still completely unknown in many other European countries. Most of them had played on the high school team during their senior year, competing against two other schools in the area and using indoor courts. Rolf, at sixteen years old, had served as the team coach and captain. Their main challenge in the summer months, with the school courts no longer at their disposal was that they had no place to continue honing their skills. Rolf searched the fields in the area and finally found one that was level enough and relatively free of trees, weeds and shrubs to work as an interim court. With surplus supplies obtained from Ernst via the artillery laboratory, Rolf constructed posts, boards and baskets for the goals and marked off lines. In spite of his hard work preparing the field, however, it became apparent after only a few practice sessions that it was far from an ideal basketball court. The field was transformed into a sea of mud in rainy weather, uneven ground prevented them from perfecting their dribbling skills, and they still would have no place to play during the colder months of the year. But for these young men, any opportunity to play basketball was better than none at all despite the primitive conditions.

Encouraged by his previous success securing the workspace for the model glider club, Rolf contacted the commanding officer on base, requesting that they be allowed to play in a nearby, partially enclosed pavilion with wooden floors that was used in the summertime for picnics and special events. When approval was granted, they were delighted at the prospect of being able to improve their running, dribbling and shooting techniques as well as conducting their games under more sheltered conditions during all but the coldest months.

The Games of the XI Olympiad were slated to take place in Germany that summer and each participating country including Latvia was invited to choose thirty of its most promising young male athletes to attend as spectators. Selection was to occur from high schools all over Latvia on the basis of athletic participation and performance, personal character and the ability to pay a portion of expenses. Even though Rolf was well qualified, as the captain of the basketball team and the star freestyle swimmer at his school, his German ancestry once again proved to be an impediment. Initially rejected by the selection committee, they later reconsidered and chose him after all as one of the two young men to represent his school at the Summer Games in Berlin.

In June, Rolf and the other young athletes were sent to a preparatory camp at a beach resort near Riga, where they slept in tents and dined in the cafeteria of a local school. They spent their days engaging in sports, listening to lectures about the trip to Berlin, and absorbing information about proper behavior as representatives of Latvia. They were also measured for uniforms specially designed for their attendance at the Olympics.

Finally the day arrived for them to board the train to Berlin. Since food was expected to be scarce in Germany, their group took along a fifty-kilogram barrel of Latvian butter (over one hundred pounds). At the Berlin station, they were picked up by a military bus and transported to a camp where each nation's youth were accommodated in their own large tent furnished with bunk beds. Meals were served in an immense mess hall. To their surprise, food of all kinds, including butter, was both plentiful and varied.

For two weeks, they were granted free admission to Olympic events of their choosing as well as free time for sightseeing in and around Berlin. Each day began with a flag-raising ceremony followed by breakfast and then departure for the stadium area by bus or subway.

On most mornings, only half of the US team attended the flag raising. One morning, several of the US participants turned their backs when the German flag was raised. This so incensed the German camp authorities that they requested that the US team leader send the offending members home. In order to avoid creating an international incident, the team leader complied, dispatching the offending young men back to the US. Rolf and his Latvian companions considered the US team members to be undisciplined by European standards, only later learning that their breach of manners was a protest against the Nazi regime's banning of non-Aryan German athletes from participation in the Games—a position condemned internationally as a violation of the Olympic code of equality and fair play.[4] Once he came to understand this, Rolf admired the US team's refusal to accept injustice and discrimination. In any case, Rolf observed that the shining star of the 1936 Olympics was an African-American, Jesse Owens, whose victories disproved Hitler's premise that athletes of "Aryan" blood were superior to non-Aryans.

While in Berlin, Rolf traveled to and from Olympic events by train. One day a man and woman sat down next to him and, noticing his uniform, began to engage him in conversation. Once they found out that he was in Berlin to observe the Olympics and that he was from Latvia, Rolf noted an eagerness bordering on urgency in their manner and tone of voice that they were unable to fully disguise.

"And how are Jewish people faring in Latvia?" the man inquired of Rolf.

Rolf replied that Jews in Latvia were able to come and go unhindered and to live largely as they wished. He did not attach much significance to that conversation at the time, but after the war's end, he often thought back on it with a chill, as shocking postwar disclosures made him realize that those people may have been Jewish themselves and perhaps desperately searching for an escape route from Germany before it was too late.

Rolf spent much of his free time attending aviation events. It quickly became apparent to him that the air shows, one at Tempelhof Airfield and one at Staaken, were organized to impress foreign visitors with Germany's military might and progress under Hitler. Already the previous year, in 1935, Hitler had reintroduced military conscription, thereby violating the Treaty of Versailles. At Staaken, not only was Rolf thrilled by the aerobatic demonstrations of high-performance soaring planes, but he also witnessed the first concrete evidence of German rearmament—a squadron of twin-engine bombers.

At the close of the Olympics, the customary call was put out for athletes to assemble in another four years in Tokyo for the XII Olympic Games. But the next two Olympic Games would be canceled. In the intervening years, the youth who were the athletic pride and future of their respective countries would instead wind up butchering each other on the killing fields of World War II. [5]

At the end of their time at the Olympics, Rolf and his companions gave half a barrel of leftover butter to the German soldier who was taking down their tent—more butter than the young man had probably ever seen in his life!

The high school years also provided some very enjoyable pursuits in the form of ballroom dancing lessons with piano accompaniment by students. Rolf was surprised to find that he enjoyed dancing almost as much as swimming or playing basketball.

And then there was Anna—an attractive, vivacious girl with shoulder-length blonde hair who attended the same high school but in the grade below Rolf. He had noticed her, but had not worked up the courage to introduce himself. Walking home from school one day, he felt something in the pocket of his overcoat. It was a folded slip of paper with a handwritten message:

Dear Rolf,

>*My name is Anna Bembere. Do you know who I am? We sometimes pass each other in the hallways and I have seen you swim and play basketball. I would really like to dance with you next Saturday.*

Anna

Anna proved to be a charming companion and a graceful dancer. Rolf spent an increasing amount of time with her, not only at dances but also going for walks, bicycling along the Baltic coast or sailing on a rented sailboat. Much as Rolf liked Anna, however, there was no thought in his mind that it might be a serious relationship leading to marriage. He was much too young and had far too many plans for the future to mistake romantic flights of fancy for reality. For Rolf, the future still held unlimited promise.

In the mid-1930s, Ernst was promoted to the rank of captain and in 1937 the artillery laboratory began to work overtime to produce ammunition used in the Spanish Civil War. No one, including Ernst, knew to which side the ammunition was being shipped, but it provided a steady stream of income to the Latvian government. Nor did any of them know that the tiny nation of Latvia, along with its neighbors Estonia and Lithuania, was already doomed. Within three short years, the independent Latvian nation would cease to exist. By the end of the war, one-third of its prewar population would disappear— casualties of the war itself, as well as from executions, deportations, the Holocaust and the grim conditions in prisoner-of-war, refugee and prison camps.[6]

Chapter 9

The Final Years in Latvia

Throughout his high school years, Rolf continued to add to his knowledge of aeronautics and to perfect his model-building skills. In 1937, at age eighteen, he won both first and second prize in the national model airplane competition in Riga with his "Winkler Junior" glider and a rubber-band-driven propeller model. He had accomplished all that he felt was possible with airplane models. It was time to consider building his first full-sized plane.

The following year, Rolf and a friend, Edwins, joined a Latvian paramilitary organization called Aizsargs (Defenders), which had functioned as a sort of Latvian National Guard since 1919. A branch of that organization had motorized airplanes at its disposal and also trained pilots as a benefit of membership. Both Rolf and Edwins were hopeful of receiving the coveted pilot training. In early 1938, when a limited number of openings became available for the training, both of them applied, but only Edwins was chosen. Rolf was crushed—still more so when he discovered that Edwins himself had convinced the selection committee that he should receive preference over Rolf due to his native Latvian status and Rolf being merely a Baltic German. The old discrimination against anyone and anything German was surfacing yet again!

Undeterred, Rolf decided to build his own full-sized plane similar to those that inspired him in a special issue of the American magazine *Modern Mechanics*, to which Ernst had started a subscription. It was fortunate for Rolf that he was able to read English. He stopped receiving two German publications, *Die Grüne Post* (*The Green Post*), a newspaper which often contained plans for glider models, and *Die Woche* (*The Week*), a news magazine with commentaries. Unbeknownst to him at the time, *Die Grüne Post* ran afoul of the Nazi regime in 1934, when it ran an editorial critical of Nazi press censorship, for which its editor was sent to a concentration camp. Both of those periodicals did continue into the war years, but were just not available anymore in Latvia. Many other liberal German periodicals were forced out of circulation by the Nazi regime only to be replaced overnight by newspapers and magazines that kept strictly to party propaganda.

To Rolf, however, it still seemed that life in Latvia would go on unaffected by what was happening elsewhere in Europe. That summer, he and Edwins worked on the construction of a full-sized glider as part of their Aizsargs training. On the wings they painted the striking red crosses on white circles that were the symbol of the Latvian National Guard from the years 1937 until the Soviet takeover of 1940. Once the project was finished, Rolf volunteered to be the first to fly it. He received no specialized flight instruction, only a last minute briefing from another Aizsargs member who had already received official pilot training. Due to his familiarity with glider construction and controls, Rolf was undaunted and already knew exactly what he would have to do to fly it successfully. It was exhilarating to be airborne at last!

In the summer of 1939, Rolf worked at the Artillery Laboratory, where his father was employed, as well as at the Tosmare plant, a facility that specialized in airplane manufacture and ship repair. With the Latvian government promising a Walter four-cylinder, air-cooled engine to anyone who completed construction of an airplane frame, he spent all of his earnings on the components needed to build his first full-sized, motorized plane—chrome-moly tubing for the fuselage, wood for the wings and all of the other necessary materials. By the end of 1938, all of the ribs, the elevator and rudder were completed and most of the tubing for the fuselage was prepared for welding.

But his Aizsargs activities and the progress on his construction projects slowed down when he became preoccupied with final exams and graduation from high school. Despite earlier tribulations with schoolwork and grades, he graduated among the top five in his class and was chosen to be the valedictorian.

Rolf's friend, Edwins, had always been extremely reckless by nature. Late in 1938, while engaged in a cross-country flight assignment for the Aizsargs, he foolishly dived the plane to frighten some farmers and horses in a field. When he failed to pull out of the dive in time, the plane crashed and both he and his co-pilot were killed. He received an elaborate hero's funeral with a procession through town, including a sentimental stop at his high school, where nostalgic organ music drifted out through the open windows into the crisp, late fall air.

Early in 1939, Ernst was sent to England for two months by the Latvian government to serve as the authority for approval and inspection of a machine gun purchase from the Vickers Company. Upon his return, Ernst told Rolf of the extensive war preparations being carried out in England. Trenches were being dug in parks, buildings were being sandbagged and barrage balloons set aloft— all proof that Great Britain was taking the Nazi threat very seriously.

Rolf's energy and attention were soon too absorbed by entrance exams for the University of Latvia to ponder long the implications of the ominous developments in England or Edwins's betrayal and his subsequent premature and tragic demise. Only two exams were conducted, one in math and one in Latvian composition. Out of five hundred applicants, only fifty would be admitted to the Department of Mechanical Engineering at the university. On the day after the exams, feeling as though their entire future hung in the balance, Rolf and his best friend, Paul, who had taken the same exams, eagerly scanned the bulletin board for admission announcements. They nearly jumped for joy to find both of their names on the list. The first semester was slated to begin in mid-September.

The earliest hint that World War II was already underway came in September 1939, when Rolf woke abruptly one night to the sound of a plane circling back and forth as if desperately searching for a safe place to land. Since the Liepaja airport was not equipped with runway lights, Rolf knew there would be no visible, safe place for a stray plane to land and no opportunity to receive landing instructions during the night. He listened intently. After a short time, the sound of the engine died away and Rolf thought he heard the plane gliding to a landing somewhere to the north of Kara Osta.

The next morning dawned a cool, clear, late summer day. Rolf cycled northward along the coastal road, stopping only to ask questions of pedestrians and local residents. Every so often one of them gave an excited reply, gesturing and pointing off into the distance. Rolf rode on, repeating the stops for information until finally he rounded a bend and saw the aircraft ahead that, the night before, aided only by the light of the moon, had managed a perfect belly landing on the beach. It was a German twin-engine Heinkel 111 medium bomber. No crew members were evident, and a guard was posted near the plane to keep curiosity seekers away. Rolf walked across the dunes and approached the guard with more boldness than he felt.

"Rolf Dutzmann, from the aircraft department of the Tosmare plant. Might I be allowed to inspect the aircraft?"

The guard was reluctant, but relented when Rolf showed him his I.D. card from the Aizsargs paramilitary group.

Rolf walked around the plane and saw that there was hardly any damage, only bent props. The gas tanks were empty and so were the bomb racks.

"Where are the crew members?"

"Captured, all four of them."

Later news releases revealed that the plane had taken off from Germany to carry out a bombing raid on Warsaw and then turned northward toward an airbase in East Prussia. Due to a navigation and radio failure, the crew had flown too far north and ended up on the Baltic coast of Latvia at Skede. The four crew members were interned in Riga, where they remained until 1940, when the Soviet occupation forces released them to return to Germany—the two countries still being on friendly terms at the time.

For Rolf, that incident was a first small brush with the war, but one that did not yet affect his own life or threaten his future happiness. It was still not clear to him at the time whether the war would ever threaten his family or anyone in Latvia directly, but as Hitler continued the march on Poland and as ominous rumors about Soviet expansion into the Baltic States grew, his optimism began to falter. As September of 1939 wore on with the surrender of Warsaw to the Nazis and the heartless carving up of the country of Poland between Germany and the Soviet Union, the question on every mind in Latvia including Rolf's was, "Where will the Soviets strike next?" Hitler was considered a much less tangible threat. Yet in only two years' time, the dunes at that very beach—the dunes at Skede— would bear mute, agonized witness to acts of unspeakable horror perpetrated against Latvian citizens in the Führer's name.

By the end of 1939, as the *Oceana* carried Rolf and his family toward an unknown destination, he sensed that he was being irrevocably drawn into circumstances that would permanently alter the course of his life. And once in Germany and at the whim of the Nazi regime, he would discover that he no longer had control of his life or his future at all.

Chapter 10

Delaying the Draft

*F*inally word arrived that the Dutzmann family's permanent resettlement would be to Litzmannstadt (Lodz), a city located in the middle of Poland. It was an announcement that was met with considerable misgivings. Not only did this news dash their hopes to be reunited with Maria's family members in the Rhineland, but they also knew that Poland in 1940 was a place of great strife, tragedy and danger due to the dual occupations of Germany and the Soviet Union as well as the fierce resistance of Polish partisans. Moreover, Litzmannstadt was far too close to the Soviet occupation forces for comfort. However, they had no choice in the matter since the Nazi regime was in total control of their resettlement.

They once again traveled by train, followed by another sojourn in depressing, primitive and camp-like conditions. They were relieved to find out that those crude accommodations would be only temporary.

Advised to search for an apartment in the city, Rolf and Ernst boarded a streetcar to look for a place to live. Eventually they passed by a long, dismal-looking, fenced-off section of the city with armed guards posted at intervals.

"What kind of place is this?" Rolf asked his father.

A man standing next to them overheard and spat contemptuously, "Juden!

This is where they put them all to keep them from contaminating everybody else! Serves them right!"

"How long can they survive?" asked Rolf, gazing in startled disbelief at the crowded, slum-like buildings that rose like grisly specters behind unsightly wooden fences, the tops of which bristled with barbed wire. Rolf had no way of knowing that within the previous month, over two hundred thousand of Litzmannstadt's Jews—those who had not managed to flee—had been forced into that ghetto, and in the coming years, twenty-five thousand additional Jews and Gypsies would be sent there from other countries. Still less could he imagine that it would serve as death row for all its inhabitants, merely one of three hundred ghettos in Nazi-controlled areas, holding their human cargo by the millions for eventual transport to extermination camps.[7]

"Who knows and who cares? A year, a month, a few days. Any way you look at it, much longer and much better than they deserve!" Then surveying Rolf's startled expression, he added with a sneer, "You would do well to get used to it!"

"Just for being born Jewish they have been brought to this?" Rolf thought to himself with revulsion.

His thoughts turned to the Jewish people the family had known over the years in Latvia, many of them friends and acquaintances from the yacht club. He wondered how they would fare in the years to come. He would have been shocked and disheartened had he known that, in only two years' time, on the heels of Latvia's "liberation from Communist tyranny" by the Germans, most of the country's sixty-five to seventy thousand Jews would be brutally and heartlessly exterminated. Those from his former home town of Liepaja who had not already been deported or murdered during the Soviet occupation would be rounded up in groups, with the largest and final transport being sent to the dunes at Skede, the very beach where Rolf had inspected the off-course German bomber. Nearly three thousand Jews, mainly women and children, would be shot there in the freezing sand at the edge of huge mass graves in the month of December 1941; their parting view a wide, frigid expanse of the Baltic Sea.[8]

Thinking back to the undisguised scorn, prejudice and ill-will with which he had been received at the university registration office in Posen, Rolf contemplated the fact that a mere slip of paper stood between his destiny and that of the people confined in the Litzmannstadt ghetto. He was unable to stifle the instinctive shiver of relief that passed over him that he and his family had been spared whatever fate might await the Jews there.

When the man disembarked at the next stop, a woman with a brown scarf partially covering her face and a bundle under her arm moved closer to Rolf and whispered, "We do not know much about the conditions over there. No contact is allowed. Recently our next-door neighbors disappeared very mysteriously. Shortly after, a military family moved into their apartment." She paused and sighed. "We think they may be over there now." She nodded in the direction of the ghetto without looking at it and then, after checking surreptitiously to see whether anyone else was within earshot, added in a resigned tone, "He was right about one thing. You will be much better off if you get used to it."

She moved away abruptly and then got off at the next stop. Rolf looked at Ernst, who shook his head, a warning look on his face. They spoke no more, each lost in his own thoughts for the duration of the ride.

After looking at many shabby apartments in ghetto areas, they finally found a fully furnished apartment in a new, two-family building in the suburbs. To their acute discomfort, however, the previous occupants were Poles who had been evicted and forced to move upstairs into cramped quarters with other tenants. Rolf was apprehensive, remembering the surreptitious streetcar exchange, but there was no time for the luxury of excessive thinking. The demands of everyday living encroached, and Rolf was soon busy helping his family move into their new quarters. While unpacking a box of books, Rolf came across several photo albums from the years in Latvia. Ernst had always been an avid photographer, and few family occasions went by without photos being taken to commemorate the events. Rolf opened one of the albums randomly and found himself in a more carefree place and time. On the spread was a group of photos that Ernst had taken of him starting at the age of ten with a succession of model gliders, some of which had been first place award winners in Latvia. In early 1940, he was not yet aware of how critical his passion for airplanes would be to his chances of survival in the years to come.

After the Dutzmann family's arrival in Litzmannstadt, Ernst searched in vain for employment in the area. Try as he might, no opening could be found that matched his technical qualifications. He was subsequently sent to Berlin, where he obtained a job at Rheinmetall Borsig, a company that manufactured bombs and bomb fuses, as well as also solid fuel rocket boosters and missiles later in the war. His responsibility was to oversee the layout and equipping of a new production facility for large-caliber aircraft bombs. By that time, Germany had already occupied Belgium, Luxembourg, the Netherlands and much of France, ruthlessly crushing their feeble resistance, but the Nazi regime was secretly setting its sights on much larger prey that would necessitate vast reserves of munitions.

Maria and Ruth followed Ernst to Berlin and were promptly issued temporary housing. Shortly after that, a decree from the Führer was broadcast over the radio that repatriates were to receive preferential treatment in the assignment of housing, and a comfortable and spacious first-floor apartment promptly became available to them.

Rolf finally received the anxiously awaited letter of acceptance to continue his college education and was ordered to report for the second trimester to the Technical University of Danzig (Gdansk), a key port city with a large German-speaking population situated on the Baltic coast in northern Poland. The city had been designated a "Free City" by the Treaty of Versailles after World War I—that is, a largely self-governed city under the auspices of the League of Nations.[9] Now it was under Nazi control.

Rolf was both surprised and gratified to find upon arriving in Danzig, that he had been awarded a scholarship that would provide him with one hundred marks per month in addition to covering his entire tuition and providing meal tickets to the Mensa, the student cafeteria. Nevertheless, since he was a stranger in a strange city and had only limited funds at his disposal, he took refuge for several nights at a local homeless shelter until he was able to find an inexpensive furnished room near the university.

For his aeronautical engineering curriculum, Rolf was assigned one of twenty drafting tables in a large study hall that was located on the topmost floor of the main building, from which there were bird's-eye views of the nearby runway. All students in that hall were members of the fraternal group Akaflieg, Akademische Fliegergruppe (Academic Flyer Group), a group of students who carried out aviation design, research and development motivated solely by their mutual love of flying. As the war dragged on, the groups would be increasingly ordered by the regime to engage in projects with a military purpose.

During an obligatory initiation ceremony for freshmen, each new student was expected to not only supply unrationed baked goods for an afternoon coffee hour, but also to entertain the upperclassmen by telling a series of jokes. When his turn came, Rolf told a series of jokes that failed miserably. He got the thumbs-down and was unceremoniously stuffed into a large, lidded wicker basket and pushed under a table, where he suffered in acute, cramped silence for a time. When he refrained from complaining or begging to be let out, he was rewarded upon release by being enthusiastically slapped on the back and deemed worthy of acceptance as a new member of the Akaflieg.

With that initiatory hurdle overcome, Rolf took to his studies with great energy, enthusiasm and exactitude, spending long hours into many a night at his drafting table. He engaged in frequent debates over technical issues with the other students, many of whom were young fanatics caught up in the Nazi ideology. Rolf found himself drawn instead to several like-minded students who were not in agreement with the prevailing extreme National Socialist sentiments. In this way, he was also able to maintain a greater degree of freedom of speech and expression since he did not have to be as careful to guard his speech with those who mostly thought as he did. His best and closest friend was a fellow student by the name of Ludwig Schlott who later became his roommate and thereafter would remain a steadfast and loyal lifelong friend.

In view of the ever-worsening fuel shortage, Ludwig tried to convince Rolf one evening that sewer gas should be used as fuel in the war effort.

"In Copenhagen, sewer gas is already being used to run buses!" he stated with great enthusiasm.

When Rolf expressed his doubts as to the efficiency of such a fuel source, Ludwig handed Rolf a book of matches and exclaimed, "I can prove how efficient it is!" Bending over and pointing to the seat of his pants, he continued, "When I give the signal, light a match back there."

Silence and a concentrated effort were followed by a loud emission.

"OK—now!"

Rolf struck and extended the match. Immediately, a burst of flame singed the seat of Ludwig's pants followed by a puff of smoke.

"You see," he exclaimed gleefully while jumping around to extinguish the flames, "it burns beautifully!"

All students were required to engage in sports in addition to their academic pursuits. Rolf was chosen to be captain of the university basketball team. He had a great advantage over the other players since basketball had already been popular in Latvia for many years while remaining virtually unknown in Germany until the 1936 Olympics. His participation in basketball allowed him to be exempt from gymnastics, a sport for which he knew he lacked aptitude.

The Akaflieg boasted exclusive use of a clubhouse on the university grounds consisting of meeting rooms, a large machine shop and a hangar to store the group's airplanes. Shortly after classes began, however, the students were informed that the war effort had requisitioned most of the Akaflieg's motor planes, with only two remaining: a "Junker Junior," one of the first all-metal planes, and a "Klemm 35." Moreover, they were informed that there was no longer any fuel available to fly them.

Rolf's initial reaction to this news was disappointment that he would not be able to receive pilot training in a motorized plane, but his thoughts were interrupted by a nudge and stealthy mirthful glance from Ludwig. Rolf could not help but grin at the memory of his eccentric friend dancing around to extinguish his smoking pants.

Since motorized planes were of limited usefulness in view of the fuel shortage, the students worked jointly on the design of a high-performance sailplane called the Penguin, each student taking responsibility for a specific aspect of the plane's design. Rolf's job was to design a retractable landing gear, the successful completion of which earned him additional credit towards his degree.

During the summer recess, when all students were expected to work in some aspect of industry for the Third Reich, all of the aeronautical engineering students including Rolf were assigned to design and assemble a special test wing for a sailplane under the auspices of the Deutsche Versuchsanstalt für Luftfahrt (German Aircraft Development Center). Since his scholarship funds were not available during the summer recess, he gave up his furnished room, and was allowed to take up residence instead in the drafting hall, where he spent the next six weeks sleeping on a wooden bench and washing up in the facility's public restroom. But that suited him just fine because it enabled him to spend long hours on the task, often laboring late into the night gluing ribs and spars and building assembly fixtures.

That summer, the news came that Rolf had been hoping for. He received notification that he was to report to a soaring camp in East Prussia, northeast of Poland, where he would receive official glider flight training and certification. It was news that he greeted with great excitement and enthusiasm. At long last, he hoped to be able to fulfill his dream of obtaining his soaring pilot's license.

En route by train, he witnessed long transports of cement and sand heading eastward towards the Soviet border. Rumor had it that Germany was fortifying her borders with Soviet-occupied territories, but in actuality, as later events would demonstrate, those materials were being used to construct airfield runways in preparation for the invasion of the Soviet Union that was secretly planned to commence in 1941. It would be a stab in the back to Stalin and the Soviet regime—Hitler's brazen violation of the German-Soviet Non-Aggression

Treaty that had enabled the two totalitarian regimes to carve up Poland as well as allowing Nazi Germany to boldly march into Belgium, Luxembourg, the Netherlands, France and Norway unopposed and without fear of provoking a second front in the east. Even as the Soviet Foreign Minister, Molotov, visited Berlin in November of 1940 to try to gain German consent for Soviet expansion into the Balkans, Hitler had already developed secret plans to attack the Soviet Union.

Upon arrival in Drachenberge (Dragon Hills), the small town where the soaring camp was located, Rolf and twenty other students learned to fly gliders launched by ropes from the surrounding hills. He easily earned his glider "A" certificate that fall, which required several successful takeoffs and straight-line flights followed by smooth landings. He felt a sense of great elation and accomplishment at making headway toward fulfilling a cherished lifelong goal.

Chapter 11

May I Have This Dance?

During the Christmas break in 1940, Rolf was visiting with his family in Berlin. By that time, his sister Ruth had resumed her high school education in Germany, and the family had moved into their new apartment on Tile Wardenberg Strasse, where Rolf's mother had employed her considerable flair for needlework and decorating. All of the familiar furniture and other belongings, including collections of china, crystal and handmade, embroidered linens that had been loaded into a furniture van in Latvia a year earlier, now graced this new home. It was unmistakably Christmastime. In the front room, a *Tannenbaum* (Christmas tree) was already set up and waiting to be decorated with ornaments and real candles, and the kitchen was redolent with the wonderful aroma of Maria's cooking and baking. In addition to baking sheets of Christmas cookies, other delights appeared from the oven, including *Stollen*, a Christmas bread with raisins, nuts and candied fruit; *Nusskuchen*, a moist cake made with finely ground hazelnuts and almonds; and his father's favorite—*Speckkuchen*—savory pastries filled with chopped bacon and onions. After the spartan university quarters and fare, Rolf was especially appreciative of the comforts of home, and he was only too happy to postpone thinking about the perils of a war that, for the time being, still seemed far removed.

One day, while out and about in the city, Rolf saw people being rounded up outside a large synagogue and wondered what was happening. Due to the location, he wondered whether they were all Jewish, although at that time in 1940, Jews were not yet required to wear the Star of David. When the local media questioned the round-up, they were told by the Nazi authorities that those people had been slated for "relocation" to farms in Poland. Rolf, like so many others, failed to grasp the implications. There were rumors, but nobody wanted to believe them, nor could they be substantiated.

The weekend after Christmas, Rolf attended an afternoon dance at the Olympic Stadium Cafe on the outskirts of Berlin. With him were Vera, a young German woman he had met several years previously while she was vacationing in Latvia, and her boyfriend Otto. They were sipping coffee—still real coffee although perhaps a bit watered down—and using their ration coupons to buy slices of *Buttercremetorte* (buttercream cake) and *Schwarzwälder Kirschtorte* (Black Forest cherry cake), which they ate while carrying on an animated conversation about the differences between life in Latvia and that in Germany as well as about the changes wrought by wartime. Rolf told them about his experiences at the University of Danzig, his successful avoidance of the draft to date, and his confidence that the war would be over before he finished his university education.

The atmosphere in the room was equally high-spirited and optimistic. The orchestra was in full swing playing the popular dance music of the day—foxtrots, tangos and English waltzes. Rolf surveyed the room full of young, unattached people of both sexes as well as couples. Here and there a young man, usually in uniform, approached a young woman to ask for a dance.

Rolf had already engaged in three indifferent dances with three partners in the first hour, when he noticed a young, blonde woman who entered the room and sat down at a table by herself. She had brought along a stack of postcards and was alternately writing and gazing off into space, her nonchalant disinterest in the surrounding festivities adding to her unique appeal. Rolf's attention was riveted.

"What do you think? Over there?" he nudged Otto, pointing to the young woman. "Something about her strikes my fancy."

"Nice figure, nice legs," Otto commented appreciatively, giving rise to an annoyed elbow nudge from Vera. Rolf rose from his chair and walked boldly over to the young woman's table.

"Fräulein, may I have the honor of the next dance, please?"

The young woman, startled out of her reverie, turned a dreamy-eyed gaze upon a very tall, handsome young man with startlingly translucent blue eyes. She hesitated at first, but then smiled and agreed to dance with him. He briefly introduced himself at the beginning of the first dance and found out that her name was Lilo, short for Liselotte. A self-conscious silence followed, dispelled only by the lively dance music. Rolf, suddenly tongue-tied, remained mute until the end of the second dance, then awkwardly invited her to join him at his table.

When Lilo accepted, Rolf went back to her table and, wanting to impress her with a grand gesture, picked up the chair in which she had been sitting, sweeping it nonchalantly overhead to carry it over to his table. Unbeknownst to him, however, the seat was loose and startled him by coming down on his head. There was amused laughter from surrounding tables as he rubbed his head, picked up the chair seat and sheepishly made his way back to where Lilo and his friends were sitting.

"So far it is not an auspicious beginning," Rolf mused to himself.

He was glad that bending down to reassemble the chair at his table gave him the opportunity to cover up his acute embarrassment.

Rolf could tell by the way that Lilo politely covered the awkwardness with a smile that she was not at all favorably impressed so far. When Rolf finally managed to swallow his wounded pride and found his voice again, he began asking tentative questions. He found out that her full name was Liselotte Wassull and that she lived in the Wilmersdorf section of Berlin with her mother. Lilo found out that Rolf was able to talk after all and they discovered that they both had Russian ancestry. Relieved and mutually pleased that they had found common ground, they agreed to meet again—same place, same time—the following week.

The next weekend, Rolf was half an hour late in arriving at the cafe. As he got off the subway, he saw Lilo, also late, stepping off a train ahead of him and hurrying to the exit. He was both amused and flattered that she was in such a hurry to see him again. Since she had not yet seen him, he let her run for a while, but then made an effort to catch up with her. Her smile upon seeing him spoke volumes. They enjoyed dancing together and getting to know each other—the details of their early lives, their current daily routines, friends and interests, their favorite foods, books, music and more.

Despite the awkward first impression he had made, Rolf found himself thinking about Lilo more and more between their meetings. On their last date before his return to the University in Danzig, he kissed her and they both promised to correspond by mail.

Rolf had no inkling that for Lilo, life had changed dramatically upon meeting him—that it was suddenly glowing with new and exciting possibilities. Like the tender shoots of late-winter flowers sheltering beneath the snow, Lilo's feelings for Rolf were already taking shape, as yet blissfully unaware that there might be bitter disappointments ahead. But then, she had always had the gift of believing in her dreams.

Maria, Rolf
(age five),
Ruth (age two)
and Ernst,
Latvia, 1924

Rolf (right) with his first girlfriend (center)
and Ruth (left), Latvia, 1924

Ruth and Rolf, 1924

Dutzmann Family Album 63

Paula Dutzmann (Aunt Paula), 1921

Costume party with Rolf (left, age eight) as a cowboy and Ruth (second from left, age five) as a Biedermeier girl, 1927

Ruth (age four), Maria and Rolf (seven), 1926

Right: Rolf and Ruth wearing clothing handmade and embroidered by Maria, 1927

Maria (back right), Ruth and Rolf (front)
with friends on the family boat, 1927

Maria, Ruth and Rolf ready to play tennis, 1932

Ruth (front left) and Maria (back row, second
from right) visiting Maria's sister Käthe and family,
Krefeld, Germany, 1935. Photo courtesy of
the Siemes and Dietel families.

Rolf (center front, age 14) and Ruth (right,
age 11) with friends in Latvia, 1933

Right: Rolf, Ernst and Ruth on
the boat that Ernst built and
named after his daughter, 1934

Left: The Dutzmann family in Latvia, 1934

Front from left: Rolf's Aunt Paula; grandmother, Julia; Maria; Ruth (age 12)

Back from left: Rolf (age 15), Ernst, Aunt Ada

Rolf, Ruth and Maria having a picnic on Lake Liepaja, 1935   Ernst in his custom built kayak, 1935

Maria in Latvia, 1933 and 1935   Maria crocheting, 1935

Rolf skating (age 14), 1933

Ruth skiing (age 12), 1935

Rolf, Ruth and Maria, 1935

Rolf (age 15-18) with model gliders, Latvia, 1934-37

Rolf at Liepaja Airport, 1938

Rolf with one of his award-winning model gliders, 1939

Rolf (right), 1939, with a full-sized glider bearing the symbols of the Latvian National Guard

Rolf piloting his first glider with the Aizsargs, Latvia, 1938

Left: Rolf (age 18)
and Maria, 1937

Right: The former Russian
Orthodox cathedral that was
converted to a Lutheran church,
Liepaja, Latvia, 1930s

Berlin Street scene at the time of the 1936 Olympics

Rolf's physics class in Liepaja, Latvia, 1939. Rolf is center front with friend, Paul Liepins, at far right.

Ruth's confirmation day, 1938

Note: In all three photos on this page, Maria, is wearing a dress that she custom tailored and embroidered in the 1920s. It is still in the family collection today and is worn by the author on the back cover.

Left: The Dutzmann family shortly before the flight from Latvia, 1939

Latvian Artillery Laboratory officers and wives, 1939
(Maria, front row, second from left. Ernst, back row, far right.)

Left: Friend,
Vera, with Rolf
and Ruth,
Latvia, 1939

Maria leaving Latvia on board the
Oceana, December 1939

Arrival in Swinemünde, a city on
the Baltic coast of Germany,
December 1939

Ruth (age 17), Maria and Rolf (age 20), shortly before
the flight from Latvia, 1939

German Army band
at Swinemünde

The von Wedel house in the resort town of Seebad Bansin, 1939

Below: Rolf reading on the balcony of the von Wedel house, December 1939

Above: Seebad Bansin street scene with the von Wedel house at front left

Right: The Christmas dinner table at the von Wedels, 1939

Boarding the train to Posen,
Poland, March 1940

Rolf writing in his
diary on the train
en route to Posen

Maria (left) on the train
to Posen, wondering what
lies ahead for her family

Ernst sleeping on straw at
the dismal barracks in
Posen, March 1940

Rolf (right) reading at
the barracks in Posen

The city of Danzig
(Gdansk), 1940

The Akaflieg building at the
University of Danzig

Rolf (#3 center front) in University of Danzig
basketball tournament, 1941

Dutzmann Family Album   73

Ruth (left) and her cousin Erna with Ernst in front
of the Brandenburg Gate, Berlin, 1940.
Photo courtesy of the Siemes and Dietel families.

Below: Maria and Ruth in Berlin, 1940

The soaring camp at Drachenberge, East Prussia, where
Rolf earned his first glider pilot certificate as part of
his aeronautical engineering curriculum at the
Technical University of Danzig (Gdansk), fall 1940

Part II

FAITH

(Lilo's Story)

"To believe in the things you can see and touch is no belief at all; but to believe in the unseen is a triumph and a blessing."

— Abraham Lincoln

Chapter 12

A Girl Who Dreams

*L*ilo woke up with a vague sense that something important would happen that day, but what? Rays of sunshine streamed in through the open window and she heard a chorus of bird song outside. It was a quintessential spring morning. She allowed herself the sweet luxury of a few more minutes of semi-sleep, trying drowsily to grasp the remnant of a dream that lingered on the periphery of her waking consciousness. She knew that moving even a single muscle could make it vanish like mist in the morning light, so she lay very still.

But then there was another sound from a bit farther away, the sound of church bells. They were louder and clearer than ever before, and Lilo suddenly remembered that this was a very special morning, one that would bring a new adventure that she had been planning for some time—a secret that only she and her best friend, Rotraut, knew about. That morning, the bells from the little village church, just a ten-minute walk from where she lived, were beckoning her with a very personal invitation.

She jumped out of bed and ran over to the large wardrobe that stood on the other side of her room. One of the best things about being nine years old was that she was finally allowed to choose the clothes she would wear each day without asking for help or approval. But this was not just an ordinary day. The choice was an easy one: she put on a silky slip, pulled one of her two "best" dresses off a hanger and quickly slipped it over her head. Clean socks and her good shoes came next. A splash of water on her face and she was ready to go downstairs. In the hallway, she gave herself a quick glance in the mirror near the coat rack. She saw that her hair looked a bit disheveled from having been left in braids overnight, but it would have to do, because there was no time to re-braid it now.

In the kitchen, her father was reading a paper while having his morning coffee, and her mother, Gertrud, was engaged in an animated conversation with the family's hired maid, Gretel. At Lilo's unexpected entrance, their conversation stopped abruptly when they turned to survey her, arrayed in her Sunday best.

Lilo's father, Walter, looked up from his paper briefly, his eyebrows creased together in a worried furrow. Young as she was, Lilo knew that the news in Germany was not good. Since 1924, when post-World War I inflation ended, the German economy had spiraled steadily downward, culminating in the Great Depression that sent markets all over the world into a disastrous tailspin. Unemployment rates in Germany continued to rise at an alarming rate and many businesses and banks were failing. Amidst all of these pressures, the German democratic government was floundering. Of course, Lilo did not know or understand most of what was going on, but her sensitive emotional radar frequently picked up on the additional tension in the household caused by the family's worsening financial situation. Dinner conversations often revolved around the dire economic situation in Germany and the family had been forced to drastically cut back on expenditures. But most frightening for Lilo was when her parents' conversations escalated behind closed doors into heated arguments.

Lilo broke the suspense by boldly declaring, as if expecting parental resistance, "I am going to church this morning, the one down the street that I hear the bells from every Sunday morning."

"By yourself?" inquired Gertrud.

"No, Rotraut is going too. We decided this many weeks ago."

Lilo ignored the exchange of amused glances between Gertrud and Gretel and the barely suppressed smiles. Between them there was a very special sort of friendship, and Gretel was treated just like one of the family except that she had her own small room off the kitchen instead of down the main hallway where Lilo and her parents slept. She also received regular, weekly pay. Gretel's room was visible from where Lilo was standing: the neatly made bed, the simple wooden chair and table, the curtain across the far corner with the clothes rod behind it that served as a wardrobe. As always, it was spotlessly clean and everything was in its place.

Gretel had been a trusted figure in the Wassull home ever since Lilo was two years old. For as long as Lilo could remember, Gretel had been the one to clean, wash and cook as well as to care for her while her parents were tending to their business. Just after World War I—shortly after they got married, and a few years before Lilo was born—Gertrud and Walter ran a shop that sold postage stamp collections, a lucrative business while inflation raged in Germany and people were looking for an alternate investment. However, once the German currency stabilized in the early 1920s, stamps were no longer such a desirable commodity and business declined, at which time they converted their shop into a women's and children's clothing store. That also did not profit for long. By 1930, with the deepening depression, rising unemployment and growing competition, they were forced out of the clothing business as well.

During all of Lilo's grade school years, needy children at her school were fed daily by the same Quaker relief organization that fed children in Latvia after World War I—the American Friends Service Committee. Since Lilo was not considered to be in need, she did not receive food daily, but she and the other children not receiving daily meals were treated to a warm roll and a cup of hot cocoa once a year on their birthday. Biting into the aromatic, delicately sweetened roll was a special and memorable delight. Those rolls were different and somehow better than any other rolls Lilo had ever tasted.

There were indications that things would be changing soon in Germany. In previous months, Lilo had heard her parents and other adults talk about a new political party that had gained popularity in recent elections amidst promises of employment, prosperity, social harmony and a restoration of Germany to its former glory. Lilo didn't know about all of that, but she hoped that somehow it would help her parents to be happier with each other.

Lilo sensed with growing alarm the rising tension between her parents, especially since her father's recent attempts to launch a new career in the insurance business amidst ever worsening economic conditions and the struggle to continue to support his family in the comfort to which they had become accustomed. He was often away, and when he was home, the relationship between her parents was extremely strained. Her mother's spontaneous, forceful personality and her father's more cautious outlook often seemed to Lilo like a disastrous meeting of fire and water. Gertrud's fiery temperament and sometimes wild and unconventional ideas often set her father's more conservative nature sizzling. Their frequent arguments filled her with alarm, and she often feared that she herself was the cause of their disagreements.

Lilo's relationship with her mother was very close and nurturing. It was her mother who listened to her troubles, who cuddled and comforted her, and who enthusiastically celebrated all of the milestones of childhood with her. When Lilo was much younger, it was also her mother who usually read stories to her. During long winter evenings, her mother would often snuggle up with Lilo and her favorite teddy bear under a warm blanket near the ornate *Kachelofen* (tile stove) in the living room. Sometimes Gertrud read fairy tales, but frequently also stories from an illustrated book entitled *Der Struwwelpeter* (*Shock-Headed Peter*), that she herself had grown up with and that Lilo found particularly amusing. Only the story of the *Daumenlutscher* (*Thumb-Sucker*) was a bit frightening to Lilo at times. At age four, when she was old enough to understand the stories but not yet ready to abandon the thumb-sucking habit, she secretly fretted about that story. Was it really possible that an angry looking man with a top hat and tails, brandishing an immense pair of shears, might suddenly burst through the door of her room and cut off both of her thumbs if she was caught in the act? She had tempted fate many times since then, and it hadn't happened. Nevertheless, she was relieved when, at age five, the attraction of thumb-sucking waned and she no longer had to worry about "the man with the shears."

By contrast, Lilo's father seemed much more distant, almost as though he were an uncle rather than her father. Since she had no siblings to help shoulder the burden of the problems she experienced in the family, Lilo was often glad that Gretel was there as an additional confidante and sounding board. But soon Gretel would no longer be there for her. She was soon to be married, and besides, the family could no longer afford her services.

After making sure that Lilo had a glass of milk and a warm roll, Gertrud and Gretel saw her off, smiling at each other and shaking their heads at her sudden fancy. It was a household where faith in God was a given and prayer habits were regular, especially at mealtimes and bedtime, but regular church attendance had not been cultivated.

"Just remember not to go anywhere near the park by yourselves!" warned Gertrud as she waved goodbye to Lilo.

With unemployment on the rise in Germany, the main parks in Berlin and in other large cities were overrun with men out of work. Groups of men with nothing better to do were occupying the park benches, playing cards, drinking beer and using foul language. Crime was on the rise and the parks were no longer safe places for children to play. Just a year or two previously, Lilo had finally been allowed to go by herself to the local park in Berlin-Lichtenberg, the part of greater Berlin where the family lived, to play in the sandbox, swing on the swings, play ball or to take her dolls and stuffed animals for a ride in her doll carriage. It had been a wonderful place then to play and make friends, but those times were gone and all had changed. She and her friends were no longer allowed to go there without at least two mothers or guardians accompanying them. Lilo hoped that if the new Nazi party accomplished nothing else, it would at least empty the parks so that she and her friends could once again play without restrictions.

But on that day, Lilo was exultant. She alternately walked, skipped and ran up the street to the building where her friend Rotraut Friedenberger and her parents had their apartment.

Lilo and Rotraut had been close ever since Lilo's first day at school when Rotraut boldly walked up to her, took her hand and asked, "Would you like to be my friend?"

Lilo, always quiet and painfully shy, felt her heart lurch with joy that of all the thirty girls in the class, Rotraut had chosen her, Lilo, to be her special friend.

Rotraut was also an only child, but at her house, things were very different from the Wassull household, and Lilo spent much time there. Rotraut's father was a teacher at a boys' high school and kept regular hours at his job, usually returning home in time for the midday meal. He also spent most evenings at home or in a large garden plot not far from their apartment that he cultivated faithfully, taking great pride in the fruits and vegetables raised there. The girls enjoyed spending time in the garden, both eating the delicious produce and helping to harvest it by putting it into five-pound baskets that they hand-delivered to small neighborhood markets. For each basket delivered, they were paid five cents, after which they would run off to their favorite store to buy penny candy.

On that spring day Lilo and Rotraut hurried without delay to the little church, where they arrived just in time for Sunday school. They were given a warm welcome by the members there, who regarded them with wonder: two children entering voluntarily and unaccompanied by an adult. From that time on, they attended almost every Sunday and took part in many events. They even proudly played "cuckoo" flutes in the *Kindersymphonie* (*Children's Symphony* by Joseph Haydn) at a concert put on a year later for the benefit of parents and the local community. There was much about the teachings and activities there that made Lilo feel good, and helped to soothe an empty ache inside.

Another consolation and inspiration to Lilo was the time she spent with her friend Ursel, who lived in the same building. There was an atmosphere of love, peace, cooperation and mutual respect as well as a sense of ease between Ursel's parents that Lilo missed in her own home life. She deeply enjoyed being able to share in their family life, and spent time there as often as possible, soaking up the ambience like a thirsty young traveler in the desert.

It was a great tragedy for everyone including Lilo when, after nursing her family through a severe bout of the flu, Ursel's mother contracted the illness herself and suddenly died. For Lilo, the example set by Ursel's family was a valuable one. The experience of being in such harmonious surroundings was one that she would never forget, and upon which she would deliberately and consciously model her own future.

Chapter 13

Learning to Walk

*E*ver since Lilo was born in 1921, Gertrud had to curb the tendency to be overprotective of her. Problems were not so apparent when she was an infant, but by the time she was one and a half years old, Lilo had yet to walk. She was in obvious pain with every attempt. After a series of tests, it was determined that she had been born with dislocated hips, necessitating that her legs be put into casts from the waist down in a straddle configuration. Since she was an otherwise healthy and growing baby, every six weeks the cast had to be removed under light anesthesia and a new one put on in order to allow her small frame to grow normally. This continued for a whole year, during which time, with Lilo's father, Walter, often away on business, the burden of carrying Lilo around and caring for her rested on Gertrud. She would routinely take her to the clinic on a streetcar since the family did not own an automobile, a luxury in those times affordable only for the very wealthy in Germany.

One day, after entering the streetcar for a scheduled clinic visit, Gertrud overheard a woman whispering to another passenger, "There is that poor woman again carrying her two children with only one head!"

Upon hearing that, Gertrud had to laugh out loud so hard that she almost dropped Lilo. But that remark from a total stranger made her realize that the actual situation was not nearly so bad after all, and that Lilo's physical crisis was one that she would no doubt grow out of. When the cast came off at age two and a half, Lilo emerged thin as a twig and had to learn to walk for the first time. But by the time she started school at age six, she appeared to be a normal, healthy child with a lot of energy.

Thus it was all the more upsetting when at age eleven, just two years after she started attending what in Germany was considered high school, Lilo once again started having symptoms of pain and stiffness in one of her hip joints. She regularly took part in a strenuous high school gym class and had taken up skating, a sport that she enjoyed immensely, but which was accompanied by unavoidable falls and spills. What was at first only a dull ache with accompanying stiffness progressed to outright pain that was getting worse with each passing week. The family consulted many doctors. One doctor recommended massage, which—to Gertrud and Walter's acute worry and dismay—rendered Lilo unable to put weight on the leg at all.

Finally x-rays revealed the dreaded diagnosis. Not only was Lilo's hip dislocated again, but the massage had caused it to break away completely, leaving her leg dangling by the ligaments. This necessitated another eight weeks in a cast, this time in a hospital with weights hanging down from the foot. Visiting hours were only three days a week for two hours each day. Gertrud came to see her at every opportunity and her father dropped in when he could, but no children under twelve years of age were allowed to visit, not even her best friend Rotraut. Lilo often felt homesick and looked forward to the day of her release with great eagerness and longing. If the leg failed to heal in the cast within the allotted eight-week time period, then surgery would be the only option, a prospect that aroused such fear and dread in Gertrud that she prayed more fervently and more often than ever before in her life.

Eight weeks later, everyone heaved a collective sigh of relief when the x-rays showed good, though not total, improvement and Lilo was spared the dreaded surgery. Upon her release, she had to be careful to do very little walking at first and no stair climbing for a couple of months. She was warned to refrain from jumping for the rest of her life.

The Wassull apartment was located on the fourth floor, which meant that upon being released from the hospital, Lilo had to be carried up and down four flights of stairs. When her father was home, the task fell to him, but he was often away on business. Sometimes friends and relatives were on hand to help, including Rotraut's father, who sometimes rushed over to carry Lilo up or down on his back. The weight that Lilo had gained from goodies received while in the hospital, coupled with the enforced inactivity, had packed additional pounds onto her eleven-year-old frame and made her much too heavy for Gertrud to carry. But more often than not, Gertrud insisted on carrying her anyway if no one else was available to assist.

Fortunately the approaching summer vacation made it possible for Lilo and Gertrud to travel to the home of Lilo's grandparents and great-grandmother in Havelberg, the small town where she had spent most of her summer and Easter vacations from age five on. It was a lovely, picturesque, historic locale with its ancient cathedral, built in the twelfth century, standing watch like a silent, stone sentinel high above the sleepy village. Below its protective shelter, the buildings of the town spilled haphazardly down the hillside, surrounded on all sides by the Havel River and town canals.

Of all the places that Lilo frequented during her childhood, Havelberg was the one of which she was most fond. Her grandparents' apartment house was located on a high plateau just outside the town. The windows overlooked gardens in the back, which were tended by the tenants. Across from the apartment house were a dairy where local farmers brought milk to be processed and a small store where milk, butter and cream were sold.

But the most beautiful thing about the location of her grandparents' house was that it was situated on the Lindenallee, a street lined with linden trees. There had been a tradition in Havelberg before World War I that whenever a young woman got married, she would plant a linden tree on the Lindenallee; that was why there were so many of them. In the springtime, when they were all in full bloom and wafting their heavenly scent, Lilo would sometimes stand under those trees with eyes closed, breathing in the heady scent of the multitudes of white blossoms and listening to the buzzing of thousands of hard-working bees overhead. She imagined what it would have been like to be one of those young women planning her wedding day with happy anticipation.

During past vacations in Havelberg, Lilo had usually spent the time playing with her cousin, swimming and fishing in the Havel River with her grandfather, and romping in her grandfather's garden while sampling all of the luscious fruits and vegetables. The summer after her injury, however, she had to forego all of those more active pleasures in favor of more sedentary activities that would allow her hip joint and leg to heal. She delighted in the pampering she received from her grandparents as well as the attention of her great-grandmother, whom she affectionately called "U-oma." U-oma taught Lilo and her cousin needlework, board games and card games, and kept them spellbound with her keen sense of humor and the lengthy poetry she was able to recite from memory.

In the evenings, Grandpa regaled them with stories from his boyhood, something that he had shared in previous summers during regular early morning fishing trips with Lilo.

After a time of storytelling during those fishing outings, he would put a finger to his lips and whisper, "Shhhhh. Fish can only be caught if you are quiet, you know!"

Therefore, his tales during those fishing trips were always interspersed with long periods of companionable silence.

That summer, not needing to be careful of alerting the fish, he related the anecdotes from a bygone era in a booming voice with great gusto and there was much laughter all around. In that warm and pleasant family environment with people who truly cared about her, Lilo, whose curiosity was usually overshadowed by her shyness, found herself opening up to ask many questions and to join in the general hilarity, thereby greatly speeding her healing. By the time school started in August, she was largely recovered and was able to join her classmates in everything except most sports activities. Walking and swimming were the only forms of exercise that Lilo was allowed to engage in from that time forward.

On January 30, 1933, when Lilo was almost twelve years old, Adolf Hitler was sworn in as Reich Chancellor of Germany. That very evening Lilo and Rotraut attended a massive public rally and parade. Both of them were carried away by the enthusiasm of the crowds, and while marching, singing and cheering, they learned the entire "Horst Wessell Song," "Die Fahne Hoch" ("Raise High the Flag") by heart.

Set to a popular folk tune, the lyrics of that militant song were written by an officer of the *Sturmabteilung* (Storm Troopers), Horst Wessell, who was murdered by a member of the Communist party in 1930. Upon his death, Nazi propaganda elevated him to the level of martyr and his song became the anthem of the Nazi movement.[10] As Lilo, Rotraut and thousands of other children took to the streets, they marched with the naive, unquestioning ardor of young people as they sang without thinking, "Millions, full of hope, look up at the swastika / The day breaks for freedom and for bread," and "Soon will fly Hitler-flags over every street / Slavery will last only a short time longer." They sang full of hope and excitement. Could freedom, bread and an end to slavery be anything other than noble ideals? Those children did not know the true context of the song: that the phrase "Raise High the Flag" represented a calculated, brazen refusal on the part of the Nazi Party to uphold the terms of the Versailles Treaty by which the international community had sought to hold Germany accountable for causing World War I. The treaty had mandated massive reparations and extensive loss of German territory as well as severely limiting Germany's military development. The words of the song were merely one more indication that the covert rearmament that Germany had been carrying out since World War I would soon commence more openly and defiantly, seemingly with widespread support from the German people.

Shortly after that, flags displaying swastikas began appearing in front of many houses and from the windows of apartment buildings designating that the residents were members of the Nazi party. Lilo's parents did not join the party, and therefore they had no flag displayed in front of their flat.

The Nazi party brought many changes, including at school. The director of Lilo's school disappeared one day, and on the next, a man wearing an SS uniform appeared in his place. While not often or with regularity, sometimes they were also ordered as a group to stretch out their right arms and yell, "Heil Hitler!"

Lilo sometimes heard her mother expressing hopes that Hitler's rise to power would bring renewed prosperity to Germany, while her father was extremely skeptical of Hitler and all that he stood for, including his promise to turn around the desperate economic situation. Even on the subject of politics, her parents could not reach agreement, and Lilo was forced to stand by in helpless despair while their already turbulent relationship entered a death spiral.

In 1934, after years of increasing stress, alienation and tension, Gertrud and Walter finally divorced. Lilo, at the sensitive and impressionable age of thirteen, was crushed by that distressing development. The lonely sort of ache that she often felt inside could never be filled or assuaged by her mother alone, and since she was an only child, there were no siblings to help ease the longing for strong, stable and happy family ties. But out of the pain and sadness of the irreconcilable rift in her family, she began to form a new central goal for her life, nurturing the most fervent wish for a happy marriage and a harmonious family life in her future. It was what she dreamt of more than anything else—seeing it, hearing it, feeling it and living it long before it ever came to pass.

Chapter 14

School Days End

*S*oon after Gertrud and Walter's divorce, Lilo and her mother moved away from Berlin-Lichtenberg to Wilmersdorf, a western suburb of Berlin. For Lilo, with the breakup of her parents still an open wound, this marked the end of a bitter-sweet chapter in her life, but she refused to give up hope for a reconciliation and cherished a fervent vision of a future with new opportunities for lasting happiness. Gertrud, ever positive, cheerful, resilient and resourceful, set about teaching voice and piano lessons from their apartment in order to provide a more stable and supportive home environment for Lilo. There were many German people who considered piano lessons for children to be essential. Even after World War II started, it was a tradition that many parents insisted on maintaining in order to provide a sense of normalcy and continuity for their children. For Gertrud, it was an important way to earn extra income.

Perhaps most important of all for Gertrud, Lilo and the students as well, was the music itself, which had a way of lifting the spirits and creating a sense of peace and calm even when outer circumstances were chaotic. Lilo enjoyed coming home from school and hearing the beginning students tapping out their halting notes and the more advanced ones playing complex pieces with verve and gusto. When she was feeling down, music made her realize that things were not so bad after all, and when she was already feeling good, her spirit would sprout wings and soar to new, even more joyful heights. Whereas music affected Lilo in such a highly positive way, it was even more the case for Gertrud who had lived and breathed music from a very young age. The piano lessons were interspersed with voice students, so that there was a steady stream of music coming from within the apartment on most days other than Sundays which were set aside as days of rest.

Getting by was still a financial struggle for Gertrud and Lilo, but they were content. Once a month, they even managed to attend an opera or concert, always able to afford only the least expensive seats, but as Lilo often stated, "The music is just as glorious from any seat in the house!"

In the fall of 1934, Lilo began the new school year at the Cecilienschule, a girls' high school in Wilmersdorf. It was during that year that she became aware of the first sinister glimmerings of what the Nazi regime was bringing to pass in Germany, although she was still too young to realize the ultimate ramifications. The death of German Reich President Paul von Hindenburg during the previous month had paved the way for Hitler's rapid attainment of total power. Seemingly positive developments gave the impression that all was well. Economic conditions *did* seem to be improving. Even Lilo could see that the idle and unemployed were disappearing off the streets and out of the city parks and were being put to work, and all boys and girls sixteen and older were ordered to serve for six months in the Reichsarbeitsdienst (Reich Labor Service), where they planted trees to restore forests, built highways, worked on farms and performed other useful service to rebuild the ailing German economy and infrastructure. Lilo, at only thirteen, was too young to take part in any of those programs.

The fanatical political speeches, displays of military might and extremist policies of Hitler and the Nazi Party, including the regular scapegoating of Communists whenever anything went wrong, formed a general backdrop to Lilo's daily life, a sort of set design in the stage play of her existence. Most of it went over her head. She trusted her parents and other people much older than herself to take care of things. But it was against those developments that all of the personal events of her life played out, and eventually, they came to increasingly dominate her life as a citizen of the Reich.

During her school years, whenever there was a major political development or state occasion, Lilo and the other students were herded into an auditorium where lengthy speeches by the Führer were broadcast. For Lilo, they were a mixed blessing. Although they provided a welcome pretext to get out of the classroom for a while, Hitler's speeches were always overly long, at least two and a half to three hours; extremely boring, especially for someone Lilo's age; and always accompanied by escalating histrionics and shouting that made her extremely uneasy. She always wondered, "Why does that man need to shout so much?"

But for Lilo, most sinister of all at the Cecilienschule were her classmates, whom she considered in general to be a bizarre and fanatical group. What alarmed her most was that approximately half of the girls there, while still too young for compulsory membership, had joined as voluntary members of the BDM, Bund Deutscher Mädel (League of German Girls), a young girls' branch of the Hitler Youth movement. Their attitude was what Lilo considered to be one of brainwashed idealism, and they engaged in regular drills as part of their BDM membership. Lilo also found that concepts of God and religion had no place in their vocabulary and way of thinking. The religious fervor that had appeared to be a hallmark of Nazi leadership in earlier years was rapidly falling by the wayside, now revealed as a mere shallow facade for a pervasive underlying nihilism. The prevailing attitudes in the BDM were a reflection of that shift. Put off by the militant activities and cynical, indoctrinated attitudes of the BDM members, Lilo refused to have anything to do with them or with the organization.

When Lilo considered her options for friendships in the other half of the class, she found that most of them were either aristocratic snobs who associated only with others in their own social class, or Jewish girls who, while friendlier than the others, tended to keep their distance for obscure cultural reasons. Nevertheless, it was within the latter group that Lilo managed to strike up a few casual friendships during her years at that school.

Another source of unease for Lilo at the Cecilienschule was the teacher of one of her classes, who had a sadistic habit of singling out certain girls, most notably those of Jewish descent, and ridiculing them in front of the class for irrelevant and arbitrary reasons. One day, Lilo and three of her Jewish friends decided to play a prank on the teacher by ignoring the bell that signaled the end of recess. They remained on the playground instead of joining the class. At length, the teacher ordered them inside and singled out Lilo as the object of her fury, ordering her outside the classroom for a reprimand.

"How could you do such a thing, Liselotte, and with those Jewish girls!" she lashed out at Lilo.

"But one of them is a Christian now!" Lilo objected in a futile attempt at appeasement.

"No matter, she is still Jewish. Conversion cannot change that!"

Despite her general shyness and the teacher's deliberate intimidation, that experience left Lilo feeling more indignant than frightened. She was not aware that shortly before that incident, in September of 1935, the highly anti-Semitic Nuremberg Laws had been put into effect by the Nazi regime. Unfortunately, the persecution would not stop at verbal slights and ridicule.

Lilo's overall negative experience at the school in Wilmersdorf served mainly to elicit a deep longing for her former friends, especially her best friend, Rotraut. In April of 1936, just a month after Nazi troops marched into and occupied the Rhineland, in open defiance of the Treaty of Versailles signed at the close of World War I, Lilo vowed to bid farewell to the Cecilienschule and marched to a different one, transferring instead to the high school in Rummelsburg, East Berlin, where Rotraut and other friends attended. All of them were jubilant to see her again. This entailed three hours of travel per day—half an hour on foot and one hour on the subway each way—but she considered it time well spent. Classes were held on Saturdays as well as weekdays, with Sundays being the only day off. Gertrud, as usual, was concerned about Lilo wearing herself out too much during the back-and-forth routine six days a week. But it worked out well, with Lilo able to do much of her homework on the subway. In view of the nightmare left behind, she never regretted her decision.

The following summer, Lilo's father remarried, thereby permanently uprooting the secret hope that she still cherished deep inside that her parents might reconcile. However, her father remained a significant part of her life, and

Lilo was often invited to the new family home. When a daughter was born to her father and his new wife, Lilo paid frequent visits to play with the baby and to crochet outfits for her new half-sister.

Lilo's father also paid the tuition for her twice-weekly *Tanzstunde* (ballroom-dancing lessons) that commenced at age fifteen. In Berlin society of that time, *Tanzstunde* was a coming-of-age experience that exposed girls and boys to each other's company for the first time—young people who had been segregated into separate schools for all their growing-up years. It was also considered a prerequisite for entrance into polite and refined society. The dance lessons, although closely chaperoned, were undertaken by most young people, including Lilo, with a proud sense of their emerging maturity and responsibility.

Lilo noticed that even the boys seemed to enjoy those lessons. Never having had brothers, Lilo found her first real exposure to boys very surprising. Instead of confirming that they truly were "the enemy," as she and her friends used to regard them, the dancing lessons convinced her that they were human after all, and that their attentions, for the most part, were tolerable and sometimes even highly agreeable. There were many times when Lilo and her partners burst out in irrepressible laughter and merriment as they trampled on each others' feet in an attempt to learn English and Viennese waltzes, the Foxtrot, Tango and Polka. Those lessons came to be a highlight of her weekly routine during the last year of high school.

At age sixteen, Lilo reached another major turning point in her life. It was necessary to make a decision whether to continue for another three years of schooling in order to graduate at the *Abitur* level, which was mainly for students planning to go on to college. Although her grades were good, for Lilo it was a simple decision motivated by financial considerations. She realized full well how difficult it was for her mother to support the two of them on the limited income from the piano and voice lessons along with the modest supplemental income from her father, much less to pay for her ongoing tuition. She decided, therefore, to take early graduation at age sixteen and, after a last summer of freedom spent in Havelberg with her grandparents, she enthusiastically launched herself into the working world to help out with daily expenses.

Lilo's first job was with a large construction company, Hermann Streubel GmbH, where she trained to work in the payroll department. It was a company that received contracts mainly for highway construction and employed several hundred construction workers and about twenty office workers. The pay started out low, but Lilo was very proud when she received her first raise after only six weeks. As part of that job, she was excused from work twice a week between eight o'clock in the morning and one o'clock in the afternoon to take courses in typing, shorthand, bookkeeping and other office skills. Whereas she liked the work, her bosses and the training, she was uncomfortable with the office intrigues, crude jokes and incessant gossip among coworkers. She quit after less than a year, but with few regrets since she had succeeded in polishing her professional skills and boosting her confidence level.

Just before Lilo left that post, in early November of 1938, the infamous Kristallnacht (Night of Broken Glass) was carried out across Germany and parts of Austria, a systematic, two-day pogrom primarily perpetrated by Gauleiters (regional Nazi party leaders), SA storm troopers and SS men armed with sledgehammers and axes, mostly dressed in civilian clothing. Jewish homes, shops, department stores and cemeteries were ransacked and destroyed and over one thousand synagogues were plundered and many set ablaze. Thirty thousand Jews were sent to concentration camps, and at least ninety-six were killed during assaults and beatings. The blame for the destruction was assigned to the victims themselves. Jewish citizens were collectively fined and even more stringent economic and social hardships were imposed on them. Kristallnacht would later come to be considered the beginning of the Holocaust.[11]

After Kristallnacht, Lilo and Gertrud saw that storefronts of local Jewish-owned businesses had been smashed. They heard nothing about beatings, deaths, or concentration camps. They had no idea how widespread the attacks were. German media coverage downplayed the outbursts of violence as isolated, spontaneous pockets of violence rather than the malevolently well-orchestrated, nation-wide anti-Semitic campaign that it actually was. Lilo and Gertrud knew there must be party propaganda mixed in with the news, but it was difficult or even impossible to separate fact from fiction.

Later in November, Lilo secured a new job at the office of Richard Mietke, a Berlin representative for two large companies that supplied paint and lacquer as well as bundles of rags for construction clean-up projects. The family-owned-and-run work environment was much more suited to Lilo's preferences and temperament. She worked hard and quickly made herself indispensable to the Mietke business operations.

At first, Lilo was intimidated by Richard Mietke, who had a tendency to spontaneously lose his temper and yell at her. In the early days of her employment, after listening to Lilo's attempt to deal with a difficult vendor in her usual polite manner, Mietke exploded, "Wassull, you have to put more steam under those guys! You are too 'plum-soft (*pflaumen-weich*)!' With a civil tone like that, you will never get anything accomplished in life!"

But once Lilo noticed that he extended his brusque manner to everyone including customers, vendors and even his wife, it finally dawned on her that his outbursts were not to be taken personally. Sometimes she would even grin to herself over his amusing, albeit unabashedly blunt choice of wording.

The Mietke family business was Lilo's place of employment for the first four and a half years of the war, a time period that she would recall forever after as both a sweet memory and a pervasive and forbidding nightmare.

Chapter 15

On Wings of Song

Music played a central role in Lilo and Gertrud's life in those days. Gertrud not only taught piano and voice lessons, but was engaged in a voice training program herself. Their apartment resounded not only with the simple, halting tunes of the beginning voice and piano students and the more fluid attempts of advanced students, but also with Gertrud's own piano and voice practice sessions.

One of Lilo's favorite leisure time activities was accompanying her mother to her voice lessons. Gertrud had cultivated her exceptionally lovely and well-developed voice from an early age, already singing solo parts in church and school as a child. Formal lessons started in her early teens in German-occupied Poland when an opera conductor from the city opera house in Posen took an active interest in her and began to train her for the opera.

But in 1912, tragedy struck: Gertrud's mother passed away very suddenly from the flu. At the tender age of sixteen, Gertrud found herself in increasingly demanding and restrictive circumstances, with a grieving father to console, three younger sisters to help raise, and a household to oversee. With those responsibilities resting heavily on her young shoulders, she voluntarily postponed her dream of becoming a professional singer and shelved her own grief in order to provide the strong support that her father needed and to help raise her three sisters.

Two years after the bitter blow of her mother's death, the worldwide tragedy of World War I broke out. With four beautiful and vulnerable daughters between the ages of ten and eighteen, all of whom would potentially be in great danger from the Russian forces that had already advanced into East Prussia, Gertrud's father, Carl Röhrich, insisted that they flee westward to Berlin. There, he eventually remarried and family life stabilized. When the Russians in East Prussia were defeated by Germany, the family ventured back to their home in Posen and were able to resume much of their former life including Gertrud's voice training. But the war was still raging and the Russians advanced again. It soon became apparent that the Röhrich family would have to flee yet again. The family lost everything when they fled to Berlin for the second time, never again to return to Posen, which by the end of World War I had become part of Poland.

Singing remained a source of great joy and deep consolation for Gertrud. For many years it served to fill the growing void in her marriage and then assuaged the pain of her divorce. Singing also provided a creative outlet for her high energy and remained a goal towards which she would continue to aspire throughout her life.

After years of lessons from a fellow voice teacher in Berlin, it was in 1936, when Lilo was fifteen years old, that Gertrud met her master teacher. At the time, Gertrud was employed as a door-to-door saleswoman for a company that manufactured girdles. One day in a new neighborhood that she had not solicited before, she walked up to a door and noticed a small sign next to it: "Madame Frieda Henke, *Opersängerin*" (Opera Singer). She rang the bell and a tall, stately woman answered the door. After confirming that the woman was indeed none other than the opera singer, Frieda Henke, Gertrud commenced a verbal sales pitch not only for the girdles, but also to promote her own ability as a singer. As two free spirits joyfully recognized one another, a bond was established almost instantaneously. Frieda invited Gertrud in and even asked her to sing something for her.

Gertrud soon discovered that Madame Frieda Henke was a highly gifted singer who had commanded the Düsseldorf Opera as soprano prima donna with her powerful, well-trained voice in the first two decades of the twentieth century. When her husband passed away, about twenty years prior to the meeting with Gertrud, Frieda found to her dismay that her financial situation was not as stable as hoped, and she began to supplement her income by accepting voice students.

When Frieda heard Gertrud sing for the first time, she commented, "You have what I would describe as a lyric coloratura soprano voice. Very lovely. With additional training and better breathing technique, it could be even better. Do yourself the favor of not singing or speaking for two full weeks. This will give your vocal chords a chance to rest and recover."

Upon receiving Gertrud's promise to follow these instructions, Frieda led her to a hassock and made her sit, personally placing Gertrud's feet together and her hands one over the other in her lap.

"Now, you are no doubt already feeling more concentrated, yes? Tell me, what would you do if you were in a large, very noisy hall and you were supposed to be a speaker?"

Gertrud replied without hesitation, "I would say as loud as I could, 'Pssst, silence, please!'"

"Very good! So now, I want you to only do the 'pssssss' without the 'tee' and breathe it out with a smile on your face for as long as you can, but do not force it. Like this!"

She demonstrated the technique herself, breathing out the "pssssss" for over one and a half minutes while maintaining a radiant, unwavering smile.

Gertrud tried it, but was only able to breathe it out for twenty seconds and without smiling.

"Do this faithfully three times in the morning and three times in the evening, always in a room with the windows open for fresh air, and I guarantee that your breathing will improve very quickly."

Gertrud faithfully followed instructions, even though two full weeks without speaking was a formidable test of her discipline and self-restraint as well as a serious hindrance in her work as a salesperson. During those two weeks, she managed to sell very few girdles. But it was a testimony to the strength of her determination and desire to advance her singing that she managed to follow the orders of this new teacher, whom she already recognized as a vital, emerging force in her life.

When Gertrud returned after two weeks for her first official lesson, she was able to sustain the breathing technique for almost a minute. Frieda praised her for her rapid progress and then gave her some voice exercises to perform daily. After that initial chance meeting, Gertrud became a regular student and soon was sought after for solo parts in concerts at local churches.

By the time Lilo accompanied Gertrud for the first time to meet Frieda Henke, her mother's remarkable voice had become her teacher's pride and joy: Gertrud was Frieda's star pupil.

A still beautiful widow who adamantly refused to divulge her true age, Frieda Henke was dramatic, artsy and somewhat bohemian. Her typical style of dress— long, flowing skirts, a white silk scarf tied at the neck, and long gray hair coiled in a chignon—was romantic, though old-fashioned for the 1930s, and Lilo's impression was that she might have been in her sixties at the time of their first meeting. Frieda was friendly and welcoming towards Lilo, happy at last to meet the daughter of her most gifted student.

Lilo strolled around the apartment looking at all of the mementos while listening to her mother sing. The large, sunny rooms were full of photos and memorabilia from Frieda's years in the opera. On a side table was a photo from the early 1900s depicting her in the lead role as Elsa in Wagner's romantic fairy-tale opera, *Lohengrin*. Her dramatic pose and expression in the photo, along with the elegant gown and long, flowing hair, evoked a more romantic, bygone era.

Gertrud was first put through three repetitions of her breathing exercises as usual. After a few vocal exercises as a warmup, she began singing an aria from

La Boheme by Puccini while Frieda accompanied her on the upright piano. Lilo sat down to listen. Of all the pieces that she heard her mother practicing between voice lessons, it was her favorite.

As Gertrud finished the piece, Frieda gave the final note on the piano a triumphant flourish and stood up, applauding.

"Bravo, Trudelchen!" using an affectionate nickname for Gertrud. "We will hear you singing major solo parts somewhere soon, mark my words!" And then, looking in Lilo's direction, she added, "Next, we have to see about training Lilo to sing as well. Beautiful voices often run in families!"

Lilo smiled and nodded, even though inside, she was not at all sure, due to her innate shyness, that she was cut out for singing. But she already liked and respected *Omi* (Grandma) Henke, and wanted to make her, as well as her parents, proud of her.

For Gertrud, a few small singing engagements came through once in a while, but not the "big break" that she was hoping for to establish a singing career. But the near future would bring major upheavals far more devastating than those that Gertrud experienced during World War I, and within a few short years, all such hopes and dreams would once again need to be indefinitely shelved.

Chapter 16

When Sirens Sound

On a beautiful, late summer day in September 1939, Lilo and Gertrud were helping Lilo's great aunts, Hedwig and Hanna, get settled in their new apartment in Berlin. Lilo was enjoying the feel of the sun shining through the large windows as she carried boxes and small items from the back porch into the apartment. She set a box down on a side table and pushed a strand of hair from the side of her face. In anticipation of an active day, she had pinned her hair up, but a few wisps and tendrils of her long blonde hair kept obstinately insisting on their freedom.

Each item that Lilo carried in and arranged in the new residence, an imposing luxury apartment in a building with an elegant stucco exterior, was already invested with memories from the many wonderful times she had spent with her great aunts in their previous home in Lübeck with its stylish terrace overlooking beautifully landscaped and manicured gardens. Now, at age eighteen, Lilo had a wealth of happy memories from times spent with them and the pleasant anticipation of many more to come.

Lilo carried a box of china and porcelain from the back hallway to the dining room, and began carefully removing the pieces from their packing to place them in a glass-front china cabinet. In an adjoining room she could hear her mother and her two aunts laughing and talking animatedly as they arranged furniture and household items. There was the sound of furniture being dragged, laughter, then more dragging.

Next she heard the sound of the radio. Not everyone was able to afford a radio in those days, but both women had worked for many years in the German postal service and were financially comfortable. For as long as Lilo could remember, they had retained a live-in cook and housekeeper, and even hired a cleaning woman for heavier jobs twice per month. Unimaginable luxury! And every time the great aunts came for a visit to Berlin, they invited Lilo and Gertrud out for dinner at a fine restaurant, knowing that the younger women were not often able to afford such a treat.

The aunts had finally both retired, and Hedwig, the older of the two, had developed a heart condition that required travel at regular intervals to see a specialist in Berlin. It was upon his advice that they moved from Lübeck, a city close to the Baltic Sea with a harsh climate, to Berlin, a city graced with much milder conditions beneficial to someone in failing health. For her part, Lilo was very glad that they had moved closer. Ever since age thirteen when her parents divorced, Hanna and Hedwig had been part of the extended family that gave her a sense of security and belonging.

Lilo unwrapped another mystery bundle to find one of her favorite items from her aunts' collection, one that always delighted her with its fanciful pose and attire—a Meissen gypsy girl figurine. The languidly reclining porcelain figure had flowing dark hair held back by red flowers. Her dress was exquisitely crafted—a lacy pink crinoline skirt with a snug-fitting red and green bodice topped with white ruffles. Defiantly shaking a tambourine over her head, the gypsy's attitude always struck Lilo as one of unrestrained joy and freedom. Lilo often wondered whether she could ever feel so free, so joyful and so unrestrained. Perhaps someday? A tantalizing possibility.

As she reached forward to place the figurine in the cabinet, she came dangerously close to dropping it as Aunt Hanna, the younger of the two aunts, burst in exclaiming breathlessly, "Come quickly, Lilo! The Führer has invaded Poland! We are at war!"

That moment would remain indelibly etched upon Lilo's memory for her entire life—her feelings and expression at that moment, the attitude of her outstretched hand holding the Meissen gypsy girl—a moment frozen in time as if captured by a cosmic camera. Within a mere instant, an overwhelming certainty washed over her that life as she had known it would never again be the same. She was not yet aware that the figurine would also never again hold the same fascination for her, and that the longed-for feelings of unrestrained joy and freedom would not be a part of her future for some time to come.

Later that afternoon, Lilo allowed herself to luxuriate in the large, elegant tub in her aunts' spacious and very modern bathroom. It was the most modern bath that Lilo had ever seen, and, ah, what a pleasure to soak in that tub! It was partially sunken into the floor and had hot and cold running water. Where Lilo and her mother lived, there was only a much smaller, less comfortable tub with a spray attachment for washing hair and a large cylindrical water heater lit manually from underneath—not a tub like this one that welcomed her, enfolded her and invited her to stay a while. Lilo settled back with a sigh of deep contentment and reflected on the day's events.

War had been declared, it was true, but the Führer had clearly stated, "No planes will reach Berlin." At that moment, relaxing in the warm, scented bath with the late summer sun streaming through the tall, open window, it did not seem at all possible that Germany could be at war.

That very night, Lilo awakened with heart pounding from a deep sleep as the deafening sound of sirens shattered the dead-of-night stillness. She thought at first that it was only a bad dream, but the sound of feverish activity and rapid footsteps in the hall and on the stairs told her that this was not the sort of nightmare from which she would awaken. She lurched panic-stricken out of bed just as the clock struck two in the morning, and stumbled around to find a coat to throw on over her nightgown. As she grabbed a pair of shoes and a few nearby belongings, she could hear her mother trying to do the same in the dark. The statements from German leaders—"No planes will reach Berlin!"—had lulled them both into thinking that it was not necessary to pack any bags or make preparations.

Gertrud was already standing at the doorway and yelling, "Mach schnell, Lilochen! Mach schnell!" ("Hurry up!")

Within a few minutes they joined throngs of people on the stairway, heading down to the cellar—a cheerless, cold and barren place, though still a refuge. Families were already huddled together on the floor and on wooden crates hurriedly placed around the shelter area to provide makeshift seating. At first there were nervous whispers, then silence as they settled in for what they hoped and expected would only be a brief, unwelcome interruption of their night's sleep.

Occasional talking in low tones could be heard. In one corner there was the sound of brief, nervous laughter. Most were taking the air raid lightly. There was no sound of planes overhead or bombs dropping, and rather than fear, the general attitude was one of annoyance for the loss of precious sleep. Less than an hour later, the "all clear" sounded: it had been merely a drill. Tired but relieved, people collected themselves, their children and their possessions and trudged back up the stairs from whence they had come. Gertrud remarked to Lilo that they should make it a point to pack suitcases with their possessions before another day went by.

Once again in their apartment, Lilo was dimly aware of the clock striking three as her head hit the pillow. The air raid alarm was behind her, but the other alarm, the one to wake her up for work, would go off all too soon.

None of Berlin's citizens—least of all Lilo and Gertrud—had any inkling of the growing nightmare that these air raids would become and the dark threat that would soon descend on the populace of Berlin.

Chapter 17

The Crossing Letters

Despite Rolf's promise to correspond with Lilo after his return to military service, weeks went by in January 1941 without a letter from him. Every day when Lilo returned home from work, she inquired of her mother whether there was any mail for her and every day the answer was no—at least, nothing from Rolf.

One day Lilo was in the middle of a voice lesson at the home of Frieda Henke, lessons that she had finally begun despite her shyness a few years prior. Lilo had come to view Frieda not only as an exceptional voice teacher, but also as a trusted confidante and friend. Frieda was adept at inspiring her and encouraging her to identify and strive for what was most important in her life rather than investing herself, her time and her precious energy on goals that were beneath her.

Lilo was singing while Frieda accompanied her on the upright piano, providing frequent prompts and pointers. They started over several times due to mistakes by Lilo. When the mistakes persisted, Frieda banged a sudden sour chord, stood up from the piano and walked over to Lilo. Taking her by the hand, she led her gently to the sofa.

"Now Lilochen, I have known you long enough to know when something is wrong and I'm afraid that a sick bird can't sing very well. So tell Omi Henke what is bothering you and then perhaps we can resume our lesson with greater success."

Lilo spilled out her story about Rolf and how she was quite sure she had met the man that she hoped to marry. However, in spite of his promises to correspond, she had received not a single letter and she felt that social convention prevented her from initiating the correspondence.

"Not so fast," Frieda interrupted. "Whatever happened to that other young man you were dating, Krafft Jäger-something-or-other? The young man with the title? I know you were not particularly impressed by his family's nobility, but as I recall, you had been seeing each other for quite some time."

"Oh, yes, Krafft and I were an item for two and a half years, but I broke it off just shortly before meeting Rolf. It was a mutually agreed-upon parting of the ways with no hard feelings."

"But you always spoke so well of him."

"Yes, I suppose I did. I liked many things about him. He is handsome and romantic with an outgoing nature and so forth. But he could also be pretentious what with all his talk of nobility and wanting to get the family title back that was dissolved after World War I."

Lilo paused.

"I think partly my fear was that Krafft would eventually become like his father—totally pretentious, theatrical and snobbish. But even if he didn't, I would still have a snob for a father-in-law. That was not to my liking. Besides, something was missing with Krafft."

"And this Rolf, are you so sure after only a few meetings that he is the right one?"

Lilo nodded.

"How do you know?"

Lilo placed her hand over her heart, "I know here. Whenever I think of him, my heart sings."

Frieda responded with a mischievous and enigmatic smile, "Well child, there are many ways of initiating things that are not so obvious. Let me tell you of a few from my own experience."

Later that afternoon, Lilo was occupied at her writing desk.

"Better to do something and know the answer, rather than to do nothing and forever wonder," Lilo murmured to herself as she drew a large question mark on a piece of paper, added a dramatic touch with a red colored pencil, and inserted it into an envelope addressed to Rolf.

The very next day she received a long letter from Rolf that had obviously crossed her question mark in the mail, in which he boldly addressed her by her first name and requested permission to use the familiar pronoun "Du."

She waited. A second letter arrived:

Dear Fräulein Wassull,

I must apologize for addressing you by your first name and "Du" in my previous letter. It was an assumption on my part that you would be willing to continue our friendship. I see by now from your very deliberate question mark that I was sadly mistaken.

Regretfully,
Rolf

Lilo immediately took out pen and paper and wrote him a long letter of explanation and reassurance in which she also related some recent experiences:

Dear Rolf,

All is a misunderstanding due to ill-timed letters crossing in the mail. After hearing nothing from you for several weeks after our last meeting, the question mark was my way to find out the reason for your silence. Your first long and descriptive letter that crossed with my question mark answered all of my questions and more. I am happy that you are not meant to be "crossed out" of my life and thoughts.

My life has been busy too, but unlike you with your interesting and absorbing studies, my preoccupation has increasingly been with the air raids that are robbing us of energy and sleep. Thank goodness, even though bombs sometimes drop, the air raids are more of an annoyance than a real danger so far.

Lilo once again awoke from a fitful sleep to the wail of sirens. In the cold and dark, she and Gertrud, both disheveled from sleep, scrambled without speaking to grab the clothing and suitcases that now stood packed and waiting in front of the door. Lilo's suitcase contained the letters from Rolf, which had become much-prized possessions, as well as jewelry, clothing, important papers, shoes, toiletries and other necessities that she would need if their apartment were to be completely bombed out. They could barely see as they struggled into shoes and coats and then scrambled down four flights of stairs to the basement shelter. It was already crowded with fellow tenants quickly sinking into the few mattresses, chairs and other odds and ends of furnishings that were now left in place around the clock to provide meager comfort for the nightly air raids.

Children, cranky from being so rudely awakened, whimpered and complained; a baby cried; someone coughed uncontrollably. All were huddled, shivering. Lilo read her watch by the light of a match. It was thirteen minutes past ten; still early. She settled in to listen and wait. They could hear the bombers flying overhead and an occasional explosion in the distance, but nothing nearby.

With a reassuring tone, Lilo said, "All right, Mother, it is all for a good cause. We have to trust our leaders and hope that in the end, all of this will be worth it."

Leaning against each other, she and her mother closed their eyes and tried to sleep. The "all clear" sounded. It was just past midnight, a much earlier reprieve than usual. They returned to their apartment and fell exhausted into bed, but the sirens went off again an hour later, signaling a repeat trip down to the cellar. By the time the final "all clear" sounded, it was almost time for Lilo and Gertrud to prepare for the workday ahead.

Later that morning, Lilo headed via subway to Berlin-Steglitz, and arrived at the three-story residential villa that housed her boss's offices as well as the residence he shared with his wife, son, daughter, son-in-law and grandson. Lilo was cheerfully and efficiently answering the telephone, taking care of correspondence, inventorying, billing, placing orders and performing general secretarial tasks when Richard Mietke walked in, followed by his faithful German Shepherd Arno.

After giving the dog a friendly scratch behind the ears and promising him a walk during her lunch hour, Lilo looked up at Richard and told him the shipment of paint supplies from the factory in Munich was late again.

Mietke grabbed his hair and proceeded to pace back and forth while pouring out a vocal tirade: "Didn't you tell them how critical that shipment is? That we have an important contract to fill by the end of the week?" he demanded. "You have been working here for almost two years, Lilo! You should know how to handle these unreliable vendors by now!"

Lilo handled the situation calmly but firmly, and, as expected, Mietke was soon on to the next item on the agenda, the tirade all but forgotten and Arno continuing to follow him about like a shadow.

His wife entered, smiled at Lilo and shook her head. "Is he in a shouting mood again?"

With her was her grandson, Peter, a little boy of about two and a half years old.

"Tatta Rulle Appi!" he cried in his baby-lisp, the nickname he had adopted for Lilo, and ran to her with arms out-stretched.

Lilo took him briefly on her lap and allowed him to play with the pencils and other supplies on her desk before resuming her work.

Lilo was treated like one of the family, and in the summertime, she was often invited out to the terrace to join the family for ice cream, a luxury that, although diluted, was not yet rationed. For Lilo, ice cream was already a rare pleasure that would become only a tantalizing memory in the years to come.

Chapter 18

The Zoppot Idyll

In mid-summer of 1941, Rolf invited Lilo to travel to Zoppot, a stylish spa and resort town on the Baltic coast near Danzig, to spend some vacation time with him and Hans Dieter, one of his university friends. Lilo rented a room from a local family, only a five-minute walk from the beautiful, sandy beach. This was, by her standards, an extravagant expenditure, but one that she considered worthwhile, given that the time spent together might help to establish how she and Rolf felt about each other. Each day, after his daily lectures and classes were over, Rolf rode over on his bicycle to meet her. They spent twelve memorable, sun-drenched days swimming, sunbathing and sailing on Hans's sailboat.

Since Lilo's room did not come with kitchen privileges and neither she nor Rolf had much cash to spare, meals were simple. A bratwurst or some smoked fish purchased from a street vendor and eaten at the beach or on a park bench was the norm, but they managed occasionally to have a sandwich or a bowl of soup and a roll at a restaurant or open-air cafe.

During the sailing trips, carefree afternoons spent on the beach and meals taken together, Rolf and Lilo finally had the leisure to find out more about their common interests and backgrounds. They found cause for laughter and merriment in the fact that not only had they both been raised on stories from the children's picture book, *Der Struwwelpeter* (*Shock-Headed Peter*), but they both had worried about the *Daumenlutscher* (Thumb-Sucker) story. Rolf in Latvia, Lilo in Germany—both anxious about the same evil man with shears bursting into their rooms and exacting cold-blooded vengeance on their defenseless thumbs!

Rolf and Lilo began to open up about their hopes, dreams, fears and aspirations. It was an exhilarating time of deepening their relationship, reveling in each other's presence and allowing the feelings for each other to grow. Those days were made even more memorable by the glorious sunsets and the changeable surf—some days raging, other days just lapping the shore with a gentle, soothing rhythm. And beyond the sparkling white sand, the dramatic surf and the watercolor sunsets, the horizon beckoned soft and sultry, offering promises of adventure and yet-to-be-revealed mysteries.

One day while they were on Hans's boat, Lilo told Rolf that she had been born with dislocated hips, which necessitated her being in a body cast from the waist down at age one and a half for a whole year and then again at age eleven for eight weeks. She commented that as a result of those unusual circumstances in her early life, along with the trauma she suffered as a result of her parents' unhappy marriage and eventual divorce, her mother had a tendency to worry too much about her. She explained to him that due to the troubled home life and her parents' frequent disagreements, most of her experience of normal family life had been from times spent with friends and her extended family of aunts and grandparents.

"I long ago decided that there is nothing more important to me than a happy home life," she stated, in a tone of voice that was at once firm, but also held a note of shyness.

Rolf listened attentively to Lilo's story with his arm around her. When Lilo envisioned that "happy home life," did she see him in it with her, he wondered? He felt protective of her and sensed that something important was happening. A turning point of sorts had been reached. Was it love?

For Lilo too, the still waters of affection for Rolf were deepening. One afternoon, Rolf was exhausted after pulling an all-nighter working on a class project and fell fast asleep on the beach. Dark clouds appeared and it looked as though a storm was brewing, but Lilo did not have the heart to wake him. As it was getting chilly, she tenderly put her beach towel over him and let him sleep on. Sitting there watching the dark clouds move in, she was overcome by an overwhelming sense of certainty that their futures would be intertwined. The thought left her feeling almost giddy with happiness, but underneath the giddiness flowed a calm, peaceful river of contentment.

As it turned out, Hans was also interested in Lilo and had developed quite a crush on her, but Rolf's positive, unsuspecting nature made him oblivious to his friend's romantic dilemma. During one of their days on the beach, Hans handed his camera to a passerby and asked him to take a photograph of the three of them. He was acutely aware of Lilo sitting between Rolf and himself. Her face glowed with the most beautiful, radiant smile and he had a hard time taking his eyes off her even though he was painfully aware that, while kind and considerate towards him too, Lilo had eyes only for Rolf.

When the vacation was over, Hans gave Rolf a print of the photo, saying with a smile, "A rose between two thorns, Rolf, a true gem. I would make every effort to get to know her better if I were you. And it's too bad I'm not you, because if I were, I would not want to let her go!"

The Walter Wassull postage stamp store (Gertrud and
Walter standing behind two employees), Berlin, 1920

Gertrud at the park with Lilo (age one),
Berlin-Lichtenberg, 1922

Lilo (age two) with Gertrud and Walter, 1923

Gertrud and Lilo at the park, 1924

Lilo (age three) sitting near the
family's *Kacheloffen* (tile stove), 1924

Lilo (age four), 1925

Gertrud and Lilo (age five) at the park, 1926

Lilo (center, age ten) with school friends including Rotraut (third from right), 1931

Lilo in a harlequin costume at the photography studio, 1931

Lilo at the beach (age ten), 1931

Lilo at the photography studio, 1931

Lilo on her confirmation day (age 15), 1936

Lilo (right) with Rotraut (age 14), 1935

Lilo's official *Kennkarte* (Reich ID), September 1940

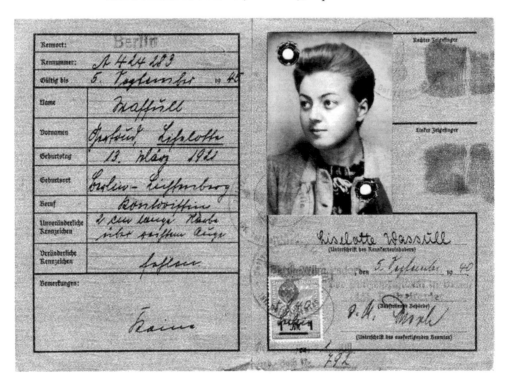

Gertrud Wassull, 1940

Liselotte (Lilo) Wassull (age 19), 1940

Left: Madame Frieda Henke, Gertrud and Lilo's voice teacher and former soprano prima donna of the Düsseldorf Opera, shown in the lead role of Elsa in Wagner's *Lohengrin,* early 1900s

Hans Dieter, Lilo and Rolf at the beach at Zoppot, summer 1941

Part III

SURVIVAL

"Though I sit in darkness, the Lord shall be a light to me."

—Micah 7:8

Chapter 19

Drafted into the Luftwaffe

In June of 1941, at an auxiliary landing strip at the University of Danzig, Rolf and the other members of the Akaflieg were receiving additional soaring flight training. There were a number of tense moments. One day, a tow plane barely got off the ground fast enough to clear a power line at the end of the runway. It was a close call. With only a moment to spare, the pilot released the rope to send the tow plane gliding under and the sailplane passing over the power line. They both landed safely in a nearby farmer's field.

One day they stopped their activities to witness massive formations of bomber squadrons flying northeastward. Shortly after that, nighttime air raid warnings began to be heard and finally, the news of the invasion of the Soviet Union by Germany was broadcast over the radio with great fanfare. The invasion was carried out under the code name of "Barbarossa," a reference to "Red Beard," the nickname of Emperor Frederick I, who had attempted to unify the Germanic states in the twelfth century.

About a month later, when German troops finished driving the Soviets out of Latvia, there were also vivid reports of the atrocities committed by the Soviets against Latvian citizens, including in the Dutzmanns' home city of Liepaja, confirming Rolf's worst-case-scenario fears of what might have happened if he and the family had stayed in Latvia. Hundreds of Soviet dissidents and prominent Latvian citizens had been executed and many more were exiled to Siberia. Those reports were soon confirmed by a letter received from Aunt Paula. She reported that the relatives were all safe, but many friends and acquaintances had simply disappeared. As for the family home, most of it had been requisitioned by the occupying Soviet forces, reducing the family's quarters to two cramped rooms on the second floor. What Rolf did not hear about until after the war's end were the atrocities carried out by German troops against Latvian citizens, most notably the systematic annihilation of the country's Jewish population.

Rolf spent his last university break at home in Berlin. By that time, his father had been drafted into the Wehrmacht (German Army; literally, "defensive force") with the rank of captain due to his previous engineering officer status in the Latvian army, and was assigned to an artillery proving ground with offices in Berlin. His duties kept him occupied away from home for six days a week.

One afternoon Rolf and Maria were sitting in the parlor. Maria, who had mastered the art of creating exquisite needlework from a young age, was engaged in crocheting an intricate lace table cover while Rolf, in between questions from his mother, was reading the *Berliner Illustrierte* (*Berlin Illustrated*), a popular Berlin newspaper.

"She works for a living?" asked Maria, after hearing of Lilo's daily trips to an office in Berlin.

"It is something for her to do in these times to get her mind off the war," replied Rolf, turning a page and not raising his eyes from the paper. "It is not her intention to work indefinitely."

"And her mother?" asked Maria, allowing the needlework to fall to her lap. "What does she do and how are they supported?"

There was an awkward pause, as Rolf looked up from the paper. The conversation was going badly and he struggled to disguise his discomfort.

"Lilo's parents are divorced and her mother is forced to work also, but I understand that she is a gifted soprano. We will see her on stage someday according to what Lilo tells me. In addition she is a talented pianist. There is no lack of cultural pursuits between them, with Lilo also studying voice under the same teacher."

"I see," was Maria's only reply as she turned her attention back to the table cover in her lap.

Her lips were set in a thin line, and it was obvious not only that she disapproved but that her thoughts were far from her needlework.

An awkward silence followed, interrupted only by the rustling of the paper and the occasional clicking of the crochet needle against Maria's rings.

"I feel that I need to touch on the subject of Berlin women, Rolf. My impression of them is that they are exceedingly shallow and just out to get married to any eligible man."

Not able to summon up a suitable reply, Rolf remained silent. He knew by his mother's tone that the subject would not be open to further discussion in any case.

In late December of 1941, when Rolf finally graduated from the university with a bachelor of science degree in aeronautical engineering, it was a time of mixed emotions rather than celebration. His only opportunity to avoid the draft had run its course. Worse still, the Axis powers had attacked both Soviet Russia on the Eastern Front and the United States at Pearl Harbor, further casting doubt in Rolf's mind of the wisdom or purpose of the German war effort.

Rolf's lifelong dream of an engineering degree at last fulfilled, the future, which should have looked full of promise, stretched ahead with menacing uncertainty, and the war that he had hoped would be over before he completed his studies was only showing signs of escalating.

Rolf was at his parents' apartment in Berlin when his draft notice arrived. He ripped open the letter, then sat down hard, staring in shocked disbelief at the notice. It stated unequivocally that he was being drafted into a Luftwaffe light antiaircraft unit that would be supporting and defending ground troops. The assignment not only violated the Führer's orders that members of the NSFK, especially those with glider training, were only to be drafted into the flying branch of the Luftwaffe; it also dramatically increased the likelihood of Rolf being wounded or killed.

He immediately asked Ernst to find out who was responsible for the Luftwaffe draft choices, and made an appointment. During the meeting, after hearing Rolf's story and finding out about Rolf's father's officer status, the officer in charge tore up the draft notice and called the draft office in Danzig from whence Rolf's order had been issued. He told the officer there in no uncertain terms to assign Rolf to the Fliegertruppe, the flying branch of the Luftwaffe. Afterwards he commented to Rolf that he suspected the misassignment might have been a deliberate retaliatory action by someone at the Danzig office in response to his previous success in postponing the draft with his student status. Rolf thought of the hostile registration official at the university, but kept those suspicions to himself.

A few days later, Rolf met with Lilo. In a halting manner that he realized was not very convincing, he told her that life seemed precarious to him since the receipt of his draft notice and that all of his time and energy would henceforth have to be directed to surviving his military service. He stated that he was afraid to get more seriously involved with her due to the war, not mentioning his deep-seated fear of commitment or his mother's objections. Lilo stared at him in stunned, heartbroken silence as he broke off their relationship.

Shortly after Rolf's abrupt announcement, Lilo received a letter from his university friend, Hans Dieter, asking if she would be willing to see him now and then. Lilo, her emotions still in turmoil, responded politely but firmly, stating that she did not feel free to do so. Lilo was living her daily life on automatic, going through the motions, trying not to allow the sadness to penetrate too deeply and keeping a glimmer of hope alive that Rolf might eventually change his mind.

With the drastic impending changes due to the draft ever present on his mind, Rolf did not dwell on the situation with Lilo for long. He received his revised draft notice with orders to report to an airbase northeast of Berlin.

The barracks were new, with clean restrooms and six to eight bunk beds per room. Basic training started with drilling, weapons training, and endless sets of pushups and squats. Rolf fell into bed exhausted each night, only to be roughly awakened before daybreak each morning to start the routine all over again.

Especially harsh treatment was reserved for college graduates, most of whom, like Rolf himself, were ill-suited and ill-prepared for the physical and psychological rigors of military life. A fellow college graduate who failed to hit the target at the shooting range was punished by being forced to stand with his knees bent and his carbine held on his outstretched arms until he collapsed from exhaustion. He was then immediately ordered to attempt shooting at the target again. He missed again due to fatigue, stress and overexertion, upon which the disciplinary action was repeated. Rolf's observation was that such callous mistreatment never improved performance, but rather caused fear and resentment, thereby rendering improvement even less likely. He considered that an eye examination or special attention to this recruit might have been more useful in improving his performance. He felt totally alienated and out of place in the military, disagreeing with much that he saw and experienced.

Eight interminable weeks were required for basic training, and Rolf marked off each day on a calendar. No Christmas leave was allowed; it would be his first Christmas away from home and family. He contracted laryngitis and felt despondent, homesick and trapped.

In late January of 1942, as the time approached for Rolf to be transferred elsewhere for specialized training, scarlet fever broke out in his barracks. He and the other recruits were quarantined for four weeks. Not allowed to leave the building, they had nothing to do but eat, sleep and reflect. For the first time since being called up for military service, Rolf had the leisure to reconsider his feelings for Lilo. He read and reread her earlier letters, thought about their times together, and decided to resume correspondence with her. He was delighted and relieved at her gracious responsiveness and began to eagerly await mail call, the only daily event that served to alleviate the monotony of his enforced inactivity.

Once the quarantine was over, Rolf left for specialized aircraft mechanic training at a Junkers engine assembly plant in a town 120 kilometers (75 miles) southwest of Berlin. After an initial training period learning about Junkers JUMO 211 fuel-injected and supercharged gasoline engines and JUMO 205 diesel engines, he and the other fifty recruits were put to work on the assembly line, where an engine per hour was produced, as well as in the engine-testing protocol conducted prior to government inspection. In addition, they were enrolled in aeronautics and basic engine theory classes. Due to Rolf's prior college education in aeronautical engineering, he was also assigned to the training department to take part in special equipment design.

In general, life at the training facility was reasonably pleasant even though the accommodations were primitive. Rolf and the other soldiers were housed in a former school gymnasium in the center of town. On workdays, meals were taken in the plant cafeteria; on Saturdays and Sundays, dinner was delivered from the local airbase kitchen. But in early 1942, food was still plentiful, and being quartered in the center of town afforded the advantage of a variety of activities during weekend leave.

Rolf finished the specialized training at the top of his class, upon which his unit received orders to proceed to the Adlershof airbase near Berlin for assignment to combat units. Upon arrival, about half of the men in his group were assigned to the Africa Corps and were issued tropical gear and uniforms. By this time, Germany had won decisive victories in Africa under General Erwin Rommel.

To Rolf's immense relief, he was assigned instead to the Höhere Fliegertechnische Schule (Advanced Flight Technical School) at Jüterbog, southwest of Berlin, where he was to be employed as an instructor in aircraft engines. After undergoing additional training at Leipzig, he was assigned the task of teaching aircraft design, aerodynamics and engine theory as well as supervising the work of trainees. He regularly reported back to the Advanced Flight Technical School about student progress. This was work well-suited to Rolf's interests and abilities, but unfortunately his circumstances would soon change for the worse again as the German war effort itself deteriorated.

While on Christmas leave in Berlin, Rolf met Lilo's mother, Gertrud, for the first time. She immediately warmed to him with her unique blend of friendly enthusiasm and motherliness, and he appreciated that she actively sought ways to engage him in conversation and to put him at ease.

Lilo, in turn, was invited to meet Rolf's parents and his sister Ruth, who had arrived home from a medical training center east of Berlin where she was studying to be a lab technician. Rolf warned Lilo that his mother could be difficult, but after finding out that his father's birthday was the same day as her own—March 13—Lilo decided that must be a promising sign. Still, she could not help but wonder what to expect from the meeting. Warm welcome, worst nightmare or somewhere in between? Endless scenarios played like motion pictures through her mind.

Chapter 20

A Second Serving of Käsetorte

As usual, Maria had outdone herself. The table was beautifully set with Rosenthal china—a yellow and gray rose pattern specially ordered for her by Ernst many years before as a gift. Silverware engraved with the family initials and a hand-embroidered linen tablecloth with matching napkins rounded out the table decor. From the very first introductions, however, the occasion was strained due to Maria's marked silence and cold, disapproving attitude. It was Ernst who was friendly, gallant and accommodating and who sought to ease Lilo's distress with his dry humor and endearing manner.

Real coffee, not ersatz, was served, and Maria had baked *Käsetorte*, a delicious cheesecake that was one of her many specialties. Lilo had not had *Käsetorte* in a long time due to wartime rationing. In fact, she could not recall ever having had one so delectable. She finished the first piece rather too quickly, berating herself afterwards for having displayed exceedingly bad manners. She felt acutely how each mistake in etiquette must be viewed by Maria as a strike against her.

When offered another piece, Lilo awkwardly declined, saying, "Oh, I believe I could not—"

Sensing the hesitation and longing behind the refusal, however, Ernst enthusiastically plopped another piece down on her plate, remarking with a benign smile, "Belief really has nothing to do with it!"

The ensuing laughter dispelled the awkwardness for a time.

After they finished eating, Rolf's friend Vera and her mother paid a surprise call to the Dutzmanns, adding even further to Lilo's discomfort. By that time, Vera's boyfriend, Otto, was away in the military and Vera was playing the field. She made it very obvious that she had designs on Rolf as she chattered away about her imminent move to Latvia, where she would work for the German occupation forces in a secretarial position, and the special wardrobe that was being tailored for her just in time for her departure.

"My seamstress told me that she obtained some beautiful silk material to make a gorgeous gown for me with a wide, wide skirt!" she stated proudly. Beaming, she twirled around in a circle, moving her arms around her body in a wide arc to suggest the extravagant skirt, tossing her thick blonde hair and smiling coquettishly at Rolf, who showed only mild amusement.

Once Lilo and the other guests had departed, Rolf did not need to ask his mother what she thought of Lilo. Maria barraged him with questions, implying that Lilo was not a suitable candidate for a life partner. Not only was there no money in her family and the status and pedigree of that family questionable, but she also worked at an ordinary secretarial and bookkeeping job, her parents were divorced and, good heavens, she was Lutheran rather than Catholic!

"Yes, Lilo works to help support herself and her mother, but even my own sister is in training to support herself someday!" Rolf objected.

"Ruth's future work is different because it involves specialized training and will pay much better," Maria replied, unruffled. "All of these things matter," she told Rolf, reaching forward to stroke his hair. "And you, mein Liebling, are the one who must carry on the family name."

Drama on a much larger, even catastrophic scale was playing out across Europe and in Soviet Russia. Between September 1942 and January 1943, the

German war effort suffered a crushing blow in the snow and ice on the Eastern Front at Stalingrad, from which it never managed to recover. And after two years of intensifying German air attacks against British cities, the tables were turned. Allied bombers commenced the catastrophic destruction of German cities with the leveling of Lübeck and Rostock. All across Germany, but perhaps especially in Berlin, the effects of these disasters were immediate and drastic. Rations, already greatly reduced, became even scantier. Coal for heating was scarce, and for Lilo and Gertrud, it was a terrifying time of increasingly destructive and devastating air raids that left the already-fatigued and frightened citizenry in Berlin dazed and reeling, though not defeated. Even for Rolf, who was farther removed from the worst bombing, the Allied threat was looming ever larger.

Throughout the final years of the war, the hopes of German people were continually shored up by reports and rumors of secret weapons that would turn the tide of the war in Germany's favor. On October 3, 1942, on the shores of the Baltic Sea at a place called Peenemünde, the first completely successful A4 rocket test launch took place, a fact known to only a few insiders at the time. That rocket, eventually renamed "V-2," soared an impressive eighty-four and one-half kilometers, over fifty miles, into the air—a feat that came to be described as the "first leap into space" by rocket pioneers.[12]

As for the genocidal designs of the Nazi regime, ominous signs were present, but with outside communications on the subject effectively blocked, the only news available to most German people was what the regime wanted its citizens to hear. Radio reports from the BBC, Radio Moscow and the Voice of America were forbidden while interminable, glowing Nazi propaganda served to keep many people in a state of ignorance about the true status of the war as well as the hideous atrocities perpetrated in the name of the Fatherland. The first concentration camps in Germany held mainly political prisoners and opponents of the regime including common criminals, but between 1939 and 1942, the number of camps quadrupled and between 1939 and the end of the war, death camps were established in Poland for the industrial-scale extermination of millions of innocent people. Already in April of 1940, Himmler had ordered construction of the Auschwitz concentration camp. In 1941, the first victims were killed there using Zyklon B gas. In January of 1942 at the Wannsee Conference, Nazi officials discussed and formalized the Final Solution—a plan of systematic, state-sanctioned mass extermination which involved moving victims from all of the occupied countries to a gruesome network of ghettos, camps, sub-camps and finally to the death camps in Poland—a plan that resulted in the murder of approximately six million Jews as well as five million other victims from across Europe.[13]

Meanwhile, after the genocidal famine in the Ukraine from 1932-33 known as the Holodomor, that killed as many as ten million people due to disastrous Soviet policies surrounding the collectivization of farms, Joseph Stalin had brutally secured the reins of power via the Great Purge of 1936-38, during which at least 700,000 people were executed. Many of his personal enemies numbered among them, but also countless ordinary Soviet citizens who were arrested indiscriminately under false pretexts. Mass deportations of millions of people under deplorable conditions followed during and after World War II with entire ethnic groups disappearing from many regions including from Latvia. Millions of relocated people died of starvation or disease. By the time of the decisive Soviet victory at Stalingrad in 1942-43, Stalin was firmly established in his role of absolute despot, with few if any detractors left to restrain his murderous abuse of power.[14]

Rolf's teaching position with the Advanced Flight Technical School came to an end when he received orders to attend an officer candidate training course in Westphalia, a region of Germany on the east bank of the Rhine River. The mid-winter course was grueling and the trainees spent much time performing field exercises in soaking-wet clothing. Rolf despised the harsh physical regimen, and sorely missed being engaged in technical pursuits. He had no ambition to become an officer anyway and harbored no illusions about the reality of military service in wartime, observing that most officers were deployed at lightning speed to the front where they were expected to feel honored to die a gruesome death. Where was the glory in that? Nevertheless, he was apprehensive about the immediate future. What negative repercussions would descend on him, he wondered, for his failure to excel in the officer candidate training, to say nothing of his general ambivalence along with a lack of cooperation and enthusiasm? Would his superiors assume he had deliberately failed the course? Would he be in for a slap on the wrist, a tongue lashing, or something far more disastrous?

Chapter 21

Terror in the Night

When Rolf returned to the base where he had previously worked as an aeronautical instructor, he was immediately summoned by the commanding officer for a severe reprimand. His failure to excel in the training course reflected in his grades and eliminated his opportunities for promotion. But what he feared most—deployment to the Eastern Front or to Africa—did not come to pass. His instructor status was revoked, however, and he was sent back to Jüterbog for assignment to an aircraft maintenance crew. The dismay that he initially felt over that development was quickly dispelled by the recognition that he could have fared much worse.

A letter arrived from Lilo dated February 12, 1943:

Dearest Rolf,

Mother and I are doing as well as can be expected under the circumstances. After being drafted and assigned to a job at the Wehrmacht-Auskunftstelle (Army Information Center) here in Berlin to provide information to people looking for their missing relatives, Mother suffered a nervous breakdown and was sent to a spa for recuperation. That job was hellish, as you can imagine, with very little good news ever to impart to anyone. Since her recovery, she has been assigned to a less gruesome post.

Back in January, a "Luftmine" exploded three blocks away from us, destroying two five-story apartment buildings. We are told that these bombs explode in the air over their targets, causing total damage underneath and gradual damage over a widespread area. People in the basement shelters were buried alive under an avalanche of smoking rubble and there were not enough rescue workers available for the grisly search afterwards. No one in those buildings survived. People still come from all over Berlin to look in abject horror at those mountains of rubble, and then walk away dazed by the magnitude of the destruction.

My great-aunt Hedwig died last year and my other great aunt, Hanna, moved away to Seesen, where we are glad she is safer. Although we miss her, there is very little time and energy for family get-togethers anyway. The leisure time that we would normally have in peacetime is now non-existent, what with almost nightly air raids and being constantly tired in the daytime in addition to needing to carry on with our jobs and other daily tasks. Mother is the one who mostly runs the errands to obtain our food, going first to the baker, then the butcher shop, the creamery and finally the grocery store for vegetables, fruit and staples.

Probably to reassure us and relieve some of the stress that we are feeling in a small way, there was a ration of real coffee issued after the Luftmine attack, something that we had not had the pleasure of in years. Mother and I each got enough for about two days, a special delight compared to the flat, tasteless, ersatz coffee! Unfortunately this gift has not gone very far to restore high spirits and optimism here in Berlin.

There is a housing shortage now, and anyone with a larger apartment has been asked to rent out one or two rooms to help accommodate all those who have been bombed out. Rather than rent out a portion of our four-room apartment, Mother and I recently sold our large, bulky furniture, bought smaller pieces and moved to a two-room apartment in another building located within walking distance of our previous flat. This way we are able to preserve a bit of our independence and privacy.

What sustains me in the midst of the waking nightmare that has become daily life for all here in Berlin is my unshakable conviction that we will survive and that there is a beautiful and very different future awaiting us.

Lilo and Gertrud found themselves once again in the basement air raid shelter. The walls of the shelter were shaking furiously from the falling and exploding bombs, and avalanches of dust and debris were coming down everywhere. The sound of detonations, deafening crashes and splintering glass resounded from outside. Inside people were screaming, crying, praying and wailing hysterically. They shook uncontrollably as they tried to protect themselves by ducking with pillows over their heads and vainly attempted to shield their children by covering them with their own bodies.

Lilo and Gertrud huddled together, terrified amidst the chaos. Lilo's nails dug heedlessly into her mother's arm as she implored, "*Lieber Gott*, be merciful and help us to survive!"

Afterwards, they emerged dazed and shaken from the basement to find that the walls of their apartment had partially collapsed. The windows were all shattered, including the large floor-to-ceiling window in the living room. What was left of the blackout blinds hung in dreary tatters across the gaping holes where glass had once been. Heaps of plaster, broken glass and debris were everywhere, and settling over everything was a layer of thick dust that penetrated even into cupboards and closets, into their food supply and into their eyes, noses and mouths. Lilo choked on the dust that hung suspended in the air like a deadly shroud. Outside the broken windows they saw the jagged remains of destroyed buildings eerily illuminated against the night sky by the flames of other burning buildings behind them. The night resounded with frantic, raised voices—shouting, wailing and moaning—and with the sounds of running footsteps both inside the building and out in the street.

Lilo tried to take it all in, then collapsed into a dust-covered chair, laughing hysterically as she realized how close they had come to annihilation.

Jumping back up, she exclaimed to Gertrud, "We are alive!" They hugged each other in relief bordering on delirium, feeling as though they had personally achieved a major victory.

Lilo, famished, found a crust of bread in a cupboard, and devoured it dust and all, wondering aloud whether others also experienced the same kind of post-air raid hunger pangs.

After a silence while they took stock of their situation, grimly surveying the devastation, Gertrud remarked in a matter-of-fact tone, "Tomorrow we replace the windows."

Morning dawned to the sound of rescue teams all over Berlin working frantically to find victims, the drone of power shovels and drills alternating with silence to listen for knocking, shouting, moaning—any sign of life amidst the smoldering ruins.

Lilo made a trip on foot to the home of her boss and his family to see how they had fared, picking her way carefully along the rubble-strewn streets, which in some areas were nearly impassable.

Little Peter saw her approaching from a window and excitedly called out her nickname, "*Tatta Rulle Appi!*"

The Mietke family was unhurt and everyone greeted and hugged Lilo ecstatically, amazed that she had managed to walk all that way amidst the destruction. The back wall of their house had fallen away from a bomb blast that had also left a huge crater in the back yard. Some rooms in the house were partially destroyed, but the office area was relatively intact. Within a short time, business resumed and Richard Mietke began a determined quest to obtain permits to have his home restored.

"I do not think we can win this war," he stated, "but after it is over, it will be even harder to obtain permits and supplies. Better to get the job done now!"

Officially, Lilo and Gertrud were members of the Evangelical Church of the Hohenzollerndam in Berlin, but like most protestant churches in Germany, it was a state-controlled church. Although the minister occasionally preached against the Nazi regime in a token sort of way, neither Lilo nor Gertrud were able to warm up to what seemed to be an underlying pro-Nazi political agenda. Across the city, there was another Evangelical church, the Bekenntniskirche, that they preferred but it was too far away to attend regularly and was often very crowded as well. The minister of that church before the war, Pastor Martin Niemöller, had frequently expressed his opposition to the Nazi regime. Despite the fact that he had been a decorated and celebrated U-boat captain during World War I, he was arrested in 1937 for his criticism of Nazi policies and interned in Sachsenhausen and Dachau concentration camps from 1938 to 1945.[15]

Lilo especially yearned for a deeper and more authentic spiritual approach than the one offered at the Evangelical Church of the Hohenzollerndam. Whereas Gertrud had never been a regular churchgoer, she *had* encouraged Lilo from an early age to trust in God and to believe that God would always hear her and be there for her. At such a time of widespread destruction and uncertainty, instead of the more traditional German denominations, they found themselves drawn to the ethereally beautiful music and unintelligible liturgy of a nearby Russian Orthodox church where they were occasionally able to forget for a time the hardships and perils of daily life in wartime. For Lilo, the church services were not only a consolation for the increasing adversity they faced daily, but also a source of new hope for the future.

One day while scaling a fence, Rolf's foot caught in the barbed wire causing him to land on his right hand and breaking his wrist. Laid up with a cast on his arm for ten weeks in a military hospital, there was little else to keep him occupied other than daily physical therapy. He practiced and became adept at writing with his left hand, sending letters almost daily to Lilo in an irregular, though still legible, script.

Hideous reminders of wartime were everywhere. In the bed next to him was a soldier whose toes had been amputated. He told Rolf they had been frozen off during the Russian winter while he served on the Eastern Front. Supply shipments had not been able to get through, and in the brutally cold conditions, his unit had only been supplied with summer-weight boots, socks and uniforms.

Lilo considered the recent correspondence from Rolf to be encouraging and was hopeful about the sincerity of his change of heart. She decided to set aside her past disappointments and pay him a visit at the military hospital. It just so happened that her visit coincided with a visit from Rolf's parents and his sister, Ruth. It was another strained occasion with Maria's cold reserve once again creating an uneasy atmosphere and getting in the way of meaningful conversation. To Lilo's dismay, there was no opportunity for her to speak privately with Rolf.

After Lilo, Maria and Ruth had left to return to Berlin, Ernst, who needed to catch a later train back to Peenemünde, lingered for a while.

He told Rolf with a reassuring look, "In spite of the stiff resistance from your mother, I will support you in whatever you decide about Lilo." After a pause, he continued, "There is much about your mother that neither one of us will ever know. You might as well sit down. What I have to say will no doubt come as a surprise, perhaps even a shock to you."

Perplexed, Rolf perched on the edge of the bed, the only seating available in the spartan hospital ward.

Ernst paced back and forth slowly while gazing down at the floor, hands clasped behind his back, and continued, "I have never told you or Ruth about this, and for your mother, it is far too traumatic to ever bring up to you. Even to me she has said very little, so what I have to recount to you will be sketchy."

Rolf shifted uneasily, wondering what secrets there could be to impart.

"As you and Ruth already know, I met your mother here in Germany after the end of the Great War, once my service in the Czarist Russian army had ended and I had spent several years in a German prisoner-of-war camp. What we never told you is that you are not the first child that your mother has had."

He paused for a moment to let the fact sink in.

"There was definitely one other, a daughter, who died during the time of the Great War. I know of this only because I walked into our bedroom one day shortly after we were married. Her back was turned to me, her jewelry box was open and she was sadly stroking something in her hand. When I asked her what it was, she reluctantly showed me a small lock of hair tied with a pink ribbon, something that she usually kept hidden in a compartment of the jewelry box, a keepsake taken from the daughter who died at a very young age. I could tell that it pained her greatly to speak about the subject, so I did not want to press her further."

Ernst stopped pacing, sighed deeply and looked directly at Rolf, "So you see, when you came along, it must have seemed to her that her lost child had come back to her. And, having once lost, she is afraid of losing again—afraid of losing you to Lilo, someone whom she does not know or understand and who will doubtless not allow herself to be controlled."

Rolf remained silent until Ernst gave him a considerate look, clapped him on the back and added, "But, mind you, her general low opinion of Berlin women still plays a large part too!"

At this, Rolf burst out laughing, but the laughter was only a cover up for the mounting sense of tension and frustration that he felt inside.

After that visit, Rolf found himself in a deep quandary. He spent a number of days thinking about what to do. Finally he sat down and composed another letter to Lilo in his ragged, left-handed script in which he broke off the relationship with her yet again, stating as his reasons that he was not only nervous about his future assignments in the Luftwaffe, but also about all the uncertainties of life during a war that showed no sign of ending soon. There were other reasons; reasons that he was not certain how to voice and did not know whether Lilo would understand. Moreover, he was not sure that he understood them fully himself.

Rolf's letter came as a bitter blow to Lilo. When she once again began receiving correspondence from Rolf's friend, Hans Dieter, Lilo agreed to see him, especially as he was by that time in the military and stationed near Berlin. They went dancing a few times, but for Lilo, the spark that had been there with Rolf was lacking with Hans. To his immense disappointment, she made it clear to him early on that she could regard him only as a friend. Out of a sense of compassion for Hans, Lilo tried to set him up with her friend, Rotraut, but there was little rapport between the two of them, so Lilo was forced to abandon the matchmaking attempt. To all who knew Lilo, it was clear that a source of great joy had gone out of her life and that her heart had stopped singing.

Chapter 22

The Bombing of Peenemünde

Messerschmitt BF 109 fighters were taking off at night from the Jüterbog airbase where Rolf and his fellow recruits had just finished stringing temporary runway lighting. They were the Wilde Sau (Wild Boar) night-fighter squadron as identified by the logos on the sides of the planes. As soon as the planes were all up in the air, the runway lights were promptly turned off in order to keep the airbase from being detected by enemy planes. Allied bombers shortly appeared on the scene, illuminated in surreal detail by searchlights from below. The Messerschmitts dived in for the attack, picking off some of them. Bombs hitting a target a mile or so away lit up the sky, suddenly blowing the Jüterbog hangar doors from their hinges.

The Wilde Sau technique of using high-flying, single-seat, day fighter planes to engage British night bombers was a new technique that emerged after Operation Gomorrah—the devastating British firebombing of the city of Hamburg less than a month earlier, in July 1943. About fifty thousand civilians were killed, most of them in the resulting firestorm that raged with 150-mile-an-hour winds and searing, 1,800-degree temperatures—so hot that even the asphalt burst into flame.[16] Which German city would be next?

While on night duty, Rolf and the other servicemen slept standby at the hangar area. Their job was to remove debris from the runway and to operate the runway lights that were only turned on when a plane needed to take off or land. The lights were removed each morning around dawn and replaced again each night. In addition, Rolf's team assisted in rescuing crashed pilots, both German and Allied. When Allied pilots were taken prisoner, as in the case of five pilots who parachuted out of a doomed bomber during the time Rolf was on duty at Jüterbog, they were held locally for only a short time before being transported to the nearest German prisoner-of-war camp.

The men carried loads of debris from both Allied and German planes to a junk pile that grew to immense proportions. When they inspected the Allied bomber fuel tanks and realized that they were made of a rubberized fabric, they used the material to make soles for slippers and thong sandals. Since it was summertime, all fuel tanks were soon cut up for that purpose and before long, soldiers could be seen casually flip-flopping around the base sporting custom-made sandals.

However, there was relatively little time or inclination for lighthearted pursuits. In the distance, the nightly bombing raids on Berlin were clearly visible from Jüterbog, providing a spectacular, though dreadful, aerial display. Rolf and the other soldiers watched the spectacle with awe, each of them silently pondering the extent of the damage and casualties. Rolf could not refrain from thinking of Lilo and Gertrud, and how they must be struggling to lead their daily lives despite multiple exhausting attacks each night.

One Sunday while Rolf was on leave, he met with his university friend, Hans Dieter. Hans divulged to Rolf that he and Lilo had met several times in Berlin after Rolf's last breakup with her, but that all of his attempts to win her over had failed because of Lilo's continuing feelings for Rolf.

"You are a fool if you let her go, Rolf. You don't want to lose a gem like that, someone who loves you heart and soul," Hans remarked. He then added ruefully, "The most romantic response I managed to get from her was when she accepted me as a sort of older brother figure. I wish it had been otherwise. That photo I sent to you, the one at Zoppot, where Lilo is smiling that beautiful smile? That smile is meant for you and only you, my friend!"

The conversation with Hans, along with Rolf's own musings, gradually worked to once again resurrect thoughts about the relationship with Lilo. He found himself wishing that he had not given all of his photos including the Zoppot photos to his parents for safekeeping during his last visit home. He vaguely recalled that "smile meant for him," but wanted to see it once again for himself. He had never thought of it in quite those terms. He finally decided to write a letter to Lilo in August 1943:

Dear Lilo,

In looking back at your past letters to me and giving much thought to our relationship and all the good times we had, I have wanted for over a month now to reestablish contact, but have hesitated due to my fear that you would refuse to resume where we left off. I fear I have made a callous and unforgivable mistake and I am hoping that you will be lenient with my lack of certainty about our future together, caused in no small part by the possibility of a grim ending to this war. Your firm faith in the future, in our survival and in a God who watches over all of us, even in wartime, is a quality that I admire but do not possess in such great abundance.

What we may not be told about the war effort is what concerns me now. The only good news I have to report is that my mother and sister have been evacuated from Berlin and are now living in Wiegandsthal in the Riesengebirge, where they are safer. I will travel there to see them during my furlough this fall. I am hoping that you will allow me to come visit you during that leave.

Aside from your own welfare and that of your mother, it is my father about whom I am now most concerned. He was transferred some months ago from the artillery proving ground in Bourges, France where he was previously stationed to some sort of development center on the Baltic Sea. He is living at the installation full time, and will be able to go home only when he is granted special leave. The last time I saw him he would say very little, only that he had been promoted to the rank of major and was working on a classified project of great urgency.

It was nighttime on August 17, 1943 at the top-secret weapons installation of Peenemünde located on the barrier island of Usedom in the Baltic Sea. Ernst was sleeping in the barracks where all of the army personnel were quartered, when he awoke abruptly to the blare of air raid sirens and the unmistakable drone of approaching four-engine bombers. Pandemonium broke out with men yelling in panic and running for the doors while bomb blasts in the immediate vicinity and the sound of anti-aircraft artillery added to the terror. Suddenly there was a very close hit. Ernst jumped out the nearest window and raced for the underground shelter. Another violent blast from behind threw him to the ground. Looking back, he saw a man just thirty meters behind him torn to pieces by a bomb, and the barracks vacated just moments before leaping up in flames. He scrambled to his feet and continued running through the artificial fog that was wafting everywhere across the installation. Searchlights from the ground and flares dropped by the bombers to illuminate their targets added to the wild confusion and mayhem. It was only after he reached the shelter, that he realized he had managed to escape with only the pajamas on his back.

After the bombing, Ernst found out that over seven hundred people had been killed, most of them foreign forced laborers from the nearby Trassenheide Labor Camp. Feverish preparations were soon underway to move the assembly and inspection facilities for the A4 (V-2) rockets to an underground location deeper in the heart of Germany. Papers and blueprints with the words "GEHEIME REICHSSACHE" ("STATE SECRET") stamped on them in large, bold letters were spread out on a conference table. While making notations on a chalkboard, Dr. Wernher von Braun was explaining details of the A4 rocket assembly and inspection sequence to an elite group of officers and civilian engineers when a debate broke out regarding a step in the assembly process.

After a period of deliberation back and forth, von Braun signaled to an aide, "Please place a call requesting that Dutzmann, *der Major mit dem Schraubenzieher* ('the Major with the Screwdriver'), join us. He is likely to be making the rounds at the F1 assembly facility at this time of day," he added, checking his watch. Turning back to the others present, he explained, "Major Dutzmann is in training to serve as chief inspector for the A4 rockets once our new underground installation is completed."

They resumed the debate and after a short time, Major Ernst Dutzmann was ushered in. He clicked his heels, bowed slightly towards von Braun, then shook hands with the civilian engineers present.

"We need your opinion on a detail regarding the assembly sequence we are currently using for the A4," von Braun continued. "From your past experience designing and overseeing the operation of automatic assembly equipment, is it your opinion that we might be able to forego the leak test scheduled during the assembly sequence?"

Ernst replied, "*Meine Herren* (Gentlemen), whereas leak testing is not essential in all cases, I am of the opinion that it is advised for the A4 due to its complexity and the fact that the quality control and inspection methods require further refinement."

He proceeded to draw a diagram on the chalkboard to illustrate his point and then elaborated his stance by taking a screwdriver out of his pocket and using it as a pointer. The debate continued as the others in the room challenged him with questions, but Ernst's solid reasoning and level of experience finally convinced the others that the planned facilities must accommodate the proposed testing.

That very month, Italy had broken the "Axis" and signed an armistice with the Allies, thereby further taxing Germany's resources and rendering even more important the swift development of the planned secret weapons. Ernst's time at Peenemünde was about to come to an end, but in the final years of the Nazi regime, his military duties would take on a much more sinister aspect and a vastly heightened intensity.

In November 1943, Britain officially launched the Battle of Berlin, causing widespread damage to residential areas in Germany. Around that time, Rolf was on leave with a pass to travel into the city. As the train approached the outskirts, he stared in disbelief at the smoldering ruins that now lined both sides of the tracks for mile after endless mile as far as the eye could see. After disembarking and finding there was little or no public transportation still operating, he picked his way through a hauntingly desolate urban landscape to Lilo and Gertrud's apartment. Passage along many of the streets was made treacherous and even impossible by mountains of rubble. The few people he encountered looked war-weary and resigned, but still not beaten.

Rolf was uneasy that he had received no response from Lilo to his last letter containing the request to reconcile. To his way of thinking, her silence was probably due to one of two reasons: either she and Gertrud had become casualties of the Allied bombing or Lilo had no intention of allowing him back into her life and affections. While the former possibility made his heart lurch with anxiety, the latter one was even more disquieting in some ways. Had he forever ruined his chances of resuming the relationship? To never see her again was a terrible thought, but to never see her again due to his own ill-advised behavior and indecisiveness was unbearable.

As he approached their building, Rolf's heart beat faster at the sight of the blackened ruin that had been the top floor, jutting up into the sky like charred, broken teeth. The floor housing their apartment was the one directly below that. Were Lilo and Gertrud still there? Had they survived the hardships and devastation of the recent months or was he too late?

Chapter 23

Berlin Amidst the Ashes

Once Rolf climbed up to Lilo and Gertrud's floor, he saw that the hallway ceiling was still supported, although barely, and the door to their apartment still relatively intact. He hesitated only briefly before knocking, steeling himself against the possibility of bad news. Ah, but there was Gertrud answering the door! He received the usual hugs, kisses and enthusiastic exclamations from her. When Lilo came into the front hallway to see who was there, Rolf's emotions lurched painfully. He wanted to take her in his arms, thankful that she was alive, but her attitude was reserved, almost disinterested, and she was avoiding eye contact. There was an uncomfortable moment, dispelled only when Gertrud invited him in.

Initially distracted both by the warm greeting from Gertrud and the chilly reception from Lilo, Rolf finally took in the dismal surroundings. It was very cold in the apartment. Windows were nailed shut with plywood or covered with blankets, old carpets, cardboard and any other available material. The once-intact blackout blinds were hanging in shreds or missing altogether. Mortar had fallen from the walls and a futile attempt had been made to sweep loose plaster from floors and furniture into piles to be removed. Dust was everywhere in spite of valiant efforts to remove it. Gertrud told Rolf that they were arranging to have most of their possessions moved to a storage space outside the city for safekeeping. They planned to keep only a mattress and a few other bare necessities at the apartment so that they could continue to sleep there, making their daily trips to work easier.

It was a strained, low-key meeting with no opportunity for Rolf and Lilo to talk privately. And in any case, Rolf realized that Lilo's reserve would probably have discouraged any meaningful communication between them. Other than knowing that she was alive, his questions would have to remain unanswered.

It was around three o'clock a.m. in November 1943. Lilo and Gertrud were once again in the air raid shelter when a sudden very loud blast directly above them caused people to scream loudly and to cling to each other in abject terror. Dust and debris rained down on the panic-stricken tenants. When Lilo and Gertrud finally emerged from the shelter and returned to their apartment, they found that the floor immediately above theirs was finally completely destroyed, and a torrent of water was pouring into their unit from broken pipes. Even the plywood covering the windows had cracks and holes from falling debris and was pitted with anti-aircraft shell splinters.

For the rest of that night, there was nothing to do but to drag a mattress and blankets to the driest corner of the apartment in the hope of catching another hour's sleep. The following day's news revealed that the attack the previous night had killed two thousand Berliners and rendered 175 thousand homeless. The very next night, one thousand people were killed and an additional one hundred thousand were left homeless.[17]

The day after the destruction of their living space, Lilo and Gertrud needed to come to a decision. Spurred on by desperation and the realization that not only might the bombings continue to worsen, but also, that without heat, running water or other comforts and conveniences and winter just around the corner, their living space was already uninhabitable, they decided to move themselves and the rest of their possessions to the storage space they had rented outside the city. The conditions there, though cramped and primitive, would still be preferable to the ruined apartment and the multiple nightly air raids that were increasing in frequency and intensity with each passing week and causing widespread devastation and loss of life.

When they arrived at the house in Berge with the rented storage space, they received a warm welcome from the landlady, Frau Geisser. In spite of the fact that she was young with three small children and a husband serving on the front, her general attitude was one of motherly solicitude and concern for Lilo and Gertrud, and she made every effort to ensure their comfort.

As they rearranged their possessions in order to create sleeping space for themselves on the floor of the cramped attic quarters, Gertrud mused aloud to Lilo, "Who could have known that this small room would become our refuge!"

After offering prayers of gratitude for arriving at a safe haven, they fell asleep that night to the drone of bombers passing overhead like angels of death winging their way to the city for the nightly raids. They slept soundly for the first time in many months, waking up in the morning to the welcome sound of children's voices and ordinary household activities coming from the floors below rather than in the middle of the night to the dreaded wail of air raid sirens. A short distance away from where they now slumbered peacefully through the night, regular raids on Berlin continued to kill hundreds of people each night and rendered between twenty thousand and eighty thousand homeless each time.

Every weekday morning, Lilo and Gertrud faced a long trek into the city to get to work, and every evening a long journey back to the house in Berge. But they were both in agreement that the time they sacrificed for the daily commute was more than compensated for by the rest and peace of mind that they were able to enjoy during the night.

Lilo received a hopeful letter dated December 14, 1943 from her grandfather informing her of an impending job opening at the Silesian Steamship Company in Havelberg, a company that transported munitions, coal and food supplies to the Eastern Front and that also helped to relocate refugees. After receiving consent from her boss, Richard Mietke, to release her from her job in Berlin,

Lilo and Gertrud traveled to Havelberg at Christmastime. Lilo interviewed for the job and received a letter of agreement from the Silesian Steamship Company stating that they would like to hire her as of March 1, 1944, providing that she could obtain permission to move away from Berlin. Armed with that letter as well as a letter of release from Richard Mietke, in which he stated that he was loathe to let her go but realized that her work with the Silesian Steamship Company would be much more essential to the war effort, Lilo made numerous trips to the employment bureau in Berlin to plead for authorization not only to switch jobs, but more importantly, to move out of the doomed city.

Each time she was refused with the same statement belted out in a grim staccato, "No working person leaves Berlin!"

Not even phone calls placed on her behalf by her boss or bringing up her mother's recent breakdown and difficult recuperation helped Lilo's cause. By mid-February, she admitted to Gertrud that she had given up and that they would have to resign themselves to remaining in Berlin for the duration of the war, which now seemed as though it might never end. Even that disappointment, however, along with the increasing ferocity of the bombing and the deterioration of living conditions in Berlin, did not lessen Lilo's inner conviction that she and her mother would survive whatever ordeals still loomed ahead.

"Odd," she told her mother, "All I can think about are our immediate concerns—what we need to do in the next few hours or the next day. How can it be, with all of the destruction around us, that the reality of this war hasn't fully sunk in for me? In spite of everything, I have a strong conviction that we will not die here in the city."

"The optimism of the young!" Gertrud thought to herself.

Rolf was promoted to the rank of corporal and soon faced a pivotal decision. There were only two choices offered—to train for the position of a fighter pilot or a navigator in the Luftwaffe. It was made clear to him by his superiors that should he fail to volunteer for one of those two positions, he would end up in a Luftwaffe Field Division, an assignment that was almost certain to entail a swift dispatch to the front. Rolf made further inquiries about the two options and decided that the navigator training intrigued him since it involved math and science as well as subjects unfamiliar to him such as Morse code, celestial and radio navigation, flight planning and the use of the new Lotfe 7D bomb sight that was used in most Luftwaffe bombers. Moreover, the navigator training course would occupy an entire year, thereby providing a further welcome postponement of his assignment to a combat squadron.

"A lot can change in a year," he thought to himself, nursing along a tiny mustard seed of hope.

Rolf and a group of other trainees were boarded onto a train and told that they were being transferred 250 miles east of Berlin to the navigator school in Thorn, located in German-occupied Poland. Housing was in a complex of old Polish army barracks, and since navigator training was not to begin until almost two months later, the trainees were to receive further glider training. Rolf was immediately advanced to "B" level flights since he had already achieved his "A" certificate. The "B" certificate flight requirements consisted of mastering a set of complex maneuvers such as S-curves, ninety-degree turns, flying parallel to the landing strip and landing close to the takeoff point. Rolf was jubilant when he disembarked from the glider after executing all of the required maneuvers for the first time. It was with great pride that he received his "B" certificate at the end of the first week of training.

Not all were so fortunate, however. On one side of the runway there was a tall, solitary tree. One day, following a good takeoff and reasonably good execution of the first two turns, a very nervous trainee headed straight for the lone tree. The others looked on in abject horror as the glider crashed head-on into the tree with a tremendous noise, debris flying everywhere. As the trainees and instructors on the ground ran towards the shattered glider, the pilot emerged shakily and sheepishly out of the wreckage without a scratch. He was alive, but was never allowed to fly again.

Rolf and most of the other trainees advanced to fly the Grunau Baby, a medium-performance sailplane with an open cockpit, and the Kranich, a higher-performance soaring plane. He undertook his "C" pilot training, during which he was required to be launched to an altitude of about three hundred meters. He needed to fly once around the airfield and then perform a smooth landing. By that time, any fear that Rolf had felt during his initial flight attempts had disappeared. He felt confident and exuberant, riding the wind like the seagulls on the Baltic coast that he had often envied in his youth for their ability to drift effortlessly on unseen air currents. If only all of life could be so free, he thought as he circled the airfield. If only the sailplane could carry him beyond the limitations of the regime, the military and the war itself, to a place where he would be free to pursue his own vision for the future! Rolf's flight was successful and he obtained his "C" certificate in short order.

Upon completing their glider training, Rolf and the others were transferred to the Thorn airbase to begin their navigator training. The housing there was in single-story wooden barracks with eight men to a room. But the toilets and washroom were in a separate building 150 feet away, to which they jogged briskly through the snow early each morning.

Following aptitude tests to determine each trainee's capabilities, classes began in meteorology, visual navigation using maps, plotting courses via wind information, radio navigation using beacons, transmitting and receiving Morse code, celestial navigation, bomb-sight training, target shooting with aircraft-type machine guns and actual flight navigation on training flights accompanied by an instructor. Rolf and the other trainees received flight gear as well as a propeller insignia on their sleeves identifying them as flying personnel. Navigational training flights and bombing practice flights were ongoing.

About three months later, Rolf's group was transferred to a training base at the northern tip of East Prussia where they practiced their navigation skills during flights carried out with young, inexperienced pilot-trainees at the controls rather than instructors. On one such flight with Rolf serving as navigator, the engine suddenly stopped dead and the plane began to lose altitude rapidly. The panic-stricken young pilot looked frantically for an emergency-landing site. Rolf, equally alarmed, but keeping his head and thinking fast, suddenly realized that the pilot had forgotten to switch over to the auxiliary fuel tank. After he shouted a reminder to do so, they were able to restart the engine by diving the aircraft, thereby causing the prop to turn the engine over. Although a non-combat incident, it was nevertheless a very close call that left them both considerably shaken.

One day, all of the men in Rolf's unit were suddenly and without warning ordered to line up. An announcement was made that the Red Army had broken through to the Baltic States, making it necessary for some men from their unit to be dispatched to the Eastern Front. The Eastern Front! It was a term that struck universal terror into every man present. The stories coming back from the desolate, snowbound vastness of the Russian countryside were gruesome beyond all comprehension and now, lined up and waiting either to be chosen or reprieved, all hearts including Rolf's were wildly beating. A list of names was read and those men were asked to step forward. It was with a sense of morbid dread that Rolf heard his name called. As he stepped forward, it seemed to him that his worst nightmare was coming to pass.

Chapter 24

The War Effort Falters

R olf concealed the paralyzing fear that he felt at being chosen behind a mask of unconcern, but he was quaking inside and his knees felt weak. The large group of men who had not been chosen to step forward were then led away and only Rolf's much smaller group remained in the room. They stood at attention for what seemed like an eternity wondering what their fate would be. There was an announcement, but what were they being told? As if from a great distance, Rolf and the others still present received the news that they would be the ones to stay and continue their navigator training while the men led away were the ones who would be sent to the Eastern Front. Rolf felt a dizzying torrent of relief rush through his body, as though a death sentence hanging over him had suddenly been lifted.

Just a few days later, they received the disconcerting news that the train on which the other group of soldiers had shipped out had been captured by Soviet troops. Those men were never seen or heard from again.

The navigator training was halted shortly after that, and then entirely abandoned due to worsening fuel shortages. The trainees were instead put to work building sand revetments in the surrounding woods. During the day they shoveled sand and at night they were assigned to guard duty around the perimeter of the base. Rumor had it that an onslaught of aircraft was due to arrive at the base from areas eastward that had been recently overrun by the conquering Soviet forces.

The rumors were partly true. Field unit personnel from the Eastern Front soon began flooding the base, arriving in droves, but not by air, rather via an odd assortment of trucks, trailers and horse-drawn carts. Some soldiers even had Russian women with them as servants. They were a wild, motley and undisciplined lot by Luftwaffe standards, their unruly ways standing out in stark contrast to the orderly, disciplined conduct of Rolf's unit. Eventually, as Rolf found out more about the grueling hardships and grisly combat experiences endured by those ragged survivors of the cold and carnage on the Eastern Front, it became increasingly clear to him that the Nazi war effort was crumbling. But he could not risk voicing those observations to anyone. Since being drafted, he had sensed an undercurrent of escalating fear and suspicion underlying every conversation. Perhaps as an immigrant, he had not noticed that at first, or perhaps the prior university environment outside of Germany proper had kept him insulated. In any case, he had long ago decided the safest course was to keep his own counsel.

After the devastating air raid at Peenemünde in August 1943, Ernst was transferred to Raderach near the Bodensee (Lake Constance) where the Prüffeld-Anlage Raderach, a large, elaborate facility for testing V-2 rocket engines, was being built. Specialized test stands were erected and an entire village rapidly sprang up to house the civilian employees and their families. Since Ernst was a member of the military rather than civilian personnel, he did not have the privilege of bringing his wife and daughter to live on the premises. He was hopeful, however, that he would soon be able to obtain brand new housing for them nearby. In preparation for that, he moved them from Wiegandsthal into a furnished apartment in the town of Göppingen north of Raderach.

Shortly after moving to the area, Maria and Ruth noticed that there was sometimes a terrible stench in the air. When they inquired about the source of the odor, some of the townspeople seemed evasive, as if deliberately unwilling to divulge the cause. Their sense of unease and foreboding was increasing daily along with the desire to leave that inhospitable place. After the war ended and shocking facts came to light, they surmised that there may have been a concentration camp somewhere in the area where corpses were incinerated—on a day when the winds were blowing from east to west, perhaps even Dachau, located just under 100 miles away—but they never received any confirmation of their suspicions.

Shortly after Ernst's arrival in Raderach, rocket-engine testing began for three shifts per day around the clock. It was not long before Ernst and the other Raderach engineers picked up a Swiss newspaper to discover the headline, "What is going on in Raderach?" The article reported mysterious fires and ominous thundering sounds on the German side of the Bodensee. It was clear to those in charge that testing at the site could no longer continue, since that kind of publicity was sure to be rapidly followed by Allied air raids. Ernst's hope to establish a more settled family life was therefore dashed when, after only a couple of months and virtually overnight, they were ordered to pack up and completely abandon the test site.

Maria and Ruth, however, hoped that they would soon be leaving the secretive, sinister area in which they were living. Little did they know that, due to Ernst's military service, they were destined to be drawn even deeper into a region that would soon contain a network of up to forty concentration camps and sub-camps in order to supply labor for the German armament industry.

To Ernst it was obvious that the Nazi regime was becoming increasingly desperate in the face of devastating losses on the Eastern Front and the destruction of German cities and infrastructure by the Allied bombing. All of this was resulting in unrealistic hopes and expectations being pinned on the V-2 rocket program for which yet another relocation was already being planned deep into the Harz Mountains, an area still well shielded from Allied attention. It was a tide that would sweep him along in service to the emerging rocket technology.

Chapter 25

The Family Home in Ruins

olf received a telegram from Lilo that his family's apartment in Berlin had sustained bomb damage. The letter was very brief and betrayed no emotion, as though she were writing from a sense of duty alone. Rolf immediately obtained a bomb furlough to go and inspect the damage. Even though Maria and Ruth had since moved away to a town called Benneckenstein in the Harz Mountains, most of the family's possessions were still in the Berlin apartment and he wanted to see whether anything could be salvaged. After once again traveling by train into the ravaged city, Rolf made his way laboriously along nearly unrecognizable streets that had been reduced to mountains of rubble with hideously charred, jagged ruins rising on either side. Every so often he would see a message hurriedly scribbled on the wall of a ruined building—a hopeful attempt to pass on a new address or other information to anyone who might come searching for residents that had been bombed out and forced to move. Here and there a still recognizable object would protrude from the piles of debris—a teakettle, a kitchen sink, a battered doll still wearing shreds of dusty, dilapidated clothing— poignant remnants of lives interrupted. Rolf couldn't help but wonder how many of those lives would ever resume.

Arriving at the block where the family had once lived, Rolf found that the two lower stories of their apartment were completely blown out while the upper stories still stood, though held up only by the skeletal steel frame. He climbed pensively through the debris from room to bombed-out room, surveying what could still be seen of the beautiful furniture brought all the way from Latvia, now mostly destroyed and covered in bricks, dust and rubble.

He was able to retrieve only a few belongings, bending down to pick them up gently from the debris-littered floor. One of them was a small album of photos. As he leafed through the pages, he found the small photo of himself and his friend Hans with Lilo sitting between them taken at the beach in Zoppot. He carefully brushed the dust from Lilo's face. She looked radiantly happy, but her gaze was directed downward as if reluctant to share some closely held secret. She looked so lovely, yet so vulnerable. Rolf turned it over. Inscribed on the back in Hans Dieter's hand, "Zoppot, Summer '41."

"Only three years ago, but it seems so much longer," he thought to himself as he stood amidst the broken walls and the rubble-covered furniture.

He sat down heavily, wearily, on what was left of a broken-down sofa, heedless of the dust that flew everywhere, and put his head in his hands. He was tired and eventually fell asleep, pulling his coat closer about him against the cold. He woke up in the dark to the sound of air raid sirens and bombs dropping in the distance. There seemed to be no further interest on the part of the Allied bombers in this part of the city that had already been laid waste. He found the remains of a curtain lying in the ruins—once an elegant brocade, now reduced to a dusty rag—and wrapped himself in it. Then he sat back down on the sofa to watch the blood-red dawn breaking over the bombed-out buildings. Just after sunrise, he set out from the gutted apartment building, walking past block after block of dismal ruins. There was no life left in this part of the city.

Rolf arrived at the house in Berge where Lilo and Gertrud were living. The landlady heard a knock at the door and opened it to a very tired and disheveled-looking young soldier.

"Excuse me, please, is this the home of Gertrud and Lilo Wassull?"

The landlady hesitated, alarmed by his unsavory appearance, but the striking blue eyes peering out of an otherwise crestfallen, dust-caked face convinced her to trust him. She asked him to wait a moment while she went upstairs to knock on Lilo and Gertrud's door. That moment seemed like an eternity to Rolf. He wondered whether he had made a mistake showing up there. Would Lilo's reception be as cold and distant as the previous time, or would she show some sign of feelings for him again? For an instant, he allowed himself to hope.

Since it was a Sunday and not a workday, they were just rising, but when told that there was a filthy, tired and exhausted young soldier at the door, they quickly threw on coats and shoes and hurried downstairs. Lilo took stock of Rolf's appearance and searched his face questioningly while Gertrud stood by with an expectant look. Rolf hesitantly pulled the photo out of his pocket and extended it towards her.

He smiled, "Remember?"

"Of course," Lilo smiled too, and took the photo to examine it more closely.

She looked up again, moved closer to Rolf, who was standing dejectedly, and took his hand, her eyes not leaving his face. When he looked at her, she put her arms around him. He held her close, overcome by emotion and fatigue.

Gertrud raised her eyes to heaven and then closed them in a silent prayer of thanks.

"Young man, if you can ever get clean again, there will be hot coffee and bread with butter for everyone, perhaps even an egg or two," the landlady interjected in a kindly tone.

She showed Rolf where he could wash up and shave and also gave him some clean clothes belonging to her husband, who was still away serving on the front. The ice finally broken, they enjoyed breakfast washed down by ersatz coffee and accompanied by lively conversation and a frequent exchange of wondering glances between Rolf and Lilo.

The smiles and laughter shared during such precarious times were priceless and all the more memorable—like scattered jewels sparkling through clouds in an otherwise endless night. For the war-weary Rolf and Lilo, the future loomed vast and unknowable, but the present was inviolable, transcendent and infinitely precious.

Later that morning, Lilo and Gertrud took Rolf upstairs to show him their tiny attic room, and extended an invitation for him to stay. Even though the bulkier furniture had been sold off months before, the rest of their belongings were still stacked from floor to ceiling in order to make everything fit and to allow enough room for their beds. They explained that they were allowed by Frau Geisser to heat their food on the lower level of the house and to spend a bit of time there each evening before going upstairs to their unheated room to sleep. They took a pail of water up with them every night to use for washing the next morning. While Rolf was there, it was bitterly cold and every morning there was a solid layer of ice in the bucket.

Rolf made the daily trek into Berlin with them. He teased Lilo about all the layers of clothing she was wearing, but even the train and subway were frigid and their breath swirled in sinuous arabesques around their faces in the cold morning air. Monday through Saturday their routine was the same: up by five o'clock in the morning, a half-hour walk through the fields to the train station, a one-hour train ride, then parting ways to get on different subway lines to arrive at their respective job locations by eight-thirty or nine o'clock. The same trip took place in reverse each evening. During one of those trips from Berge to Berlin, the train suddenly stopped and they witnessed the surrealistic nightmare of an air raid in progress over the city. This had never happened before in the daytime. It was March 4, 1944. After the "all clear" sounded, the train began to move again towards the beleaguered city as if nothing at all had happened—as if "business as usual" would be conducted that day.

Every evening, Frau Geisser allowed the young lovers to spend some time alone together in her kitchen where they could talk by candlelight in relative privacy. That particular evening they heard a news report on the small box radio about the commencement of daytime air raids on Berlin in addition to the nightly raids that the populace had already endured for almost four years.

Rolf suggested that perhaps Lilo and Gertrud should get away from Berlin and move to Havelberg, where Lilo's grandparents lived and where they would be safer. Lilo smiled and told him of her vain attempts to gain permission to leave Berlin. They talked about their hopes for the future. Rolf confided that he was now focused on only one thing—survival—which, for him, meant both a life together with her and the long-dreamed-of career in aeronautical engineering. He confided that he felt unsuited to the military, had no faith in the war effort and that from the family's first days back in Germany, had been unable to countenance the fanatical policies of Hitler and the Nazi regime.

They enjoyed just holding hands and sitting in companionable silence at times, each reflecting on how the small, ordinary, everyday details of life, so often taken for granted, would never seem ordinary or unremarkable again. Gazing at Lilo across the table on the last evening of his leave, Rolf had the strange sensation that she had changed. She was not quite the same person that she had been just a few short days ago. A new quality that he could only describe as a tender joy encased in confidence and certainty had surfaced. It was there in her smile and in the loving expression she wore whenever she looked at him. There was a strength and resilience about Lilo now that not even the threatening wartime conditions could diminish.

Chapter 26

Escape to Havelberg

he following week, Gertrud marched into the Berlin employment bureau determined to speak to someone in authority. Two officials were sent to hear her request. Gertrud began a well-rehearsed pitch to gain permission to move out of Berlin, pleading valiantly, but to no avail. No tactic she tried met with success. Each new attempt at persuasion only set the two officials repeatedly and in unison shouting the same refrain in a harsh staccato, "No working person leaves Berlin! No working person leaves Berlin!"

Overwhelmed by nervous exhaustion, frustration and worry, Gertrud felt a breakdown coming on—partly legitimate, and partly staged from sheer fatigue and desperation. Trembling, gasping for air, and rolling her eyes, she broke out in a cold sweat, aided by accumulated anger, fear and frustration. At this new and unexpected development, the officials' attitude changed abruptly from suspicion and hostility to embarrassed solicitude as they offered her water to drink and tried to calm her. She was ushered into the office of their superior, a kind-faced, elderly man, who immediately sat her down and spoke some reassuring words in a gentle tone. Not comprehending at first what he was saying to her, Gertrud was stunned when she finally realized that he had promptly and without further discussion granted her request to move out of the city.

After regaining her composure and thanking the official profusely amidst tears of joy and elation, Gertrud exited the employment bureau. Once out of sight of the building, laughing exultantly, she broke into a brisk pace, nearly running, to give Lilo the good news that they were free to move away from the bombed-out city of Berlin at last.

※◆※

Rolf received a letter from Lilo dated March 18, 1944:

Dearest Rolf,

Mother and I are settled in Havelberg at last, the place where I spent many of my summers and school holidays as a child! Although it was sad for us to leave our friends in Berlin, especially our voice teacher, Omi Henke, and my boss, Richard Mietke, and his family, it is a great relief to live a more normal life without the continual threat and disruption of air raids both day and night.

After staying with my grandparents for a few days, we found first a furnished room and then a two-room apartment that was vacated by a family with four children. Hopefully they will not suddenly reappear to reclaim their apartment! For now, we are paying them a generous monthly rent that we send via the mayor's office here in Havelberg. The apartment has no bathroom, only an outhouse out back, but it has running water in the kitchen. It is not what we have been accustomed to in the past, but the hardships of wartime have systematically weaned us from dependence on any "luxuries" to which we were previously accustomed. To have a little place of our own with no broken windows, walls intact, and doors that lock for privacy now seems like an extravagance. I call it a blessing!

We are in the process of having our furniture shipped from Berge through the Silesian Steamship Company where I am now employed. Meanwhile, we are spending all of our spare time cleaning, painting and renovating since the apartment desperately needs work. Gradually we are making it feel like home.

There is currently only an old-fashioned stove in the kitchen for heat, but we have found a potter who is willing to install a tile stove in exchange for two large packages of pipe tobacco plus pay. I don't know where we will find the tobacco, but Mother has determination and ingenuity enough for both of us whenever there is a need! She has found a job as a representative for a floor wax company selling reduced-quality wartime "gook" to those who insist even in these times on having sparkling clean floors. The new job with its flexible hours suits her independent nature and even allows her to give piano lessons to local children whose parents are struggling to maintain as normal a lifestyle as possible in the midst of wartime. The sounds of music make us all feel more optimistic and cheerful, certain that better times are right around the corner.

Did I ever tell you that Havelberg is built on an island? It is completely surrounded by the Havel River and town canals and is only connected to the mainland via three bridges. On a high plateau overlooking the town and the river, not far from my grandparent's house, stands the ancient Havelberger Dom Cathedral built in 1170 A.D. There is such a sense of history here, and a comforting tranquility envelops the town like a silent benediction even in the midst of wartime. Many of the lovely red brick buildings with tile roofs have changed little for centuries. I would love for you to come and enjoy with me this beautiful place that is the backdrop for so many wonderful childhood memories.

One day at the Thorn airbase, Rolf and the other trainees saw that the officers' quarters were under heavy guard. The word was that there had been an assassination attempt on Hitler. This was the failed assassination attempt known as Operation Valkyrie masterminded by Colonel Claus Schenk Graf von Stauffenberg and other members of the German Resistance movement within the Wehrmacht. It culminated in two hundred immediate executions of "enemies of the Reich" and as many as five thousand additional executions in the bloody purge that followed.[18] A decree was issued to abandon the universal military salute in favor of the Nazi stiff-armed salute, but without the "Heil Hitler" salutation. Severe penalties were also announced for the surrender of uninjured servicemen and there were dire threats of imprisonment for their family members as well.

Although Nazi radio and newspaper propaganda frequently still boasted of secret weapons that would turn the tide of the war in favor of Germany, Rolf suspected that the war was winding to an end with little or no chance of a German victory.

Chapter 27

Perfecting Hitler's Secret Weapon

Inside tunnels dug deep under Kohnstein Mountain at the top-secret installation of Mittelwerk near Nordhausen, Major Ernst Dutzmann was reviewing and signing off on paperwork. As head of the *Heeresabnahmestelle* (Army Acceptance Office) and chief inspector of the V-2 rockets manufactured there, he was in charge of over two hundred former Peenemünde scientists, design engineers and technicians, most of whom had by that time been conscripted to the military. His department was in charge of quality control at inspection sites spaced along the assembly line as well as at the main inspection site between the two largest underground tunnels.[19] In his work, he dealt primarily with army and civilian engineers and technicians, but also with Wernher von Braun, the central figure in Germany's pre-war rocket technology, who realized that the inspection process was essential to the project's overall success and remained closely involved in all decision making regarding its functions.[20]

Starting in mid-June of 1943, concentration camp inmates, many of them political prisoners, were deployed to carry out the production at Peenemünde.[21] That protocol, rationalized on the basis of the extreme wartime labor shortage across Germany, was continued in the two main tunnels at Mittelwerk where the manufacturing was carried out by thousands of prisoners who were shipped to the Mittelbau-Dora camp from all over Germany as well as from surrounding occupied nations and countries still at war with Germany. Among them were many Soviet, Polish, French, Czech, Belgian and Dutch prisoners. Along with the civilian and army engineers and technicians, they toiled for twelve or more hours each day in the immense, arched, stone-lined tunnels, creating and assembling parts while sitting or standing at specialized machinery. They were pressed into service as mechanics, welders, electricians, solderers, carpenters, painters, draftsmen, and other specialists, but a few prisoners with more technical qualifications were also engaged as inspectors, technicians, accountants and secretaries, including three who worked in Ernst's department.[22]

The workers on the daytime shift rarely saw the light of day since it was dark when they arrived at work underground and usually dark when they emerged. Unlike the civilian and army workers, however, the prisoners' living conditions in crude barracks located in the Dora Camp outside the manufacturing complex were dismal, and most of them suffered from hunger and overwork. Yet these were the more fortunate prisoners because, as specialists, they were able to work in a technical capacity shielded both from the elements and, by and large, from SS brutality. They also received better rations and experienced better living conditions than the other inmates, some of whom were still living in the dark, damp underground tunnels. In 1944, the unskilled laborers working on construction and transport *Kommandos* (units) still fared much worse than the technical workers, but even their circumstances were an improvement over the fate of thousands of prisoners who had labored on the expansion and installation of the underground facility starting in the fall of 1943, six thousand of whom died from exhaustion, malnutrition, overwork, lack of sleep, exposure, disease and abuse by the following spring.[23]

In Ernst's department, the prisoners were generally treated well by the civilian and army engineers who worked directly with them. On one occasion, however, Ernst received a report that one of the civilian engineers was kicking the inmates whenever he walked by them. After Ernst called the engineer in for a reprimand and threatened him with removal from the department, the abusive action was not repeated.[24]

The presence of SS guards in other parts of the underground tunnels, however, was an unpredictable factor that struck universal fear into the inmates. One SS guard in particular, Erwin Busta—nicknamed "Pferdekopf" (Horsehead) due to his elongated facial features—was especially sadistic and had been known to arbitrarily beat, whip and even murder prisoners on the spot whom he considered to be slacking off on the job. He never seemed to sleep, being on the prowl for victims day and night. Even many of the civilian workers were afraid of him. However, he did not dare to perpetrate any of his excesses in front of the civilian and army engineers in Ernst's department.[25]

Although Ernst had no opportunity to ensure the welfare of inmates during their time spent outside the plant, he felt personally responsible for all of the workers while under his direct employ. He maintained particularly cordial relations with a Czech inmate by the name of Jiri Benès, who was put in charge of secretarial tasks for the department, including recording the specific characteristics of each rocket that affected firing capability.[26] Ernst was aware that some SS guards and a handful of civilian engineers took sadistic pleasure in terrorizing the prisoners, but he felt constrained to focus on his own assignments and not become involved in anything not explicitly designated as his business.[27] Fear, along with the accompanying instinct of self-preservation, were universal under those extreme working conditions. For Ernst, there was indeed a sense of satisfaction in furthering the rocket technology, but it was mainly his strong sense of duty as a military officer and the underlying impulse of self-preservation that kept him at his post.

Besides, where was he to go? Under no illusions about the war effort and perhaps more informed than most about Germany's military setbacks, Ernst knew full well that the Nazi regime was foundering, and defeat was knocking like a specter at the very gates of the Reich. In June the Allies had landed at Normandy. Paris was liberated in August followed by the wholesale retreat of German troops from other parts of France. With Soviet troops encroaching from the East, the future of Germany looked bleak indeed, even though the first V-1 flying bombs had been launched against England earlier that year and the V-2, the "secret weapon" project on which the Nazi regime now pinned all its hopes, had taken on a life and a momentum of its own that kept Ernst and the other engineers tirelessly engaged in perfecting the production and inspection process.

Ernst gathered up all paperwork from his desk, carefully locked it in a safe according to security protocol, and proceeded to the central inspection site. As an officer, he had a *Jagdschein* (hunting pass), a special pass that granted him permission to roam anywhere in the installation,[28] but he rarely needed to use it at checkpoints because he was recognized on sight by most of the guards. En route, he passed the entrance to tunnel B where rockets at all phases of assembly were pushed along on specially designed rail cars that moved along tracks installed from one end of the tunnel to the other. The rockets were assembled in three stages: first the center section that contained the propulsion apparatus, fuel tanks and top of the engine; then the tail section containing the lower part of the engine; and finally the nose cone that contained all of the rocket-guidance components.[29] The final assembly of each rocket entailed over 1,200 man-hours by a myriad of specialists.[30] The warheads were attached only after delivery of the rockets to field depots. Finally, just before launching towards Antwerp, London or some other destination, they were erected at the launch sites and their tanks filled with fuel and liquid oxygen.

In the months since his transfer from Peenemünde to Mittelwerk, Ernst had become accustomed to frequent setbacks and delays. Production schedules had been revised and pushed back countless times, wartime resources continued to be stretched to the limit, and the output of missiles thus far had been a massive disappointment. Design changes were frustratingly frequent, each time necessitating intricate revisions of the entire assembly and inspection process. Some believed that industrial sabotage was occurring, but Ernst was convinced that it was the complexity of the rocket technology itself, still merely in its infancy, that was hampering progress and causing the costly mistakes and delays.[31] He was convinced that the V-2 would not be able to turn the tide of the war, but did not dare to communicate his doubts to anyone in view of the harsh punishment meted out to those who voiced defeatist sentiments.

Ernst arrived at the main inspection site where a rocket towered majestically up to the vaulted tunnel ceiling with staging erected alongside to assist in the inspection process. This was not just any rocket, but one that marked a critical turning point in V-2 production. Efforts to coordinate development and manufacturing had finally paid off, and the facility was now operating at close to anticipated capacity. Ernst and the technicians finished their inspection, and amidst enthusiastic cheering, Ernst signed off on the six-hundredth rocket assembled and inspected during the month of September 1944.[32]

On September 8, 1944, the first V-2 rocket hit London, but with its primitive navigational systems still allowing a seventeen-kilometer deviation, it missed its intended target and struck a residential area southwest of the city instead. The following month, Hitler issued orders to launch the V-2 rockets exclusively at London and Antwerp.[33]

Rolf received his food and pipe tobacco rations.

When a fellow trainee approached him for the usual trade of food for tobacco, Rolf exclaimed, "Not this time. There is a young lady with a far greater need for it and I think I'm going to marry her!" He wrapped the pipe tobacco and mailed it to Lilo with a note: "For your tile stove."

During the approach to some of the darkest days in Nazi Germany, amidst uncertainty, death and destruction all around, Rolf and Lilo decided to sow a fragile seed of hope. In May of 1944, banishing any last misgivings regarding what lay ahead of them, they pledged their love for each other.

Filing for the marriage permit required papers to prove Aryan ancestry for at least three generations. When the issuance of the permit was delayed, Ernst demanded immediate action on his son's request. Within a few days, Rolf received the coveted permit, and soon afterwards, his leave was approved. By that time, leave was even scarcer than food, and marriage leave was the only form of military leave still available. From an old gold ring of Gertrud's plus additional cash, Rolf and Lilo had two rings made which, according to German custom, they wore on the ring finger of the left hand until the wedding day, at which time the ring would be switched to the right hand. They decided to be married in Havelberg and set a tentative date—November 24, 1944—the very month when the US forces under General Patton would reach the borders of Germany proper.

Chapter 28

Something Borrowed, Something Blue

$\mathcal{L}$ilo received a letter from Rolf dated November 15, 1944 and hastily ripped it open, her expression both eager and anxious:

Dearest Lilo,

Thanks to intervention by my father on our behalf, our long-delayed marriage permit has finally been approved and so has my wedding leave.

With an exclamation of delight, Lilo yelled for Gertrud to come hear the news, then continued reading:

A last-minute upset is that my division has been transferred to Slovakia to guard railroads and munitions factories against the partisan uprisings in the area. We are being moved from place to place as necessity dictates. One night, a partisan unit swept through the city of Banovce where we were stationed, attacking our guard post. When we retreated to a nearby school building that we were using as our barracks, they managed to surround us. There was a furious exchange of machine gun and cannon fire for an hour or so, after which they retreated, leaving one of their wounded men behind, who, alas, was later executed under martial law. No one on our side was wounded, but the walls and ceilings of our accommodations have been decorated ever since with bullet holes and damage from the shattered glass.

As you can imagine, I am very uneasy about the increasingly dangerous assignments that my division is receiving of late. In addition, I am no longer involved in technical work that is in line with my interests and abilities. I decided to send a letter to my father to ask whether he could put in a word to have me transferred to the facility at Nordhausen where he is currently stationed, but his request on my behalf was denied, so I continue to be at the mercy of my current situation.

More recently, I was sent to Ruzomberok when orders came for our unit to join a German Army "penalty battalion" to mount a general offensive against solidly entrenched partisans west of the town. On that day, I was scheduled to serve as "Corporal of the Day" at our command center to answer phones and facilitate the communications between incoming calls and the officer in charge of our unit. Although the attack went in our favor and forced the partisans to retreat into the mountains, several of my comrades were wounded, one seriously. An enemy bullet exploded the clips of ammunition in his pocket and tore a hole in his abdomen. When doctors at the local hospital called for blood donors, I volunteered since I am a universal donor with "O" type blood. His color improved, but sadly, he died anyway a day later.

In the midst of all of this chaos, I so long to see you, my darling, and to finally make you my wife! I have been granted a ten-day leave and, God willing, I will depart my unit on November 19th from Malatzky, where I am currently stationed, and will arrive at the Havelberg train station via Berlin on the 21st.

From that day on, despite her recognition of the continual danger to which Rolf was exposed, Lilo wore a perpetual smile, supported by the solid conviction that they would both survive whatever was to come. She and Gertrud immediately began preparations for the wedding and reception just nine days away. They drew up a list of those who would be invited: Rolf's mother, father and sister, Lilo's father, grandparents, a great aunt and five of her friends. They numbered fifteen people, including Lilo, Rolf and Gertrud.

Not only did they need to find a place to hold the reception, but they would also have to feed all of their guests and find housing for some of them—a huge challenge in wartime with the ongoing rationing and housing shortage. They sent telegrams to Lilo's father, to Rolf's parents and to his sister, who would all be arriving from different parts of Germany. Then they made arrangements with the owners of a nearby restaurant, where they were shown a small but attractive banquet room. The owners pointed out that, although they would make every effort to prepare a delicious and memorable feast, they would be unable to supply most of the necessary food items due to the severe rationing, but Gertrud and Lilo were determined to find a way to provide most of what would be needed.

Gertrud arranged with two of her floor-cleaning-product customers, one of them a farmer, the other a fisherman, to obtain two chickens and several pounds of fish. Thus the main course menu choices were established as chicken fricassee and baked fish. She and Lilo checked the stock of coffee rations that they had been saving as well as the available stamps for butter, sugar and flour. Along with the extra ration stamps generously supplied by Lilo's grandparents and friends, they were able to order two large *Buttercremetorten* (buttercream cakes) from a local bakery to be supplemented by an old-fashioned *Streusselkuchen* (crumb cake) baked by a family friend. They also attempted to book rooms in two different hotels for their guests. The hotels were filled with evacuated people and refugees, and therefore rooms were difficult to obtain, but at the last minute, accommodations became available.

Next, Lilo and Gertrud turned their attention to Lilo's wedding attire. They had some money to spare, but there were no dress materials or notions available for purchase. That was where Gertrud's ingenuity came to the rescue. Out of the closet, she pulled an old ball gown of Lilo's with a full, white tulle skirt. Out of Gertrud's bureau drawer, came a generous length of white voile. Working furiously, cutting and stitching by hand until late in the night for over a week, Gertrud triumphantly produced a gown with a tulle skirt and a long-sleeved, white voile bodice with tulle inserts. Gertrud had trouble with the gathers at the bust line which resulted in some undesirable puckers. She ripped and restitched the area several times in an attempt to eliminate them, but Lilo finally told her not to trouble with it further. The finishing touch was brought about when Gertrud produced an old, light-blue silk slip to be worn under the gown and bleached it until it was almost white. A brand-new pair of white stockings received from Lilo's Aunt Lotti in Berlin, a long, white, lace wedding veil loaned by friends, a smoke-topaz cross pendant borrowed from Gertrud, along with a pair of silver sandals that Lilo already possessed, completed the outfit. For the bouquet, they ordered white chrysanthemums from a local florist.

Lilo reflected dreamily to her mother after surveying the components of her outfit, "Isn't there an American saying: "Something old, something new, something borrowed, something blue?"

Long before November 21st arrived, Lilo inquired about the incoming train schedule and was told that there were four trains arriving at the Havelberg train station via Berlin daily. When the day arrived, she checked her watch frequently. At ten o'clock in the morning, a train pulled in and the passengers disembarked. No Rolf.

Lilo remained waiting patiently at the station. Finally, her watch showed two o'clock in the afternoon. The train pulled in and the passengers disembarked. No Rolf. She went home and told Gertrud that Rolf was more likely to arrive on one of the two later trains anyway.

At seven o'clock in the evening, Lilo was posted at the station again. The second to the last train of the day pulled in and the passengers disembarked. Still no sign of Rolf.

Lilo returned home again. Finally, she made the trip back to the station for the last train of the day. The eleven o'clock train pulled in. There were few passengers on that train and Lilo watched anxiously as they disembarked. No Rolf, but Lilo remained standing on the platform as the passengers straggled out of the station. She took one more look along the full length of the empty train, and noticed way at the back of one of the cars, a man struggling along with knapsack, bags and gun. It was Rolf! In their long-awaited embrace, joy mingled with relief was made all the sweeter by the delay.

Chapter 29

Flower Petals on Their Path

Early the following morning Rolf and Lilo went to see the priest at the local Catholic church in Havelberg. He told them that he would perform the wedding ceremony on the one condition that they sign a commitment form stating that any children born to them would be baptized and raised in the Catholic faith. Rolf and Lilo looked at each other in consternation. Rolf had been raised in both the Lutheran and Catholic faith, but Lilo's sole religious experience was Lutheran. It was a last-minute predicament that they had not anticipated.

Taking Lilo's hand in his, Rolf stated quietly, looking at her and then at the priest, "No, I cannot ask that of her."

They decided instead to seek a Lutheran minister at the Havelberger Dom Cathedral. Their voices were hushed in awe as they entered the vast, hallowed structure. The minister informed them that, due to the fact that it was already winter and there was no heating system in the cathedral proper, the ceremony would have to be performed in the Paradiessaal (Paradise Hall) rather than in the cathedral proper. They agreed to that and finalized the arrangements.

In the afternoon, Ernst, Maria, Ruth and Lilo's father, Walter, arrived. Amidst the joyful reunion, Ernst surprised them with a case of excellent vintage wine for the reception obtained through a subordinate at the V-2 rocket assembly plant. Ernst explained to them that the family of the young man owned a vineyard in the Rhineland and the mission to procure the wine enabled the young soldier to visit with his parents one last time before American troops occupied the area only a few weeks later. This was a sobering note in the family gathering, reminding everyone with a bittersweet pang, that underneath the happiness of the occasion, the future and even the survival of everyone present remained shrouded in risk and uncertainty. For Rolf and Lilo, however, nothing beyond the present moment existed and they did not allow themselves to dwell on the fact that they would be parted again after the ten days of Rolf's leave.

During a quiet moment in the late afternoon, Maria, who was still reserved but polite, mentioned to Gertrud, whom she had just met for the first time, "I have heard how hard you worked on Lilo's gown. If there is anything to finish at the last minute, I would be glad to offer my help."

With a perceptive glance at Lilo's future mother-in-law, Gertrud answered, "That is very thoughtful of you."

Taking her by the arm, she led her into the next room where the gown was hanging under a protective fabric sheet.

As she removed the sheet, she said in a collaborative undertone, "There was a problem with the gathering at the bust. Perhaps with your expert sewing skills, you will know better than I what to do."

Maria took one look at the inside of the bodice and set to work, deftly ripping and restitching two seams. Gertrud left the room, smiling to herself. After about an hour, she beckoned Lilo to the room where Maria had been working and requested that she try on the gown one more time. Lilo asked no questions, although her expression registered curiosity. The gown slipped over her head, the bodice was tugged into place and Lilo surveyed her reflection in the looking glass. The puckers were gone and the gown now fit her perfectly.

Maria and Gertrud only smiled conspiratorially as Lilo hugged them both.

In the evening, the family was gathered at Lilo's grandparents' house when they were suddenly alarmed by crashing, shouting and other loud noises outside. They rushed to the doors and windows in time to see friends and neighbors smashing dishes at the paved entranceway.

"Polterabend!" cried Lilo's grandfather, recognizing with delight the gleeful, pre-wedding tradition that was customary in Germany. And then, smiling at Rolf and Lilo, "Scherben bringen Glück! (Broken pottery brings good luck!) Good fortune and happiness are now being invited into your life together. But custom dictates that in order to ensure those blessings, you will have to go out and clean up the mess!"

Rolf and Lilo did as they were told amidst the teasing ribaldry of the crowd.

The wedding day dawned gloriously warm and sunny for November. At ten o'clock in the morning, the civil ceremony took place at City Hall with Lilo's and Rolf's fathers serving as witnesses. Photos were taken afterwards on the steps of City Hall with Lilo classically stylish in a wool crepe suit and felt fedora. The three men appeared in their respective uniforms: Lilo's father in a navy uniform, Ernst in his Wehrmacht officer's uniform, and Rolf in a Luftwaffe uniform.

Later that same day, a horse-drawn carriage pulled up to the Havelberger Dom Cathedral. The driver, clad in a formal topcoat with tails and a top hat, jumped down and opened the door of the carriage. Rolf stepped out, handsome in his dress uniform, and gallantly lent his hand to assist the bride out of the carriage. Rolf was unable to keep his eyes from Lilo, who looked radiantly beautiful in the hand-tailored gown, her sleekly styled hair and trailing lace veil framing a glowing face wreathed in smiles. The cross hung suspended against the bodice of her gown from a silver chain. Behind them, a young girl wearing a long white dress and a circlet of flowers in her hair carried the long train of Lilo's veil, while ahead of them two young children, a boy and a girl carrying flower baskets, skipped hand-in-hand into the Paradiessaal of the cathedral. Here and there they dropped a flower ahead of the bride and groom.

Rolf and Lilo entered the hall together to the smiles, tears and exclamations of delight from waiting friends, relatives and onlookers—twenty-one people in all, who were able for a short time to forget about the peril and destruction of wartime. The minister beckoned the young couple to the altar. Rolf tucked Lilo's hand in his arm, his blue eyes reflecting the love shining in hers, as they approached the altar and knelt to take their vows.

After the solemn yet joyful ceremony, Rolf and Lilo left the church arm-in-arm as friends and relatives on either side called out wishes and greetings and the flower girl and boy once again tossed flowers ahead of them. On the way to the restaurant where the reception would be held, Rolf and Lilo threw pennies from the carriage windows to the local children, who ran along behind, scrambling to collect the coins.

The reception fare was sumptuous by wartime standards, with the Buttercremetorten and real coffee being special treats for all in attendance. Afterwards, the bride and groom danced to music played on a gramophone. They were in a world apart, totally oblivious as to who was still present and whether others were dancing.

When Rolf and Lilo left the restaurant, strains of music were still drifting languidly out into the unseasonably warm night. They walked leisurely hand in hand through the dark, quiet streets of the town, back to the apartment that Gertrud had agreed to vacate temporarily for the newlyweds. Before entering, they lingered at the front door, looking at the stars. Rolf kissed Lilo and pointed out a constellation in the sky.

"After we part again, just look for the Big Dipper in the night sky and know that I will be looking at it, too, from a place far, far away, praying for you."

At that moment, the hardships, the food shortages and the dangers of war seemed remote and insignificant compared to the bliss of their first night together as a married couple, and they allowed themselves the luxury of dreaming of a future with no more goodbyes.

After two more exquisite days spent together in Havelberg, Rolf and Lilo traveled by train to Benneckenstein to spend the final days of Rolf's leave with his parents. En route, Rolf noticed an emaciated prisoner in a striped, cotton uniform being ushered onto the train by an armed SS officer. It was late November and the weather had turned suddenly cold, but the prisoner had no coat and was shivering in his thin uniform. Rolf wondered about the incident, thinking it unusual that a prisoner would be individually transported in such a fashion. Much later, long after the war's end, he found out that concentration camp inmates with special technical or scientific skills, some of them even respected scientists, engineers and professors from occupied countries who had been arbitrarily pressed into service, were occasionally hand picked from camps elsewhere in Germany or even from locations outside of Germany proper to work on the V-2 rockets at Mittelwerk and then transported there under SS guard. Had that unfortunate prisoner been one of those?

Since the Dutzmann apartment was very small, Ernst rented a room at a local hotel for the newlyweds. By that time, the tension between Maria and Lilo had eased considerably. Rolf smiled to himself when he overheard his mother say of Lilo that what she lacked in wealth or social standing, she made up for with an exceptional character. Maria had always had the ability to gracefully accept and even thrive amidst challenging conditions once it was clear that no amount of effort on her part would change them.

Ernst was only home late in the evenings because he worked twelve-hour mystery shifts somewhere in the vicinity, leaving very early in the morning to travel to work by train and not arriving back home until well after seven o'clock in the evening. He divulged little of his work to Rolf, telling him only that he was involved in the development of the V-2 rocket and that the work was highly classified.

On the last day of Rolf's leave, Ernst pulled him aside and, with a remark that the days ahead would become increasingly dangerous for German military personnel, handed Rolf a small pistol.

"For self defense, in case you should ever need it," he commented .

At Rolf's request, Maria sewed a special pocket into the inside of his military knapsack to help conceal the pistol in the event of a search, but also to make it easier for Rolf to access it quickly in case his life should ever be in danger.

All too soon, Rolf and Lilo found themselves at a train station again, the brief honeymoon over. They held each other and kissed goodbye amidst the deafening noise and widespread panic of another daytime air raid. As Rolf boarded the train, Lilo lingered. He looked back, blowing her a kiss. Along with masses of other people, Lilo turned around to dash for the nearest shelter, but then changed her mind and ran back to the train, struggling against the human tide, frantically scanning the windows of the many compartments, searching for Rolf.

"One more glance, one more smile, just once more!" she thought to herself with a sense of burning urgency, realizing that they might never see each other again.

All of a sudden, a window near her opened.

An arm reached out towards her. "Lilo, Lilo!" Rolf shouted above the clamor of the air raid sirens and the hubbub of the fleeing crowds.

Lilo ran towards him just as the train began to move. As it pulled out of the station, Lilo could see Rolf's arm extended out of the window in a long wave goodbye until the train was almost out of sight. Only then did she turn and run for the nearest shelter, her heart hammering in her chest as much from the pain of parting as from exertion.

After ten blissful days together, the days and months once again stretched ahead fraught with danger, and a future with no more goodbyes seemed as insubstantial as a vague and wistful dream. The double pincers of the US, British and French Allied troops from the west and the Soviet Allied troops from the east were converging in a feeding frenzy to finish off what was left of the doomed and battered Nazi regime.

Left: Ernst in his Wehrmacht uniform and Rolf in his Luftwaffe uniform, Königsberg/Neumark, Germany, 1942

Right: Rolf home on leave with Maria and Ernst, 1943

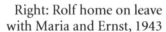

Left: Rolf in the pilot's seat of a *Grunau Baby* intermediate soaring plane at the Luftwaffe Navigator School in Thorn, Poland, 1943

Rolf reading a Berlin newspaper, the *Berliner Illustrierte* (*Berlin Illustrated*), 1943

Right: Ernst Dutzmann as Wehrmacht major, Peenemünde, 1943

Rolf with a broken wrist, 1943

Maria, Ruth and Lilo visiting Rolf, 1943

Rolf as Luftwaffe corporal, 1943

Ernst as chief inspector at the Mittelwerk V-2 rocket installation, 1944. The original photo has been donated to the Mittelbau-Dora Concentration Camp Memorial located at the former V-2 mass-production site.

The bombed-out Dutzmann apartment in Berlin, March 1944. Most of the family's furniture and other personal possessions were lost in the ruins.

The Havelberger Dom Cathedral keeping
a lofty watch over the town of Havelberg

Below: Rolf and Lilo's engagement
announcement, May 1944

Ihre Verlobung
geben bekannt:

Liselotte Wassull

Rolf Dutzmann
stud. ing. aero.
z. Zt. Uffz. der Luftwaffe

Havelberg (Mark) — Neukuhren (Ostpr.), 22. Mai 1944
Amtsstraße. 1

Right: On the steps of City Hall after the civil
ceremony with Lilo's father, Walter Wassull
(back left) and Rolf's father, Ernst Dutzmann
(back right), the morning of November 24, 1944

Lilo and Rolf arrive by carriage
at the Havelberger Dom Cathedral
for the church wedding in the
afternoon of November 24, 1944.
All wedding photos were
taken by Ernst Dutzmann.

Lilo and Rolf leaving the
Havelberger Dom Cathedral

The wedding party and guests
outside the cathedral

Lilo and Rolf,
wedding portrait

The wedding party

Lilo and Rolf dancing at the reception

Family photos taken the day after the wedding in front of the Havelberger Dom Cathedral

Part IV

DESPERATION

"Hope is not the conviction that something will turn out well but the certainty that something makes sense regardless of how it turns out."

— Vaclav Havel

Chapter 30

The Allies Advance

The events of the war continued to unfold with terrifying brutality and loss of life. From December 1944 through January 1945, the Battle of the Bulge was fought in the frigid, snowy Ardennes Forest of Belgium where as many men on both sides succumbed to the numbing cold as to the battle itself. It would prove to be the largest land battle on the Western Front, in which over nineteen thousand American and nearly sixteen thousand German soldiers lost their lives—an unsuccessful, desperate, last-ditch effort by the Nazi regime to stem the persistent Allied tide. By the time it was over, the remnant of the German military reserves was exhausted, the Luftwaffe was destroyed, and the remaining German forces in the west were being systematically pushed back to the Siegfried Line within the borders of Germany proper.[34] With the Soviet offensive across Germany's borders commencing simultaneously from the east, the foundering Nazi regime was caught in a noose of its own infamous making.

Lilo wrote a post-Christmas letter to Rolf dated January 5, 1945:

My Dearest Rolf,

It was painful for me to spend this Christmas without you, not knowing where you are and whether you are all right. I have had no word of you since our parting and, as you can well imagine, that has me fearful for your safety despite my conviction that all will be well and we will survive this dreadful and exhausting war.

Mother and I did not do much buying of presents this time, but one day in a bookstore I came across something that I just had to buy for little Peter in Berlin. I hope that it will entertain the little fellow and make these trying times seem a bit less terrifying.

It was nearing evening in Havelberg when Lilo lingered at the window of a bookstore and then stepped inside. She asked the shopkeeper a question and he motioned for her to follow him. He paused in front of a shelf, peering briefly over his spectacles, and pulled a book off the shelf, handing it to Lilo. As she opened the brightly illustrated front cover of *Der Struwwelpeter* and began to leaf through the pages, she beamed with delight, exclaiming every so often over one of the stories.

"I remember most of these stories by heart from my own childhood," she told the shopkeeper.

"You are very fortunate, my dear, to have stopped by here today. Scarcity, along with great popularity, have made that book nearly impossible to come by these days, and before long, it would have been snatched up by someone else!"

By the time Lilo left the store, night had fallen, and as she walked by the Havelberger Dom, she stopped to look up at the starlit sky. The Big Dipper twinkled luminously as if in blessing over the fervent prayer she offered for Rolf. Once back at the apartment, she wrote a greeting inside the front cover of the book, "*Frohe Weihnachten Peterchen. Deine, Tatta Rulle Appi*" ("Merry Christmas little Peter. From your Tatta Rulle Appi"), and wrapped the book in brown paper for mailing.

And so, I wrapped up the book weeks ago and sent it to Anneliese, Peter's mother. Just today I received a thank-you letter from her in which she told me that little Peter loves the book and cannot get enough of the stories. There was a sad note attached, however. She has had no word in several months from her husband, who was stationed in France, not even a Christmas greeting. Although she does not say so, I know that she fears the worst.

The very worst and most intense bombing of the city of Berlin was about to commence. From early 1945 until the end of the war, Great Britain, the United States and the Soviet Union were all dropping bombs on the beleaguered city. By March of that year, half of all homes in Berlin were damaged and around one third of them were uninhabitable. By the end of the war, approximately sixteen square kilometers of the city had been reduced to dust, ash and rubble and between twenty thousand and fifty thousand residents had perished.[35] Lilo never heard from Richard Mietke and family again, and all of her efforts to find or contact them after the war would prove to be in vain.

From the building where Lilo worked at the Silesian Steamship Company, she could see a steady stream of exhausted and destitute refugees arriving daily by train from Silesia and other areas to the east that had been previously overrun by the Soviets. She and Gertrud found out that the owners of the apartment they were renting lived in Silesia, and their concern was increasing daily that they might eventually need to move out to make way for them to return.

One day in mid-February, there was a loud series of knocks on the door of the apartment. When Lilo answered the door, she was surprised and a bit alarmed to see an SS man in uniform standing outside. Even though she did not know anything yet about SS atrocities during the war, she was sufficiently aware of SS fanaticism to be wary. He was polite enough, taking off his hat and introducing himself as the owner of the apartment. He stated that he just happened to be passing through the area and only wished to have a look at the "old homestead."

Lilo invited him to come in. He walked from one room to the next, remarking how pleased he was with the way the apartment looked, and especially with the new tile stove. Lilo and Gertrud were convinced that his next comment would be that he intended to move his family back, and that they would have to vacate the premises. But when they asked how his family was, he replied that they were well, and that they did not plan to move back to Havelberg in the foreseeable future. Despite his outward friendliness, Lilo and Gertrud were relieved when he turned to go. Perhaps it was the uniform more than anything else, but his presence left a chill that even the warmth from the tile stove could not dispel.

Soviet troops were advancing closer and closer to where Rolf's unit was stationed. There were reports of the Soviets advancing into Eastern Slovakia and also south of Rolf's unit into Hungary. Due to concerns about being overrun or surrounded, his unit was pulled back to Malatzky, where they were initially quartered in crude barracks. In the distance they could still hear the ominous daily rumbling of Russian artillery on the front near Budapest.

At the barracks a drama-in-miniature was playing out. A small, stray, black and white kitten appeared near the barracks. The nights had turned bitterly cold and Rolf noticed that the tiny creature had no collar or identification. Each evening he hoped that it would go home, but each morning it was still there, greeting him and the others with pleading, hungry eyes and a plaintive meow as they left their quarters. He started to feed it with anything he could obtain from the kitchen, including bowls of milk. Before long, he began to smuggle it out of the bitter cold into the barracks each night inside his coat.

Eventually the soldiers were dispersed to live with farm families while awaiting further orders. Rolf and one other soldier were ordered to make the journey to their assigned farm on foot. During the trek, the kitten, grateful for the free ride, was snugly stashed in Rolf's jacket pocket, from which its tiny head occasionally popped out for a view of the passing scenery.

Rolf and his comrade were each offered a couch in the farmer's living room to sleep on. During the day, they pitched in to help the farm family in the barns and stables. Rolf managed to keep the kitten indoors with him most of the time.

While he worked, it was either roaming around the stables or stashed in his pocket, and at night, it slept with him on the couch. When his unit was called away, he regretfully turned the kitten over to the farmer's wife, who promised to give it special care.

Another transfer took place. They were loaded into freight cars with straw for bedding and only a small stove in the center of each car for heat. Their destination, they were told, would be Gardelegen, about one hundred miles west of Berlin. En route they viewed hideous scenes of mass destruction. All major city railroad yards and stations were in shambles, with only the most urgent repairs carried out in makeshift fashion. The train was forced to make many detours due to bombed-out tracks. At one point, their train was moved to a siding in order to allow a short, very swift transport to pass. It consisted of a locomotive and a single flatbed car with anti-aircraft guns mounted on each end, flanking a long, covered object.

"What in the world could that be?" asked one of Rolf's companions.

Another soldier replied, "Maybe it has something to do with the so-called secret weapons we have been told about."

Rolf surmised that it was most likely a V-2 rocket, based on limited conversations with his father and the fact that the car received priority passage, but he shared none of his thoughts with the others.

Upon arrival at Gardelegen, they were quartered in unheated barracks. They attempted to gather wood from the surrounding forests in order to provide some heat, only to find, to their dismay, that the wood was too wet and unseasoned to burn. They were cold all the time and Rolf was very glad that he had left the kitten behind at the farm. He often thought longingly of his couch there and the welcome warmth from the wood stove.

Just a couple of months later, in April 1945, one of the worst known war crimes perpetrated by the Nazi regime would take place at Gardelegen. Over a thousand inmates evacuated from the Mittelbau-Dora Concentration Camp were transported there by the SS and herded into an immense barn filled with straw which was doused with gasoline and then incinerated. Those who tried to escape the scorching heat and flames were machine-gunned down. But still, about one hundred inmates *did* survive to relate the horrifying story to the Allied troops who arrived in the area soon after.[36]

Rolf and his fellow soldiers were fortunate that they were ordered away from that place before the aforementioned brutality took place. They were once again boarded onto a waiting freight car, at first elated at the prospect of abandoning their cold and cheerless quarters, but they were disappointed when the train failed to move for two days. But at least the new freight car in which they were housed was supplied with straw to sleep on and a crude stove with a supply of seasoned wood so that they could stay reasonably warm. When it finally began moving, however, fear gripped them—fear that they might be heading towards the Eastern Front. Rolf and the other soldiers talked apprehensively in low tones amongst themselves, speculating about what their destination might be, and watching feverishly for railroad station signs or identifiable landmarks. When they spied a sign for Kassel, an indication that they were heading westward, jubilation broke out among the ranks. Rolf immediately composed a letter to Lilo dated March 7, 1945, a letter that she would never receive:

Dearest Lilo,

We are on a train bound for an unknown destination. All of us are apprehensive, but by now we at least know that we are headed westward away from the Soviet threat. Please promise me that if and when the Soviets approach Havelberg, you and your mother will head west to Benneckenstein in the Harz Mountains to join my mother and sister. There you will be safe.

In early April of 1945, at the V-2 rocket assembly plant, Mittelwerk, Major Ernst Dutzmann was called into the office of his superior officer, who informed him that since the area was expected to be overrun by Allied troops at any time, he would be reassigned to a post further east. There had already been air attacks on Nordhausen and surroundings during the previous days, which had resulted in extensive destruction and many casualties. With the final collapse of the Third Reich imminent, evacuation orders were carried out with an urgent desperation bordering on panic, though accompanied by totally unrealistic perspectives as to whether the war would end and how.

"As chief inspector, your technical ability is too highly valued to keep you here, where you are in great danger. After finishing the inspection and sign-off on the rockets that are currently in progress, you will proceed immediately to Saxony." After a pause, he added, "On foot, that is. There is no transportation at our disposal anymore, not even for officers."

Just a few days earlier, expecting that such orders were imminent, Ernst had packed a bag. At the last minute, he put a photo of himself taken at Mittelwerk, as well as some assorted cards that had been hand drawn and signed for his fiftieth birthday just a month earlier, into the bottom of the bag. Normally such memorabilia would not be allowed to pass out of the installation, but with the Allies nearly at the gates, security at the plant was almost non-existent. Therefore, he was able to carry the items out undetected and bring them home to Maria for safekeeping. Each day, not knowing whether it would be their last before the inevitable evacuation orders, Ernst and Maria engaged in a tearful farewell, not knowing what the future would hold and whether they would live to see each other again.

So now, the time had finally come. After a last look around the workspace that he had occupied for fourteen months, Ernst set off on foot with a group of other officers. They immediately agreed that their best course of action would be to part ways.

"It is my conviction that Saxony, the area to which we have been ordered, will shortly be overrun by Soviet troops. I prefer to delay my move eastward as long as possible in order to avoid falling into Soviet hands," Ernst said.

"But if you stay here, you risk certain capture by British or American troops," one of his fellow officers protested.

After a moment's thoughtful reflection, Ernst replied, "I have throughout my life been faced with difficult decisions. The choice now is whether to drown in a barrel of water or a barrel of mud. I prefer to drown in a barrel of water."

Ernst continued heading eastward on foot as ordered but at a deliberately slow pace, harboring the ardent hope that he would soon be overtaken by US troops. Less than a week later, while he was resting at a farmhouse, US troops occupied the area. He was taken prisoner of war.

When the US troops arrived in the vicinity of Nordhausen on April 11, 1945, they were horrified to find over a thousand emaciated, dead and dying inmates in the sub-camp, Boelcke Kaserne, as well as another few hundred sick and debilitated inmates in the barracks of the Mittelbau-Dora camp itself.[37] They also discovered an arsenal of completely assembled rockets and enough finished parts to assemble two hundred fifty more.[38] With help from a member of Wernher von Braun's group, fourteen tons of documentation were also retrieved from a hiding place in an abandoned mine. The documents and one hundred rockets were promptly shipped to the USA for military research purposes.[39]

Chapter 31

The Russians are Coming

As the Soviet tide pushed westward, accompanied by alarming accounts of murder, rape and pillage inflamed by Nazi propaganda, the most fervent wish for thousands of displaced people was to stay ahead of the Soviets, preferring to be overtaken instead by American troops. Lilo and Gertrud were in the dark about the atrocities committed by German troops in the Soviet Union, Poland and other countries. They also did not know about the wholesale slaughter of "enemies of the Reich," including Jewish people, nor were they aware of the harsh conditions in Allied prisoner-of-war camps throughout Europe which were ill-equipped to provide for millions of captured German soldiers. Though the war was drawing to an inevitable close, some of the most trying times were yet to come.

In Havelberg, Lilo and Gertrud loaded a small wagon with the few prized possessions still left after their numerous relocations. Among them were all of the precious letters that Lilo had received from Rolf in the five years since they met, carefully tied with a silk ribbon and placed in a decorative wooden box.

The news was, "Die Russen Kommen!" (The Russians are coming!) By April 1, 1945, American troops had reached the west bank of the Elbe River. Their advance then halted to allow Soviet troops to arrive at the east bank—with Havelberg directly in their path. Lilo and Gertrud plotted their escape on foot to Benneckenstein, where, to their knowledge, Rolf's parents still had their home. Based on their calculations, it would be a journey of about 160 kilometers (100 miles), much of it in mountainous terrain. But first they had to cross the Elbe.

Lilo saw a boat coming across from the west bank carrying three American soldiers. She and Gertrud hurriedly hid the wagon in some nearby bushes and then approached the soldiers.

Trying to appear nonchalant, Lilo—grateful now for the English she had learned in school—inquired, "What would happen to civilians who attempt to cross the Elbe?"

One of the soldiers replied, "Since the war is still on, either the Germans will shoot you if they see you attempting to cross or our troops will shoot you before you make it to the opposite bank!" His tone softened a bit as he added, "Unless of course, you can find a place where no one is watching."

One of the other soldiers who had been observing the exchange offered to Lilo in passing, "I am sorry. We are forbidden to help anyone across."

Once unobserved by the soldiers, Lilo and Gertrud retrieved their possessions and resumed their trek along the river.

Gertrud said, "Somewhere there must be a bridge that is not guarded."

Every so often they managed to get a ride on a farmer's wagon, offering a rehearsed explanation that they were refugees from Berlin. At night they slept in bunkers full of displaced persons, both military and civilian. At one point they came across an area of vast destruction that Gertrud suddenly recognized as a former weapons depot. Now a blackened ruin, it had been bombed to oblivion.

"This is only twenty kilometers from Havelberg. How could we not have known about this destruction?" Lilo exclaimed in shocked disbelief as she and

Gertrud poked around in the ruins. "I wonder what else we have not been told?"

On the third day, they heard singing and laughter at midday coming from a roadside tavern.

"Poor things, they're living it up thinking their end is near," commented Gertrud, adding after a thoughtful pause, "And perhaps it is."

Later that day they gave up their quest to escape across the Elbe and headed back to Havelberg.

About a month later, in early May of 1945, an official announcement was broadcast by the mayor of Havelberg that the Soviet troops had advanced to less than twenty kilometers from the town. All women and children were advised to leave via the Elbe locks, which would now be opened to allow easy passage. Lilo and Gertrud once again gathered their meager belongings. At the last minute, Lilo rolled up a technical design of Rolf's—a "flying boat" drawing that he had entrusted to her for safekeeping with the request that she take it along in the event that she should have to escape the Soviet troops. It was a three-foot-long roll that she attached to one of her bags. All of the letters received from Rolf were once again packed securely in her suitcase. After a tearful farewell from Lilo's grandparents and great-grandmother, who had decided to stay behind—none of whom Lilo would ever see again—they hurried out of town along with thousands of other panic-stricken people, including many German soldiers who had thrown away their weapons and uniforms and were now posing as civilians.

Lilo and Gertrud abandoned their little wagon at the locks and, after a one-hour wait, were taken across on a ferry. Even German soldiers were mercifully taken across as prisoners of war by American troops in inflatable, motorized boats to get them away from the advancing Soviet troops who, it was expected, might not treat them so well. When Lilo and Gertrud reached the far side of the river, they were searched for weapons and dangerous implements of all kinds.

A soldier rummaged through Lilo's purse, found her nail file and ran it across his throat with a dramatic grimace demanding, "Kill? Kill?"

Lilo protested, horrified, "Oh no!"

When she started to giggle, suddenly seeing the humor in the situation, the soldier smiled, dropped the matter and returned the file to her purse. They were told that they were free to go, so they set on their way with a knapsack each on their backs, a blanket on top of each knapsack, and a suitcase or other large bag in each hand.

They walked for several hours amidst throngs of other refugees. With years of severe rationing, people in general had grown much thinner than in peacetime—Lilo and Gertrud included—but now they were joined by clusters of people with shaven heads who looked like mere cadavers on stilt-like legs, and who carried little or no baggage of any kind. Lilo and Gertrud were not yet aware that in July 1944, Soviet troops had liberated the first concentration camp at Majdanek. Other camp liberations followed, including Auschwitz in January of 1945, where an estimated two million people had been murdered—among them, one and a half million Jews. As they later found out, many of the emaciated people they encountered during their flight from Havelberg were liberated concentration camp inmates.

American military traffic was constantly passing them in both directions. Lilo attempted several times to get a ride on one of the slow-moving vehicles, but to no avail. Later in the day she finally succeeded, and they were fortunate enough to get a ride to a farmhouse with a US soldier. The house had been deserted in a hurry. Even an unfinished meal was still on the table. The soldier started a fire in the wood stove and heated some water for coffee—real coffee, not ersatz—which he supplied from his own rations.

He looked in Lilo's direction and said, "It's not safe for you to stay here very long because there are released Polish POWs marauding around the area at night, some of whom are terrorizing any fleeing Germans they encounter. I'm sorry that I can't drive you any farther, but let me show you where you can find shelter for tomorrow night."

He proceeded to point out on a map the direction in which they needed to travel the following day. By that time, it was past five o'clock in the evening.

At that very moment, unbeknownst to Lilo and Gertrud, Soviet troops were entering Havelberg. Although their reputation for brutality may have been exaggerated in some instances, in that particular takeover, they lived up to the worst fears of the local citizenry, raping young girls and also older women, plundering homes and businesses, smashing furniture and other personal possessions and even urinating and defecating in kitchens and living rooms. Some of the soldiers had never seen flush toilets before and used them to wash themselves. Lilo's grandparents, her great-grandmother and the neighbors who stayed behind were hiding in the cellar of their house. Once they were discovered, a fifty-year-old neighbor and her thirty-year-old daughter were dragged out of the cellar and raped. Lilo's grandparents and great-grandmother were not harmed, but her great-grandmother died the next day of a heart attack, the physical and emotional stress of the previous night's ordeal having taken its toll.

Lilo and Gertrud pressed onward. Some Poles that they met on the way spread false reports that the Soviets were continuing their advance and that they had better hurry to stay ahead of them. In actuality, the Soviet and US advance had halted at the banks of the Elbe, since there was no need for either army to press on into territory that was already in Allied hands. Nevertheless, the rumors stirred up great fear and consternation among the fleeing populace who had no way of knowing about the Allied military successes. Under the circumstances, Lilo and Gertrud decided to keep to smaller, less-traveled side roads where they felt safer.

A young refugee, carrying only a blanket and one small bag, introduced himself as Schäfer and offered to help them carry their bags. Lilo and Gertrud gratefully accepted. He confided that he had been in the German army, had returned to his home town of Havelberg, and was now pretending to have worked as a gardener throughout the war. He was en route to find his wife, who worked in Bavaria for a service unit.

Later, Lilo pulled Gertrud aside and asked her whether she believed Schäfer's story. Should they trust him? After all, he was carrying almost half of their remaining possessions, items that now were more precious to them than ever.

Gertrud replied, "With a name like Schäfer (Shepherd), how could we not trust him? My instinct tells me he is a good man."

Lilo agreed, and they resolved to help him in any way they could in return for his assistance carrying their bags. Their opportunity presented itself during the inspections that occurred on an almost daily basis, where they backed up his story, claiming that he had been their neighbor in Havelberg where he had worked as a gardener.

During the first stretch of the journey, they mostly stayed in private homes or shelters, often at farms where their rations were supplemented by homegrown food from people who sympathized with their fatigue, hunger and homelessness. Some of the farm families that they stayed with had radios and it was during one of those overnight stays that they found out that Hitler had committed suicide just a few days before their departure from Havelberg.

Eventually the conditions on their journey grew more severe as they were forced to sleep in barns, bunkers or wherever they could find makeshift shelter. One night in mountainous terrain, they found themselves among a group of refugees seeking shelter in a cave. A group of men with shaven heads spent much of the night exchanging stories around a campfire about their terrible ordeal in the "death camps"—relating how countless thousands of people were killed in gas chambers, and describing gruesome atrocities committed there, many in the name of science and medicine. In the flickering firelight, Lilo could see that they were showing each other something on their forearms. They spoke of tattoos.

"Do you hear what they are talking about?" Lilo whispered to her mother. "Could it be true?"

Gertrud replied, "Exaggeration? Rumor? Truth?" She shrugged her shoulders. "The most important thing for us now is to rest and regain our energy for tomorrow's walking."

With that, she rolled over on her side, pulling her coat over her head to block out the sound of the men talking.

Lilo tried to do the same, but the droning voices kept her awake.

She overheard one of them saying, "I was so heartbroken when they shaved off my hair. Ah, my beautiful hair! But soon it did not matter anymore. I survived only because one of the SS officers at the camp took a liking to me. He slipped me extra food now and then and also arranged to have me put on an easier work detail."

From under her blanket, Lilo peered over to where the group of men were huddled near the fire. The speaker was holding up a mirror fragment, and Lilo saw with a heart-wrenching shock that the skeletal hands stroking the tufts of new hair were definitely not the hands of a man.

At the end of each day's walking, Gertrud and Lilo consulted a road map they had brought along to plan the next day's route on their journey to Benneckenstein.

On the third day, they were stopped by the American military police as usual. The guard on duty looked at the three-foot-long roll of paper attached to one of Lilo's bags and motioned her to turn over the bag. He unrolled Rolf's blueprint of the "flying boat," looked at Lilo and then back at the drawing. Requesting that Gertrud wait outside, he beckoned Lilo to follow him to the office of his commanding officer. She was asked to sit down while the CO and a handful of other officers carefully inspected the drawing, conferring among themselves. The CO asked Lilo where she had obtained the drawing and why she was transporting it. She hesitantly replied in the British English learned during her school years that it was her husband's project from the university where he had attended before the war and that she had promised not to leave it behind. They engaged in further deliberations, and then finally, their expressions relaxing, handed the rolled-up drawing back to Lilo, saying that she was free to go.

Lilo and Gertrud journeyed on with the help of Schäfer. Several days later, Lilo suddenly sat down by the roadside, exclaiming over a sudden pain in one of her legs. She tried to get up and walk, but the sharp pain was still there and she was unable to put weight on the leg at all. From the very first steps of this journey, she had been apprehensive that the physical problems of her youth might resurface. If so, the timing could not be worse. Sitting by the roadside, with Gertrud looking on in helpless distress, Lilo gave way to bitter tears of anxiety, frustration and fear.

Chapter 32

Crossing the Harz Mountains

With a tone of the deepest concern for her daughter, Gertrud cried, "*Ach Gott*, let it not be your hips again, Lilo!"

She then insistently flagged down the very next American Army vehicle, telling the driver that her daughter was injured and that they urgently needed a ride to the nearest town.

The Americans agreed to take Lilo and Gertrud, but not their baggage, which they were forced to entrust entirely to Schäfer. While the driver waited, Gertrud made hurried arrangements with Schäfer to meet them later at the far side of the town, pointing out a location on her map.

En route, Lilo suddenly whispered to Gertrud in a startled undertone, "Mother, it feels as though the pain is going away!"

They were driven straight to the nearest hospital, and to their immense relief, the Americans did not linger, but merely dropped them off at the entrance.

"*Gott sei Dank* (Thank God), they did not insist on accompanying us inside!" exclaimed Lilo, finding the pain almost gone. "It must have only been a leg cramp."

When Lilo and Gertrud arrived at the far side of town they were relieved to see Schäfer already waiting with their bags. By that time, they felt very grateful towards him and fortunate to have placed their trust in him.

Lilo, Gertrud and Schäfer decided to quit walking early that day, since the next town was more than ten kilometers away. They stayed that night with a farm family. While they were sitting with them and a few other people in the living room, a radio broadcast came on announcing the German surrender and the end of the war in Europe. People began laughing, crying and jumping for joy that the inevitable end to the dreadful war had finally come. There was no longer any thought about being on the losing side of the conflict—or, for that matter, on the side that had instigated the war in the first place. There was only a sense of blessed relief. That day was unforgettable. It was May 8, 1945.

Later that evening, Lilo pulled down the shoulder of her blouse to examine the bloody sores from the load she was carrying daily. Blood-filled blisters had also formed on her feet and on the palms of her hands.

"We have been on the road for six days," announced Gertrud from nearby where she was bandaging her weary feet with rags. "At this rate, based on my calculations, we have about nine more days to go. But much of the walking from here on will be in rugged terrain and much harder."

The route did indeed become steeper as they approached the Harz Mountains. After struggling for hours up hillsides with frequent stops to rest, they arrived at a small town where children were playing in the street, merrily pushing their cat around in an old baby buggy. On a sudden inspiration, Gertrud offered the children some money for the buggy. The children were delighted at the unexpected windfall and ran off with their loot. Gertrud was smiling as she motioned Lilo and Schäfer to load their bags onto the carriage; then they started off again. Going uphill, all three of them pushed or pulled the carriage; on downhill stretches, it was all they could do to keep the buggy from speeding away out of control. But in that manner, they made much faster and easier progress.

It was a warm, sunny May morning in Benneckenstein. Rolf's sister, Ruth, happened to be looking out the window of the Dutzmann apartment, when she saw something unusual and remarked to Maria, "There is a very odd looking group of people out there on the street with a baby carriage loaded with baggage. Oh dear! The carriage looks like it has broken down!"

Joining her at the window, Maria exclaimed, "So, they have arrived! Quickly, get the large soup pot down from the upper shelf in the pantry and go make up the extra bed. They will be very tired and hungry!"

About an hour later, over steaming bowls of soup that Maria skillfully concocted from the scanty ingredients on hand, Lilo, Gertrud, Maria, Ruth and Schäfer exchanged stories, bringing each other up to date on recent happenings.

Maria told Lilo and Gertrud, "Rolf's father received evacuation orders by mid-April. Since then, we have had no news of him or his whereabouts. As for Rolf, he made it back here alive from the front." Then noting Lilo's expectant and hopeful gasp, she quickly added, "He walked two hundred fifty kilometers cross-country in early April to get home, but unfortunately you missed him by about four weeks."

She handed Lilo an envelope.

"However, I have this for you that he wrote when he was here. He wanted me to post it to you once the mail service resumed."

Amidst Lilo's mixed exclamations of joy that Rolf was alive and consternation at having missed him, she tore open the envelope. The date on the letter was April 19, 1945:

My Dearest Wife,

You will be amazed and very happy when you receive this letter. First I want to give you a quick kiss and then here it goes. Just yesterday I arrived in Benneckenstein and found my mother and Ruth well and healthy. Tomorrow morning I have to report to the "Ami" (the American Kommandantur or Headquarters), and so I am writing this letter beforehand since one never knows what might happen. In the worst case, I might not be able to write again so soon. I hope that by this time, Havelberg has been occupied by the Americans so that we can at least be "on the same side."

My darling, I hope that things are going well for you by today's harsh standards. You are and always will be endlessly dear to me. We will always stay firmly together and will overcome all obstacles and trials. We will remain true to ourselves and to each other and our great love will grow stronger and stronger. By now, we have persevered through the hardest times and must continue to trust in God who has not failed us thus far.

With many kisses,

Your Ever-Loyal Rolf

Lilo looked up from the letter, still troubled. As Maria and Ruth launched into relating the events of the previous months, Lilo was very quiet, only occasionally interjecting a question. She was experiencing a tumult of emotions—triumph that she and Gertrud had escaped the Russian occupation and managed to walk to the one place where Rolf would be sure to find her, excitement that she had come so close to being with her beloved again, but bitter disappointment at having missed him despite her best efforts. As the tale from Maria and Ruth progressed, however, all of those emotions were replaced by a sense of growing consternation and alarm as she realized that it might be a very long time, if ever, before she and Rolf would be reunited.

Chapter 33

Dispatch to the Front

By March of 1945, the US Army under General Patton had already advanced into Germany proper to the west bank of the Rhine River, and additional major Allied victories within Germany were soon expected to follow. Rolf, along with about a thousand other apprehensive Luftwaffe troops, was assembled on the east bank of the Rhine, directly across the river from the Allied Front near Koblenz. They had reason to be fearful. A new Führer directive was being announced for a renewed offensive—a final, though futile, unrealistic and death-defying attempt to halt the relentless Allied offensive into Germany:

"You must all fight for the Fatherland with strong hearts. Surrender is forbidden! Effective immediately, the family of any soldier captured uninjured will be punished by deportation to a concentration camp."

They were issued camouflage suits, but personal weapons were no longer available to carry out the ordered fighting. They were warned to move around cautiously since Allied Mustang fighters were already in the area strafing everything that moved. They marched northward in small groups so as not to present easy targets for enemy aircraft, dispersing to surrounding small villages at night to sleep in haylofts or in nearby woods. En route, they witnessed an Allied Mustang attack on a farmer who was out plowing his field, a violent burst of gunfire raking the ground and killing the farmer instantly. Several times at night they heard a deafening rumble and saw immense rocket plumes that Rolf knew could only be caused by V-2 rockets still being launched from somewhere nearby in a desperate effort to stem the Allied advance.

Rolf's unit was soon joined by Luftwaffe personnel in desperate retreat from France. They all had body lice, and soon the men in Rolf's division started scratching too. Eventually, everyone including Rolf became hopelessly infested.

Rolf was put in charge of a group of twelve men. One morning they overslept, which meant they had to make for the surrounding woods across a wide-open field in full daylight with Allied "Jabos" already circling overhead like vultures waiting to pounce on their prey. In small groups, they scrambled to the edge of the sheltering woods and then proceeded cautiously in the shadows of the leafless trees, taking one cautious step at a time. If it had not been a life and death matter, Rolf would have been amused at the macabre, surrealistic choreography in which he and the others were engaged—taking a step or two forward, then stopping still as fence posts and desperately trying to make themselves invisible as the planes dived in for a closer look. He and his comrades still had no personal weapons, just a few grenade throwers and a single *Sturmgewehr*—a new infantry weapon with a machine-gun-like action that would later come to be known as an assault rifle.

One night they marched more openly on the Autobahn. Ahead in the distance, they saw flashes of light and heard constant barrages of artillery fire. Towards dawn, they were ordered to dig foxholes on a hill overlooking the highway. They dug in and waited. Just before daylight, from the shelter of the woods, they watched as column after column of American tanks and other military vehicles passed them moving northward. In the evening they sent a group of men to a German supply depot in a nearby town for news and provisions. They returned with canned goods, bread and the alarming news that the area was already overrun by Allied troops. An order was issued to break up into even smaller groups and retreat eastward. Rolf and his company realized they were trapped behind enemy lines with only a slim chance of escaping. And with enemy troops already encroaching from all sides, "Escape to where?" was the disturbing question foremost on every soldier's mind. There was no longer any safe place within the Reich, especially for German military personnel. The situation was looking increasingly dire with no way out.

Finally the orders came, "Save yourself if you can," and "Each man for himself."

Rolf and the others in his unit understood this to be unofficial sanction for a full-fledged retreat.

During the escape eastward away from the front, they came across a mysterious tower—a staging area of some sort that looked very familiar to Rolf. The other soldiers walked around it, conjecturing as to its purpose.

Rolf was fairly certain that it was an abandoned V-2 rocket staging area, but he once again did not feel free to share his insight with the others. Rolf's suspicions were confirmed by news reports after the war ended: as the German Army retreated east of the Rhine River away from the rapidly advancing American, French and British troops, V-2 rocket launch sites were left behind. They were towers just like the one that Rolf, Ernst and Ruth had encountered on the Baltic coast near Seebad Bansin six years earlier—staging areas for the most advanced weapons system known to man. With rocket production grinding to a halt and the war as good as lost, no further launch sites would be established further east.

Eventually, Rolf and his unit arrived at the bank of the Lahn River. All bridges by that time were either guarded by American or German troops; they decided to avoid both. They requisitioned a metal tub from a nearby farm, placed their clothes inside and swam across the icy cold, 150-foot-wide river, pushing the tub ahead of them. On the other side, they once again donned the uniforms that had miraculously managed to stay dry.

They proceeded through the woods and found themselves on a steep hillside overlooking the courtyard of a castle previously used as a German army training base, but now overrun by American troops. They pressed on, and as they crossed a highway, they were offered a ride by a passing German convoy. Footsore and weary, Rolf and his comrades were grateful to ride in relative comfort, but their relief was short-lived. After traveling only a short distance, a volley of shots was fired at the convoy from the hills overlooking the road. As Rolf and the others fled for cover into the surrounding woods, Rolf fingered the small pistol concealed in the secret pocket of his bag, hoping that he would not soon find himself needing to use it.

Based on that experience, Rolf and the other seven men still remaining in his group decided that joining other German units had become too risky and that their chances of survival would be improved if they traveled the rest of the distance by themselves and on foot. Their intention was to make their way home. They had run out of food and were traveling via side roads and forests and sleeping in haylofts of remote farms, where they were occasionally also fed. Since their only map showed major German cities but no details, they fell back on their navigator training and plotted their course by the North Star, inquiring every so often at local farms to make sure they were still heading in the right direction. Whenever Rolf looked at the night sky, he marveled at how distant, clean and peaceful the stars appeared as they hung suspended over the wartime chaos in a remote corner of the universe on this tiny planet called Earth. He located the Big Dipper and thought about Lilo, wondering where she was and how she was, and sent a fervent prayer winging her way. He and his companions had started their journey about two hundred fifty kilometers (156 miles) from Benneckenstein. He hoped that Lilo had arrived there already so that she would be able to receive his prayer in a place of relative safety.

Three of the seven men turned off in different directions toward their homes, each fervently hoping that there was still a home and a family to return to. That left only four other men still traveling with Rolf. The ditches of the side roads were littered with horse carcasses, casualties of Allied fighter plane attacks. All usable flesh had been cut away from the carcasses by starving locals and refugees, leaving the skeletons and inner organs to decompose on the ground. The stench was overpowering and it was all Rolf and the others could do not to gag.

One night they sheltered in a barn and were awakened the next morning by the unsuspecting farm family arriving to gather eggs. The farmers froze in their tracks, startled to see five sets of eyes staring back at them from the hayloft.

"Wir sind Deutsche!" ("We are German!") Rolf called out, whereupon the family relaxed, invited them into the farmhouse and offered them a much-needed breakfast and extra provisions for the road.

While they were being fed, the farmer asked whether they had heard anything about concentration camps being liberated by the Allies. When Rolf and his companions replied that they had heard no news of any kind in many weeks, the farmer told them that there were more and more stories circulating about the horrors discovered in the camps—piles of corpses, half-cremated bodies in ovens, mass graves and thousands of living, barely moving skeletons, people more dead than alive, who were being liberated from the camps. He told them that the Allied troops were deliberately marching local civilians through the camps, mostly farmers from surrounding rural areas, to witness the atrocities firsthand and that was how the news was spreading.

Once they finished eating, the farmer stated, "Now we have a quandary, because unfortunately there is an American platoon quartered only a few houses away, and between here and the woods there is an open field where they are sure to spot you!"

He rummaged around in a closet and emerged with an armful of civilian work clothes, which he invited them to put on in place of their blue Luftwaffe uniforms. One by one they exited the house and took separate routes to the surrounding woods. Attired in civilian clothing, Rolf and his companions felt relieved that they would no longer be such obvious targets for Allied troops in the area.

Shortly thereafter, they again encountered a river with no easy way across, necessitating another frigid swim. This time they fashioned a raft out of fence posts tied together with telephone wire cut from nearby downed lines. They waited until nightfall and then tied their clothes to the raft. Rolf, still a strong swimmer from his high school and university days, entered the water first, pulling the raft behind him. Another soldier who was unable to swim held onto the raft. They were not as fortunate as in their previous river crossing. Halfway across, the strong current capsized the raft, soaking all of their clothing and panicking the non-swimmer trying desperately to hold on. They made it across only with great difficulty, losing some of their meager supplies to the swift current.

Once on the other side, they found a hay-filled barn where they hung their wet garments from the rafters. Rolf checked to make sure the pistol from his father was secure in the secret pocket in his bag. Shivering and clad only in wet underwear, they burrowed into the hay for warmth and tried to sleep. In the morning the clothes were frigid and clammy, but they put them on anyway and continued their journey.

By the time Rolf approached the Harz Mountains, only one other man was still accompanying him. In the distance they could see a small village nestled in the hilly landscape, and after rounding a turn in the road they were suddenly confronted by two British soldiers pushing a requisitioned motorcycle. It was too late to run or hide without arousing suspicion. Doubly grateful to the farmer for their civilian attire, Rolf and his companion approached the soldiers as nonchalantly as possible, struck up a conversation about why the cycle's engine would not start and offered their assistance to inspect it. The British soldiers frisked them and ordered Rolf to open the bag he was carrying. Rolf opened it and held it towards them, his hand carefully positioned over the opening of the inside pocket in which the small pistol was hidden. He felt his heart hammering in his chest and the blood rushing to his head as one of the soldiers rummaged around in the bag with one hand. To his intense relief, they did not take it from him for closer inspection or insist he empty it. Shortly, after all attempts to start the motorcycle proved futile, Rolf and his companion were allowed to continue on their way.

A short distance up the road, Rolf told his partner to wait a moment. He walked a short distance away from the roadside, hurriedly dug a shallow hole, took the pistol out of his bag and buried it with a comment that he should have disposed of it long ago. The weapon was a liability that could cause both of them to come under suspicion and be taken as prisoners of war.

Finally, the last traveling companion turned off and Rolf was walking alone. There was a lot of American military traffic in the vicinity and the roadsides were littered with German guns and ammunition. When he came to a US Army checkpoint, he was stopped and asked to identify himself and state where he was headed. Rolf, thankful once again for the civilian clothing provided by the farmer, stated that he was a Latvian forced laborer and pulled out the student I.D. from the University in Danzig that he had managed to keep in his possession.

The officials seemed to believe his story, handed back his I.D. and told him he was free to go when suddenly one of them called out after him, "Hey you!"

Rolf stopped short, alarmed.

"One last thing. What is the capital of Lithuania?"

Rolf answered without hesitation, "Kaunas!"

Waving Rolf on, he turned to his companion, "Had he said Kowno, the German pronunciation, we would have had to turn him in."

Rolf had just walked a few steps when the same guard called after him again. Rolf turned to face them once more, his heart beating a desperate staccato as he struggled to maintain an unconcerned demeanor that would not arouse suspicion.

"In case you are hungry, there is a soup kitchen in the next town on the Hochstrasse!" called the guard.

He smiled and waved and Rolf waved back, relief flooding through every fiber. Despite the gnawing hunger and bone weariness that was overwhelming him, he decided to avoid both the soup kitchen and the town, wary by now of any further questioning he might have to face there. He mustered the last few reserves of strength and determination to press onward towards home.

Chapter 34

POW in the Freezing Mud

olf had been standing across the street from his parents' apartment building in Benneckenstein for over an hour anxiously searching the windows for signs of his family. He couldn't just walk over and knock on the door, for fear of putting himself and the family in jeopardy—if they were still there. To his relief, his mother's face finally appeared at a window, and soon the door opened to admit him. Maria and Ruth greeted him at the door in subdued fashion, only throwing their arms around him, kissing him and exclaiming over his safe return once he was safely inside. His reluctance to knock on the door proved well-founded. They informed him that other people in the house were suspicious of anyone harboring former German soldiers for fear of repercussions from the US occupation forces.

"What do you hear of Lilo?" Rolf asked anxiously, upon which they sadly told him that they had heard nothing from her or from her family. "My last news of her was a letter about two months ago," he said with a regretful sigh.

"First things first. We can talk later," Maria stated firmly.

They threw away all of Rolf's clothing and he underwent a thorough delousing and a long bath. Afterwards Maria and Ruth filled him in on the events that had recently occurred in the extended family, including the fate of those who had initially stayed behind in Latvia.

After having their home in Latvia taken over by the Soviet troops in 1940, Rolf's aunts, Paula, Ada and Emily, along with his grandmother, Julia, regained possession of their home briefly from 1941 to 1944 when Germany occupied Latvia. Then in 1944, with the port city of Liepaja once again surrounded by Soviet troops, another brutal Communist takeover imminent, and Nazi propaganda predicting even more dire consequences for any Germans still remaining in Latvia, they fled via ship from Latvia to Germany. Their brother Alfons still stubbornly refused to leave Latvia with them. By that time, travel by ship had become perilous due to the presence of Soviet submarines in the Baltic Sea. They arrived safely, but just a few months later, on January 30, 1945, a large ocean liner, the *Wilhelm Gustloff*, with over ten thousand German refugees, left the Bay of Danzig and was torpedoed by a Soviet submarine. It was the largest ship disaster in history, yet one that would remain virtually unknown. Over nine thousand people perished in icy seas, nearly half of them infants and children who were being evacuated from Latvia to what should have been a more secure future in Western Europe.[40]

Of the immediate family, only Lilo, Gertrud and Ernst were still unaccounted for. The fate of members of Lilo's extended family who had stayed behind in Havelberg, however, was also unknown.

A sudden, loud knock on the door interrupted their conversation. It was one of the other tenants. He said that he was aware that their son had returned, and he had been chosen as spokesman by the other residents in the building to point out that Rolf's unauthorized presence was putting them all at risk. In order to ease the tenants' anxiety, Rolf stated his intention to report his presence and register at the Kommandantur the following day.

The next day dawned warm and sunny. After putting on a woolen overcoat, Rolf decided that it would be too warm and took it back off, leaving it behind. He set off accompanied by Ruth. As they approached City Hall where the Kommandantur was located, they were stopped by US MPs and asked to produce their papers. Rolf, of course, had none. Despite Ruth's frantic protests that he was on his way to register, he was taken into custody along with a group of other men under suspicion. Rolf's life as a prisoner of war had begun.

"We have orders from General Eisenhower to make every effort to prevent Nazis from slipping through our fingers," one of the MPs announced to the assembled men.

In the afternoon a truck arrived, and ten men, including Rolf, were loaded into the back. As the truck drove away, Rolf saw Ruth in the crowd milling around outside the building. She was yelling, waving and trying to catch up with the departing vehicle. In one hand was his coat, but she did not make it close enough to throw it on board. Shortly they arrived at an empty warehouse in Nordhausen, where they were checked under their arms for tattoos of their blood type—a sign of SS membership. A few SS men were discovered in the group and punched, kicked and made to stand for hours spread-eagled against a wall before being transported elsewhere. There were no sanitary facilities and no rations; Rolf and the others suffered through a sleepless night on a hard cement floor.

The next day they were loaded back onto the truck. In some of the towns they traveled through, people flocked to the truck and passed loaves of bread up to them, a few of which Rolf and the other men, by that time ravenously hungry, managed to grab and devour. Later that day, they arrived at an immense, open-air POW camp where they underwent further interrogation. The camp was located almost back where Rolf had started, very close to the front that he had fled more than three weeks earlier to make his laborious cross-country trek homeward. He was relieved that Ruth had been with him at the time of his arrest so that the family would at least know what had happened to him.

Rolf stated his name to the interrogating officer, who painstakingly consulted page after page of notes and then asked, "And what is your relationship to Major Ernst Dutzmann?"

"He is my father," replied Rolf.

"And what is your home address?"

"Benneckenstein, in the Harz Mountains."

Rolf was given a box of C-Rations, an eight-inch by two-inch by one-inch cardboard box.

"Make it last. You won't get anything else for two days," he was informed in a matter-of-fact tone.

He opened the box to inspect the contents while standing up since there was no place to sit. Inside were five crackers, about one-half ounce of cheese, a small piece of chocolate and a packet of instant coffee, just enough for one cup. Famished, he immediately consumed the cheese, two of the crackers and a small bite of the chocolate, his first food in over two days other than a few mouthfuls of bread. Then he looked around and saw that some of the POWs were heating up their coffee in tin cans over small fires that they built using the emptied C-Ration cartons. Rolf wandered over to one group and questioned a fellow POW about getting his coffee heated. The man took his coffee packet, emptying it into a tin can, and asked him where he was from.

When Rolf answered Benneckenstein, the man replied, "That's good. Since it is in a British-occupied area and not Soviet, you are more likely to be eventually released."

"Are German officers ever brought here?" Rolf inquired, thinking of his father.

"Yes, over there," pointing to the other side of the camp. "There is a section just for officers, but they only stay a short time before being shipped off elsewhere."

Every day, truckloads of POWs were being shipped into and out of the camp. Rolf watched all of the departing transports and also asked around about his father. One day he saw a man who looked like his father on board one of the trucks leaving the camp, but the truck was too far away for him to be sure. A few days later, he too was boarded first into a truck and then onto a freight car. It was cold, rainy and miserable, and several of the men, including Rolf, succumbed to gut-wrenching diarrhea. Worst of all, there were no toilets, only the perennial tin cans.

The train arrived west of the Rhine River and the POWs were marched about five kilometers to a large open field that had been previously seeded with wheat by the farmer who owned the land. At the time of their arrival, there was a hint of green on the field from the sprouting wheat, but soon, with tens of thousands of POWs as well as Allied troops and vehicles crushing the tender shoots underfoot, the field was reduced to a freezing mud pit. It was obvious that the

US occupying forces had managed to expend very little time, resources and manpower to prepare for the massive influx of German POWs. Tanks with armed guards were set up every hundred yards around the perimeter of the camp, forming the only barrier to escape. Since there had been no time to erect tents or shelters of any kind, the POWs were forced to sleep on the muddy ground. It was cold and rainy during the day and well below freezing at night, the harsh and dangerous conditions a direct threat to many of the men who were already weakened by combat conditions on the front and years of rationing. The POWs in uniform had their overcoats and some had tarps, but Rolf had only the spring-weight suit he was wearing the day he was shipped out of Benneckenstein. Shivering from the cold, especially at night, he often thought with desperate longing of the coat he had so nonchalantly left behind.

After several bitterly cold, miserable nights, Rolf struck upon a survival plan, gathered six other men, and set them to work helping him dig a knee-deep hole in the muddy ground with their hands.

Some American guards strolled by, joking, "No use trying to dig your way out of here!"

That night, once the hole was dug, Rolf and the members of his group sat propped up together in a tight circle with their legs and feet down into the hole. By sharing their blankets, overcoats and tarps, they were able to cover themselves while attempting to sleep sitting up as a group. The next morning Rolf's feet were numb as he pulled his legs out of the freezing mud. As he took off his boots to massage his feet, he saw rows of dead POWs being laid out nearby to be taken away for burial. The following night one of his group suddenly tipped over into the mudhole and could not be revived. In the morning the dead man was laid out with scores of others who failed to make it through the night. Many thousands of POWs died during the two and a half months that the camp was under American control. There was no sanitation and little or no medical care.

Every day additional transports of POWs arrived. Rolf overheard that the camp they were in was located near a place called Bretzenheim and that there were already a hundred thousand prisoners detained there. The American troops were working feverishly to erect a fence and to improve conditions, but each

POW still received only one box of C-Rations every two days, resulting in a high mortality rate from hunger as well as from exposure.[41]

About a week after Rolf's arrival, there was a call from the guard battalion at the camp for kitchen help as an interpreter. Since he was fluent in English, Rolf promptly volunteered for the job, and upon being tested with a few questions to ascertain his command of the language, he was appointed to the task. Early in the morning, he and the other volunteers were picked up by truck and driven to the guard kitchen in Bretzenheim. Rolf's job was to interpret the orders given by American cooks to the volunteer German POW kitchen helpers. They received plenty to eat at the guard kitchen and were even given leftovers to bring back to the camp.

Since the American soldiers at the kitchen were friendly and eager to communicate with the German POWs, Rolf made full use of his English language skills to engage them in conversation. He soon discovered that most of the Americans were concerned about being transferred to the Pacific since the war with Japan was still underway. He and the other kitchen volunteers were even given access to copies of the American newspaper, *The Stars and Stripes*, to stay informed about current events. It was during his kitchen duties that announcements were made about Hitler's suicide and the end of the war in Europe.

One day Rolf had an idea to collect all the empty cartons from the kitchen supply shipments and bring them back to the camp for a construction project. POWs all over the camp sprang into action to put his idea into effect overnight. By the following morning, housing in the form of carton shacks held together with planks from dismantled wooden US Army crates sprouted up all over the muddy field.

One day, while standing in a line of men, all of whom were from the same general area of Germany, Rolf befriended a POW by the name of Rudi. When Rudi found out that Rolf worked at the kitchen each day, he and Rolf agreed to exchange favors. In return for leftover food from the kitchen, Rudi built them a carton shack and "looked after things" during the day while Rolf was away.

Rolf's position at the camp kitchen gave him access to large amounts of leftover food on a regular basis. Initially he brought it back, gave Rudi first choice and then offered the rest to other POWs in the carton shacks nearest to their own. It was not long before the news of this spread like wildfire through the camp. Returning from kitchen duty one evening, Rolf's truck was besieged by POWs yelling for food, and a full-fledged riot ensued. After that unfortunate incident, the camp commandant issued an order that leftover food from the kitchen was no longer to be brought back to the camp.

In time, the POWs were informed that those whose homes were located in British- or American-occupied areas would be discharged shortly, so Rolf and Rudi were both hopeful that they would soon be going home. On duty at the kitchen a day later, Rolf opened the latest edition of *The Stars and Stripes* and saw an article accompanied by a map indicating the areas already in the Soviet Zone and those slated for Soviet occupation. He felt his heart sink to his shoes when he saw that among them were not only Havelberg where Lilo and her mother had last lived, but also parts of the Harz Mountains, including Benneckenstein, the town that he had reported as his home. He and Rudi soon discovered, to their acute dismay, that discharge for both of them had been cancelled since no one would be released into the areas under Soviet occupation.

On the day of the mass exodus, Rolf and Rudi watched forlornly as truckloads of POWs left the camp bound for home. Afterwards, Rolf estimated that there were only about a thousand POWs left. He also lost his kitchen duty and was back on C-Rations. Rolf, Rudi and the other remaining POWs were cold, hungry and disheartened.

For Rolf, the fact that he had received no word from Lilo in many months worried him even more than his immediate physical discomfort. Was she alive? Did she head westward in time and make it to the British or American Zone, or was she trapped in the Soviet Zone? The lack of news was like a festering wound caused by a sliver of glass under the skin. Each time Rolf thought about the uncertainties regarding Lilo, the pain became greater and the worry was driven deeper and deeper. There was no way to get answers. And yet, he could not refrain from thinking of her for long, so it was a never-ending spiral of increasing anxiety.

Rolf's time for reflection was cut short, however, when the camp was suddenly overrun by Moroccan guards. Rolf found out that it had been turned over to the French occupying forces who immediately set about erecting many more tents than seemed necessary. They also issued uniforms to the POWs, but Rolf managed to keep his civilian suit on underneath the uniform for added warmth.

Shortly after that, trainloads of German POWs previously held in Norway started arriving, quickly filling the previously vacant tents. After being processed at the camp, most of them were sent to France for forced labor clearing minefields and rubble. Rolf and the other camp inmates were assigned maintenance duties, where they were regularly in close contact with the arriving POWs. Sometimes Rolf was surreptitiously handed a watch, family heirloom, photo or other treasured item by one of the arriving prisoners that he secretly tucked into his pocket, returning it only after the prisoner had gone through the frisking process. Rolf estimated that there were once again at least a hundred thousand German POWs present in the camp.

One day during the influx of German prisoners, Rudi ran up to Rolf, breathless with excitement.

"Rolf, I have great news! About Havelberg! I just found out that there is a sixty-year-old man, one of the recently arrived POWs, who is being released shortly to the Havelberg area in the Soviet Zone. Didn't you say that your wife lives there?"

"Hopefully Lilo left there long ago, but perhaps some of her relatives have stayed behind," Rolf replied.

They discussed Rolf's options, after which he went to talk to the man, Johann Kanter, who told him that he would be happy to take a message to Rolf's relatives if they were still in the Soviet Zone. Since bearing messages out of the camp was strictly forbidden, they decided that Rolf should write just a couple of words in his own hand, something that would not look like a smuggled message in case it was discovered amongst Johann's belongings or on his person. Rolf requested that Johann go to Lilo and Gertrud's apartment in Havelberg first in case they were still there, but if not, then to Lilo's grandparents' home. He quickly jotted something down on a small piece of paper. After deciding it seemed insignificant enough to avoid suspicion even if it should be discovered by camp authorities, he handed it to Johann.

Johann glanced at it, then quickly slipped the scrap of paper into his pocket.

"That should leave no doubt about your survival," he remarked with a smile.

Chapter 35

Escape from the Soviet Zone

*R*uth stormed into the guesthouse in Benneckenstein where Lilo and Gertrud were living, her face white as a sheet. She was out of breath from running, and panic resonated in her voice.

"Everything has changed overnight! All of the signs in town identifying public buildings that were in German and English are now printed in German and Russian!"

Dismayed at the prospect of either facing or fleeing another Russian occupation, Lilo and Gertrud followed Ruth to the apartment she shared with Maria and the four of them commenced a fast and furious packing campaign. Maria had kept wooden crates on hand for just such an emergency, which they began to fill with whatever china, crystal, linens and other household items had survived the flight from Latvia, the many subsequent relocations and the bombing of the apartment in Berlin. In spite of the atmosphere of desperate urgency, Maria directed the packing with calm authority to ensure that the most cherished items would arrive at their next destination intact.

As a native Rhinelander, Maria was able to travel legally via transport bus. She was allowed to take Ruth, Lilo, and—with a small bribe to a local official—Lilo's mother, Gertrud. However, at the last minute they were forced to leave behind seven of the wooden crates containing many of the family's precious belongings as well as two rolls of exquisite, handcrafted oriental rugs.

Maria hoped to be reunited at long last with members of her family. Their destination was Krefeld, a city near the Rhine River and the Dutch border where Maria's sister, Käthe, lived with her husband and four daughters: Anneliese, Erna, Marta and Ilse.

The trip took about eight hours by bus, including a stop for "delousing" in Duisburg where the men and women were placed in separate lines. Lilo and Ruth could hardly keep from laughing out loud at the procedure for the women, which consisted of one official going along the line and tossing some powdery white substance under each skirt and another blowing the same powder down each back under the collar. Once this procedure was carried out, they were declared "louse-free" and allowed to continue across the Rhine River.

They arrived totally unannounced at the home of Maria's sister, who generously took all of them in, even Lilo and her mother, whom she had never met before. But the family's home was too small to accommodate them all for long, so Lilo and Gertrud soon found themselves inquiring about another place to live. The downtown area of Krefeld had been badly bombed, and housing even on the outskirts of the city was scarce. Lilo and Gertrud considered themselves fortunate to eventually find a room, though lacking electricity, in a small house belonging to an elderly couple. To the delight of the landlords, they hired an electrician to install a minimal amount of electrical wiring which enabled them to have a bit of light in the evenings and to be able to heat their frugal meals on a hot plate.

"Lilochen, I have something to tell you," Gertrud announced one night over their evening meal. "I think you will be very happy that I have come up with a way to express our gratitude to Maria and her family for taking us in and for helping us to escape from the Soviet Zone."

"How so, Mother?"

"The day after tomorrow I will make a trip back to Benneckenstein to retrieve the Dutzmann family possessions that we were forced to leave behind."

"By yourself?" asked Lilo, incredulous.

Even before the words were out of her mouth, Lilo had the most absurd sense of déjà vu. Weren't those the exact same words that her mother had uttered to her when she announced that she was going to church at age nine? Somehow, in the intervening years, the roles had curiously reversed.

Gertrud nodded.

"But Mutti, Benneckenstein is now in the Russian Zone! There is no way of knowing what you will encounter. It is bound to be dangerous! What if they arrest you and send you to Siberia?"

When there was no ready response from Gertrud, only a familiar look of unwavering determination, Lilo continued, "But, seven crates and two rolls of oriental carpeting! How will you bring all of that back by yourself?"

The obstinate set of Gertrud's mouth indicated that she was unconcerned about such inconsequential details.

It was with a smile on her face, but grave misgivings inside that Lilo saw Gertrud off at the train station for the first and easiest leg of her journey. Before reaching the Soviet Zone, she would have to get off the train and cross the border illegally on foot. Lilo thought of Winston Churchill's recently coined phrase, "Iron Curtain"—a chilling metaphor for the Soviet action of closing its borders with the West, initially with guard posts and eventually with actual steel. That's what her mother was challenging for the sake of retrieving mere possessions, but Lilo realized, also for the adventure. In her opinion, it was both heroic and absurd.

Confirming Lilo's worst fears, Gertrud, along with a group of other people, was apprehended by Soviet armed guards while crossing the border. Fortunately the guards were not inclined to impose severe punishment. The only penalty for the illegal foray across occupation zones was a day spent scrubbing and cleaning a factory building, after which she and the other detainees were miraculously allowed to go on their way unharmed. Lilo, of course, would only find out about this detail of her mother's trip after her return.

Gertrud continued walking and hitchhiking. Each day towards evening, she began to knock on doors to request food and a place to sleep, keeping at it until someone agreed. Overall, people were sympathetic, generous and responsive to the plight of the traveling stranger. Finally, four days after leaving Krefeld, she arrived in Benneckenstein to retrieve the two large rolls of high-quality oriental carpeting and the seven wooden crates. Just before leaving for the return trip, she decided to leave one roll of carpeting with Ernst's mother and his sisters, Paula and Emily, to use as a "bargaining chip" to eventually escape westward out of the Soviet Zone. The other roll of carpeting would serve as payment for transportation for herself and all of the crates.

Later that day, Gertrud was sitting by the roadside on one of the crates. She was still a long way from Krefeld and the last roll of carpeting had been used to pay the previous driver. Stacked behind her were six more crates. Each time a vehicle approached, she boldly jumped up and hailed the driver in an attempt to obtain a ride. Since she no longer had any means of paying for the ride, she was refused several times. Finally, the driver of the fourth truck that came along took pity on her and assisted her in loading the crates into the back. She got in, relieved at last to have secured a ride westward to the border.

One afternoon a few weeks after Gertrud's departure, Maria, Ruth and Lilo were helping Maria's sister Käthe with canning fruits and vegetables harvested from their garden. The home-canned produce included beans, tomatoes, carrots, red currants and black raspberries, and they hoped that it would help to ensure a varied diet during the increasingly severe food shortages that were expected during the winter months.

Suddenly there was the unmistakable sound of a heavy vehicle pulling up in front of the house. They looked out just in time to see Gertrud getting out of a truck, upon which they all hurried out to greet her. The crates were unloaded amidst tears and exclamations of joy from everyone in the family at her safe return and the success of her mission.

That evening, Lilo told Gertrud that she had received a tip from an acquaintance that Rolf might be in a POW camp somewhere along the Rhine River. Ever since then, she had been visiting the camps within striking distance and making inquiries at the gates for both Rolf and Ernst, but so far with no success.

"I hoped to get some news of Rolf or his father during my trip back to Benneckenstein, but there was none," Gertrud responded. "So we will just have to keep on searching for them in the camps."

"I imagine that Rolf must know that Benneckenstein has been turned over to the Russians," Lilo speculated. "So he would have been wise enough not to name it as his home town. Nor would he name Havelberg, for the same reason. That leaves only his birthplace, Krefeld, that he logically would identify as his home, especially since he still has relatives here."

So why was Rolf not returning?

Gertrud began to accompany Lilo on her needle-in-a-haystack search. They traveled by bus, eventually visiting nearly every camp in the Rhineland, always equipped with written notes to leave at each location and packages containing cookies, bread, darned and recycled socks, or any other items they could spare from their scant rations and personal possessions. At the gates of every camp, hundreds of other women were also inquiring about their husbands, brothers, sons and lovers. Lilo would attempt to get the attention of anyone at the gate willing to listen and then pass on a note and package in the hope that they might get to Rolf or to someone who knew of his whereabouts. Sometimes they were told to come back for an answer, which entailed either an additional trip or an overnight stay at a village inn nearby. They both realized that it would take nothing short of a miracle to find Rolf or Ernst in this manner.

Lilo and Gertrud saw more and more POWs arriving home, and heard stories about the dismal conditions in the camps, especially during the first few months after the war's end. With each new story, Lilo's alarm increased—as did Gertrud's assurances that all would be well. What kept Lilo's spirits buoyed up was the certainty that nothing even approaching her worst fears could possibly have happened to Rolf without her knowing or feeling it like a knife wound deep inside.

Chapter 36

A Startling Revelation

Johann Kanter approached the home of Lilo's grandparents in Havelberg and knocked on the door.

When Lilo's grandfather answered, Johann introduced himself by name and asked, "Are you Carl Röhrich?"

"Yes?" the hesitant reply sounded like a question.

"Does Lilo Dutzmann née Wassull live here too?"

"No," replied Carl. "She and her mother fled westward many months ago before the Russian occupation, but come in please!"

Sensing important news, he shouted excitedly for his wife and offered a chair to the unexpected visitor.

"I recently met Lilo's husband, Rolf Dutzmann, at a POW camp near Bretzenheim," Johann told them, and passed on the few details that Rolf had asked him to relate to them if not to Lilo directly.

"Has Rolf then received no communication from Lilo in all this time?" asked Carl in a worried tone. "We hope that she and her mother arrived safely in Benneckenstein several months ago, but of course, we have no means of receiving word."

"No, he told me he has heard nothing from her since early this year."

"And we unfortunately have no way to pass any of this information on to Lilo either. In fact, we do not even know whether she and her mother are alive. Of course, we will seize on any opportunity to get your message to her."

Johann then handed them an envelope, saying, "The central message is from Rolf himself, but you will see my scribblings in the margins regarding his whereabouts and a few details of our conversations at the camp. I hope it will be intelligible to you."

Lilo's grandparents opened the envelope to find a slip of paper inside. There were tears in their eyes as they read it. Carl shook Johann's hand with warmth and gratitude.

"Thank you so much for the pains you have taken to hand-deliver this message! We hope that we will have an opportunity to get it to Lilo. How relieved and overjoyed she would be to receive it!"

Before long, Lilo noticed that her mother was starting to act restless again. She was therefore not too surprised when Gertrud suddenly announced that she would be making another trip into the Soviet Zone, this time all the way to Havelberg to check on her father and stepmother. Since there was no mail service to or from the East Zone and no other means of communication, Gertrud was anxious to see how they and the other relatives had fared, and to retrieve additional possessions they had been forced to leave behind with friends.

Lilo's objections were more strident this time. "But Mother, it is not only prohibited to cross the borders, but much of that trip will have to be on foot— a round trip of at least four hundred eighty kilometers. It is already the end of October and getting cold! You might be caught traveling back in mid-winter, or worse, you might be trapped in the Soviet Zone permanently and I will never see or hear from you again! It's bad enough that I have to worry about Rolf and his father."

"Do not worry, Lilochen. Since I made it safely to Benneckenstein and back, God willing, I will make it to Havelberg and back too!"

It was during that perilous trip into the Soviet Zone that Gertrud found out about her grandmother's death and the harrowing experiences that her parents and the other residents of Havelberg had endured when the Soviets occupied the town.

Early in the evening about ten days after Gertrud's departure, Lilo was sitting at a window reading when there was once again the sound of a heavy vehicle stopping out front and then excited voices. She looked up and, with an exuberant cry, ran out to meet her mother, who hugged her and triumphantly handed her a dog-eared envelope. Lilo's hands were shaking as she opened the envelope and read the slip of paper inside. Her breath caught in a gasp, and she began to sob uncontrollably. On the shred of paper in the familiar hand of the man she loved were the words "Rolf lebt!" ("Rolf lives!").

"But where? Where is he?" cried Lilo, breathless with emotion and excitement.

"Keep on reading and you will find out," Gertrud replied, pointing out the additional notes hastily jotted near the edges of the slip of paper. "Some place called Bretzenheim. I don't know where that is, but don't worry, we will find out," she declared. "We must tell Rolf's mother and sister that he is alive. Then tomorrow, we go to the post office to inquire the whereabouts of this Bretzenheim!"

Chapter 37

The First Woman I See

he next morning, Lilo and Gertrud waited expectantly at the post office while the postmaster searched a large book, both of them hopeful and determined to finally locate Rolf. Lilo could barely contain her impatience and excitement.

"There are two Bretzenheims," he stated. "One is Mainz-Bretzenheim near the city of Mainz, the other is the village of Bretzenheim on the Nahe River."

Since Johann Kanter's notes had stated nothing about Bretzenheim's proximity to a large city, Lilo and Gertrud surmised that the latter one was the most likely location of the camp. It was in the French Occupied Zone, and they obtained permission from the British military authorities to travel there by train. Upon arrival, they rented a room in a small country inn near the camp. When the innkeepers found out the nature of Lilo and Gertrud's visit, they were eager to offer what little they knew about the camp protocol.

"No unauthorized Germans are allowed inside the camp, and the Moroccan guards there are not very friendly, perhaps due in part to the language barrier," the innkeeper explained to Lilo and Gertrud. "So we don't know very much. But one thing we *do* know is that early each morning, a work detail of POWs leaves the camp, attended by only two Moroccan guards, one at each end."

They told Lilo and Gertrud exactly where to be stationed in order to see the POWs pass by, whereupon the innkeeper's wife cautioned Lilo, "When the work detail passes by where you are standing, yell out loudly, asking whether anyone knows Rolf Dutzmann. But…," she lifted one finger in warning and paused briefly for effect, "you must pretend to be having a loud conversation or argument with your mother. And by no means look directly at the prisoners! Since the Moroccans do not comprehend any German, they will not suspect anything, but the POWs will hopefully understand, and this way you might get an answer about your husband."

Lilo and Gertrud left the inn well before dawn and stationed themselves at the roadside. It was an unusually chilly, late fall day, and Lilo was shivering under her lightweight coat. In time they saw a group of about twenty men marching briskly towards them in formation, with one Moroccan guard at the front and one at the back, just as the innkeepers had described. The POWs were marching in step and chanting in unison.

As they drew nearer, Lilo looked pointedly at her mother and began to yell repeatedly, "Does anyone know Rolf Dutzmann?"

When no one answered, her voice rose to a fever pitch of desperation. As the column passed directly by where they were standing, the temptation to look directly at the passing prisoners in the hope of finding Rolf among them was nearly overwhelming but Lilo managed to restrain herself.

"Does anyone know Rolf Dutzmann?" she yelled even louder at her mother.

Gertrud shouted back at her, "We need to find Rolf Dutzmann!"

The men marched on to the sing-song chant, but once the column had nearly finished passing by, a POW turned his head ever so slightly in their direction and responded in time with the singsong.

"I wi--ll ask a--round. Come back to--mor--row!"

Lilo and Gertrud looked at each other, stunned, elated and uncertain what to do next. They continued standing by the road for a time. Eventually a lone man could be seen approaching from the camp, walking very slowly. He did not look like a Moroccan, was unarmed and was wearing a uniform of sorts that did not seem to be a military uniform. As he approached, Lilo began to speak in German, then remembering this was a French camp, she summoned up what she could remember of the French lessons from her school years to ask whether he was coming from the camp.

He stopped, smiled disarmingly and answered in perfect German, "Yes, I am."

"Are you a POW?" asked Lilo, switching to German.

"Yes, I am."

"But," Lilo asked with a puzzled expression, "How is it that you can walk out of the camp without a guard?"

"I have a job to do at the railroad station and they allow me to walk there and back unattended each day."

"Do you by any chance know a Rolf Dutzmann?"

"Do I know Rolf Dutzmann!" he exclaimed. "I have come to know him quite well. He and I work alternate shifts at the station, and around noon today he will be walking down this very road to relieve me there."

"Oh, thank you, thank you!" Lilo exclaimed with joy and relief.

Heedless of the tears running down her cheeks, she pressed an apple into the man's hand in gratitude. He smiled, wished her well and turned to resume his slow walk to the station.

Rolf was finishing up a postcard to Lilo in one of the newly erected barracks that would be housing the POWs for the coming winter. Since the construction project was still underway, loud hammering could be heard in the background. That postcard was just another in a long line of postcards, none of which had received a reply. He had not heard from her since February. Now it was November.

The POWs were only allowed to send postcards supplied by the Red Cross that were to be routed via a Red Cross address in Geneva before being delivered to the family and friends to which they were addressed. Rolf and other POWs would find out only after the war's end that, for reasons unknown, few if any of the postcards ever reached their destination.

Rolf looked up and commented to his companion, Rudi, "None of my postcards to Lilo have been answered. But I refuse to think the worst." A despondent silence followed where, in spite of his proclamations to the contrary, he obviously was contemplating the worst.

Then he resumed, "Either I am sending them to the wrong place, not knowing where she is now, or they are not being properly posted. But today," he announced with a resolute tone, "I will try a different method. I am determined to give this postcard to the first woman I see and ask her to mail it for me!"

He stood up, put the postcard in his pocket and left to begin his daily trudge up the road, eyes downcast. En route to the railway station, a voice—an endearing, wrenchingly familiar voice—made him look up.

"Is this only a dream?" he wondered. But there she was! The woman he loved was running towards him, laughing for joy, sobbing, calling his name over and over again. They shared a passionate embrace while time stood miraculously still—a moment that would forever remain vividly etched in memory.

Rolf pulled the postcard out of his pocket, smiling broadly, and handed it to her saying, "Especially for you. I intended to give this to the first woman I saw today!"

Lilo found out that Rolf worked different shifts on alternate days—the morning shift one day, afternoon shift the next. For the next several days, she waited twice each day for Rolf as he walked to and from the station. In that way, they managed to steal a bit of heaven amidst otherwise dreary times, to have a few words together, to exchange a hug, a kiss and letters that they each spent their evenings alone composing, hoping to make up for some of the lost time and lost communication in the previous months.

Lilo brought whatever food items she could obtain each day—an apple, a slice or two of bread, a small chunk of cheese—whatever she felt that Rolf would be able to smuggle back into the camp undetected. A year had passed since their wedding day and both of them were considerably thinner than when they had parted ways. On November 24th, their first wedding anniversary, Lilo brought him a few cookies and a hot cup of tea that a sympathetic local couple had provided.

At their final meeting before she and Gertrud left the area, Lilo promised Rolf she would return as soon as possible. The joy of their reunion had temporarily dispelled all misgivings about the dangers that still lay ahead, but now those dangers once again cast a dark and menacing shadow over their hopes for the future.

Chapter 38

En Route to Bingen

A week and a half later, Lilo traveled back to Bretzenheim alone and waited at the road. Counting back every other day to their last meeting, she had calculated that Rolf would be working the afternoon shift that day It was very cold and snowy for early December, and she could see her breath forming spiral plumes in the brisk air.

To her relief, Rolf appeared shortly. It was another joyful reunion, but she could tell that he was tense.

"More and more of the POWs from my original group are being sent to France to perform forced labor clearing land mines. I hear it is a grisly task with very high casualties, and the risk of being sent myself is increasing daily."

Lilo was silent for a moment, then: "Tomorrow you have the morning shift?"

"Yes."

"And how soon are you expected back after your shift?"

"Shortly after it ends at noon, unless I get special permission to stay later, in which case it would be by dark, so maybe four, five o'clock. Why?"

"Just meet me here tomorrow, as soon after your shift as possible. I will tell you more then, but the more time we have, the better."

The next day, Rolf told the guards he would have to work later than usual to help inventory some large incoming shipments. After his shift, he rendezvoused with Lilo, who immediately began to hustle him away from the road, offering only the briefest greeting.

"How long before they will begin to miss you?" she asked breathlessly.

"A few hours. Four at most."

"Then we have four hours to get as far away as possible!" she replied.

They continued to walk briskly while Lilo explained in breathless gasps how she had mapped out a route to get him away from the camp, and filled him in on the details of her plan. Rolf's initial sense of caution and hesitation was rapidly replaced by hopefulness. Facing a situation of dwindling and ever-worsening options, he had everything to gain if the escape was successful. If it was not, well, he did not want to think about that—it would almost certainly entail immediate dispatch to France for the mine-clearing detail.

They stopped only long enough for Rolf to remove his POW uniform, under which he was still wearing the civilian suit that he had on when he was taken prisoner of war so many months earlier. Lilo hurriedly stuffed the uniform behind a clump of bushes. They walked to the train station at the neighboring town of Bosenheim and boarded what Lilo believed to be a train to Bingen. From there they could take a four o'clock train to Köln (Cologne). Only once they were en route did she realize her mistake with a sense of horror. The train they were on would only take them to Gensingen, about ten kilometers short of Bingen—leaving them only half an hour to cover those ten kilometers on foot! It was an impossibility. A fellow passenger who overheard their conversation, said he too must reach Bingen in that half-hour to make a connection. The three of them deliberated urgently until the train pulled into Gensingen; then they started walking.

After a last desperate look at her watch, which showed three thirty-five, Lilo asked herself what Gertrud would do. It was the right question. Without hesitation, she stepped boldly into the middle of the road and flagged down the first car that appeared, a black Volkswagen with a kindly, bespectacled, middle-aged gentleman at the wheel.

Even as she explained to the startled driver that all three of them had taken the wrong train and needed to be in Bingen in twenty minutes, she was opening the door of the car and energetically pushing Rolf and the other man inside. The kindly driver, who turned out to be a doctor, was a bit stunned at first, but responsive to the smile and sense of urgency of the pretty, blonde woman and followed her orders. The three thanked him profusely as they arrived in Bingen with time to spare. Until their train was ready to board, Rolf and Lilo moved up and down the stairs and back and forth from one platform to another to escape the notice of the French soldiers patrolling the station.

At length, speeding through the darkness toward Köln (Cologne), they heard the announcement of the border between the French and British Zones.

"Let us hope they do not check for identification tonight," Lilo whispered fervently, offering up a silent prayer.

They traveled the remaining distance to the border with bated breath, but there was no ID check that night, and they arrived in Köln around midnight. The waiting area of the station was in a former air raid bunker.

"We will have no choice but to spend the rest of the night here," Lilo told Rolf. "The curfew is still on until six o'clock in the morning."

They moved as far back into the bunker as possible to hide behind other people and then attempted to sleep sitting up with their arms around each other. Lilo asked one of the other passengers whether they could expect to have a restful night or would there be patrols of the bunker. She was told that there was usually at least one patrol nightly and often more than one. Fortunately there was no patrol that night and they were able to board the six o'clock train to Krefeld the following morning.

When they arrived at the flat in Krefeld, Gertrud was having a late breakfast. She looked up in surprise as the door opened. To her utter amazement, she saw a thin, tired, but cheerful Rolf and a radiantly triumphant Lilo walk in. Nothing could have made her mother's heart more elated than to see their faces, glowing with happiness despite their exhaustion.

Rolf still had no ID and no discharge papers from the POW camp. Wary of another trip to the Kommandantur to register, he, Lilo and Gertrud discussed what story would be most likely to persuade the British authorities to issue him valid ID papers. The Nuremberg International Military Tribunal had opened that very month. Twenty-two Nazi leaders were on trial; any man with SS connections was a suspect; a man without papers could not count on Allied leniency.

Gertrud suggested that since Rolf could prove that he had been married in Havelberg, which was now in the Soviet Zone, he could tell them that he had searched for his wife there and that his papers had been confiscated at the border upon returning. Rolf decided to adopt that story. The next day he was questioned by a British officer at the Kommandantur, checked for an SS tattoo and, to the profound relief of all in the family, officially admitted to the British Zone.

Years earlier, Rolf's love for Lilo had conquered his fear of commitment. The treacherous war years had taught him that matters of necessity and matters of conscience sometimes intersect in unexpected and fortuitous ways. His reluctance to advance himself in his military service had not only aided his survival but also prevented him from further aiding and abetting a corrupt and violent regime. Unbeknownst to him at the time the war ended, his uncertain, often precarious navigation through treacherous times was setting the stage for doors to open to new opportunities in the decades to come.

The grueling postwar years now awaited Rolf and Lilo and millions of other displaced people. But they knew that their love had survived the worst, and they felt that nothing in the future could possibly compare with the perils and hardships that they had already overcome.

Left: Rolf with the stray kitten at Malatzky, Slovakia, 1944

Below: The slip of paper with the words "Rolf Lebt!" (shown by the arrow) informing Lilo of Rolf's survival in a POW camp. It has Johann Kanter's notations and signature in the right margin.

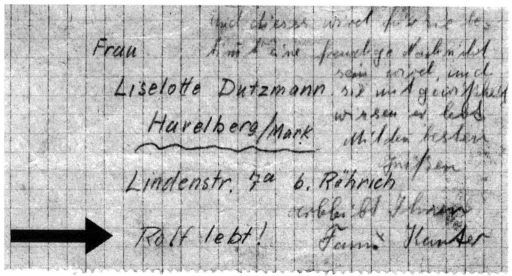

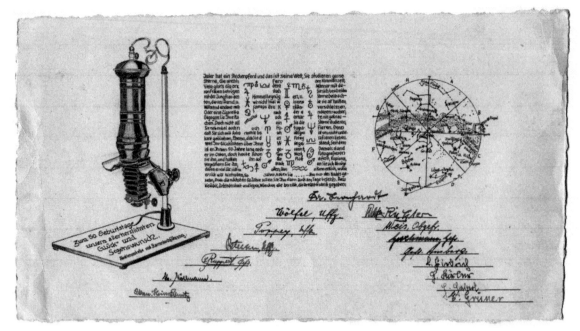

Two of the five intricately hand-illustrated cards with original signatures given to Ernst Dutzmann by coworkers at Mittelwerk for his fiftieth birthday on March 13, 1945, just days before the Allied takeover of the top-secret installation. The cards were specially designed around themes of life-long interest to Ernst, in this case, astronomy and radio technology.

All of the five original cards, along with a birthday card from 1944, a New Year's card from January 1945, and the photo of Ernst at Mittelwerk shown on page 186, were donated to the Mittelbau-Dora Concentration Camp Memorial in Nordhausen, Germany in 2011. (View the donated items at www.kirschstonebooks.com.)

Part V

HOPE

"Patience and perseverance have a magical effect before which difficulties disappear and obstacles vanish."

— John Quincy Adams

Chapter 39

Postwar Privation and Pleasure

olf received a letter from his college friend, Ludwig Schlott, who had been living in the city of Braunschweig with his parents since the war's end. He invited Rolf to come for a visit in order to look into the master's program at the Technical University of Braunschweig—the oldest technical university in Germany. Since there was no other transportation available for German citizens at the time, Rolf traveled from Krefeld to Braunschweig in the month of January via an unheated freight car. At the university admissions office he was told that his chances of being admitted were good, but that a three-month work period performing bomb-damage cleanup would be required prior to beginning studies. He picked up the necessary forms and returned to Krefeld.

Lilo discovered that she was pregnant, but she and Rolf agreed that he should leave for Braunschweig anyway at the end of January in order to complete the three-month work detail which would enable him to register for the summer term. He was put to work six days per week, eight hours per day clearing rubble from destroyed university buildings, tearing down walls still left standing and cleaning up old bricks for use in the rebuilding effort. On the work detail one day, Rolf declined to scale a thirty-foot wall to knock down loose bricks. A former submarine lieutenant who had survived the entire war in the North Sea aboard a German U-boat accepted the risky challenge and was killed when the wall suddenly collapsed. Rolf couldn't help but ponder the irony of that tragedy and the slim thread of self-preservation that had shielded him from the same fate.

Rolf and the other workers received minimal pay for their work, just enough to cover their rent and food. They were able to purchase only what was currently available on ration cards. When Rolf went to buy a week's supply of food, he stood in line first at the butcher shop, then the bakery, the dairy and the grocery store—a three- to four-hour routine, with rations sometimes running out before his turn came. A typical weekly allotment was one loaf of bread, two ounces of butter, fifty grams of meat (less than half the size of a deck of cards), one hundred grams of sugar (about one-half cup) and a few other items. It added up to only 1,300 calories per day. Ration amounts were set by the occupying Allied government and usually changed on a monthly basis depending on the availability of food items. People on the street and even a few of Rolf's fellow workers were collapsing from hunger and malnutrition.

One of the laborers on the work detail lamented, "We are being punished by the victors—our fate for initiating and then losing the war."

Whenever the topic arose, that seemed to be the consensus. Rolf was in general agreement, noting that only the Allied military personnel in Germany were adequately fed while the German people went hungry. The monumental task of rebuilding not only Germany, but much of Europe—a task that would later be taken on by the United States via the Marshall Plan—was something that the average hungry person in postwar Germany could not even begin to grasp.

Rolf rented a dark, dingy room in an apartment owned by an elderly woman, but continued to search for quarters that would be adequate to accommodate Lilo and an infant as well. He finally found a suitable apartment with a retired couple, the Franzes. A female tenant would have to pass through their room in order to access her own, but Rolf decided to take the apartment anyway and promptly sent for Lilo to join him the following month.

Probably due to the severe food shortages and other wartime and postwar hardships, Lilo suffered a miscarriage shortly after her arrival in Braunschweig—

a loss that she found hard to bear. Rolf consoled her that things would improve, and the next pregnancy would turn out differently.

Finally the opportunity arrived for Rolf to sign up for his university courses. The aeronautical engineering curriculum had been prohibited by the Allied military government, so he chose mechanical engineering courses with a major in automotive engineering. He decided to pre-pay his tuition since it was expected that the old "Reichsmark" would soon be devalued, which would reduce their savings to almost nothing overnight. Under normal circumstances, Rolf would have been discouraged about not being able to pursue his aeronautical engineering studies, but with the joint specters of food shortages, imminent financial insolvency and other survival challenges foremost on every mind, he accepted any educational opportunity as no small miracle.

The woman who rented the room next to Rolf and Lilo knocked on their door every morning at 5:30 on the way to her job in a restaurant kitchen, awaiting their consent to pass through their rooms. Every evening she knocked on the outer door to re-enter her own quarters. At that time, there were many women, including elderly women, who were forced to manage alone in Germany. So many had lost their husbands, sons, fathers, fiancés and lovers. Towards the end of the war, even old and disabled men were sent to the slaughter on the front from which many failed to return.

Rolf and Lilo's apartment had no running water and therefore no tub, shower, sink or toilet. They carried water from the landlord's kitchen into their unit, then collected the dirty water into a pail, which was later transferred into a toilet downstairs that they shared with the landlords and the tenants in the apartment adjacent to theirs. Once a week they went to the "city bathhouse" where, after standing in line for hours, they were able to share a single tubful of water. They found keeping clean to be their greatest challenge, and Rolf eventually developed a severe case of boils that broke out on his neck, buttocks and back. Due to the searing pain that rendered him unable to sit even long enough to carry out his class assignments, he was admitted to the local hospital to receive a five-day round of penicillin shots.

Their hardships were offset by a heartening letter from Maria:

Your father has finally been released after more than a year in an American POW camp situated in Mourmelon, France, where he spent his time refurbishing used military trucks. Your time as POWs briefly overlapped at an intermediate transfer camp, but not at Bretzenheim, where you spent most of your time. Since your father was in the officers' part of the transfer camp and you were both only there briefly, your paths did not cross. After his release, your father obtained a job for Friesecke & Höpfner, a US Army vehicle repair plant in Bavaria. Thanks to your father's ingenuity, we are by now settled in a small house surrounded by trees in a country setting. It is a simple, but peaceful life here. We hope that you and Lilo will be able to visit us sometime soon.

The Americans had provided Ernst with a huge wooden crate originally used to ship a bulldozer. He had applied his carpentry skills to convert it into a cottage that he, Maria and Ruth shared. From an additional wooden crate obtained the following month, he added a porch to the original structure. They now had a small but charming three-room house with a front porch. Since the rooms were tiny, Ernst built space-saving benches right into the walls of the living room, one of which also provided sleeping accommodations for Ruth. Copycat crate houses started to appear around the area after others caught on to Ernst's clever solution to the housing shortage.

Lilo soon became pregnant again, which qualified her to receive additional ration coupons. The woman from the next room moved out and they were able to add her room to theirs, happy that the awkward 5:30 a.m. wake-up calls were over and that they would have more space once the baby arrived. Slowly but surely, conditions were improving, and some semblance of a normal life was being reestablished.

But in Germany as a whole, the terrible crimes against humanity that had been committed before and during the war had to be confronted before any sort of "normalcy" could be restored. In October 1946, the Military Tribunal of Nuremberg came to an end. All but three of the twenty-two top Nazi defendants were pronounced guilty, and twelve would eventually hang. Every surviving German citizen was left to question their conscience about the extent of their own complicity in the preceding madness and brutality. As for liberated concentration camp inmates, there was a long, arduous road ahead to regain life amongst the living—a life that for many could never be fully recovered.

Amidst the ongoing tragedy and grinding hardship across Europe, a son was born to Rolf and Lilo on January 11, 1947. They named him Ingo, a name that appealed to them because it was different from any other one in their families. Despite the hunger, the cold, the scarcity of food and the other adversities that they endured on a daily basis, they never forgot that they had loved each other enough to marry at a time of dreadful wartime peril, and that after a year's separation, they had been reunited. They recognized how fortunate they were compared to so many other people, and were thankful just to be together and alive.

Chapter 40

The Harshest Winter

During the early months of 1947, the city of Braunschweig lay submerged under a heavy blanket of ice and snow. Each day in the late afternoon, Rolf was engaged in his university studies at a desk in a corner of the room that served as their kitchen, the only warm room in the apartment, while Lilo finished cooking the evening meal on a hot plate. It was an old, ceramic device with open coils that sometimes stopped working at the most inopportune times. Next to it on a wooden table was a "*Kochhexe*" (kitchen witch), a small, primitive stove with a flat metal surface and a compartment underneath into which slivers of wood or paper could be stuffed and then lit to provide heat for pots of food placed on top.

Lilo boiled potatoes. In another smaller pot, she created gravy from the only available ingredients—water, wheat flour or cornmeal for thickening, and mustard for flavoring. When available, she used a bit of horseradish instead of the mustard. There was no butter or other fat available to add calories, taste or nutrition to the gravy, and meat was a special luxury reserved only for Sundays. Even for their Sunday ration, they received only one hundred grams of meat between them. Along with the weekly meat ration, they usually received a bone, which Lilo cooked up in water to create soup, sometimes adding an onion, a carrot or a handful of greens generously provided by their landlords. On a Sunday afternoon, she often had three pots stacked one on top of the other—the soup pot with a smaller gravy pot on top of it, and the potatoes boiling in a third pot under them. This way she was able to keep everything warm until mealtime. However, on weekdays, the cooking was greatly simplified since potatoes with mustard gravy were standard daily fare for Rolf and Lilo. Fruits and vegetables, although not rationed, were seldom available for purchase.

At five o'clock every evening, the electricity abruptly went off, plunging the entire city into darkness, a measure enforced all over Germany which may have been for the purpose of redistributing power from residential areas to the industrial sector during the evening hours. They often had to eat their meal in the dark. Halfway through the meal, when Ingo began to stir and then cry in his crib, Rolf and Lilo got up and went to the bedroom that they all shared. Lilo changed Ingo's diaper while Rolf manually worked a postwar flashlight, squeezing the handle continually to generate electricity. Lilo dropped the dirty diaper into a pail of water on the floor and placed Ingo back in his crib, at which time they both returned to finish their meal. Afterwards, Rolf went to bed while Lilo made her way to the landlords' kitchen by flashlight, where she used their gas stove to heat the wash water. Then she carried the pail of hot water back to their rooms. Since she could not work the flashlight and do the wash at the same time, she washed the soiled diapers as best she could in the dark, rinsed them with ice cold water poured into a bucket from a twenty-five-liter dairy can (just over six and a half gallons), and hung them to dry on a clothesline strung across the room. It was long enough to hold at least half a dozen diapers. Lilo checked them, but they were seldom dry in the evening due to the cold, damp conditions. She put the pail of used water by the door. Then she went to bed too, taking Ingo with her to keep him warm.

The lights suddenly came back on every night at midnight. After sitting up in bed with a groan, Rolf wrapped a blanket around himself, went to the door where the pail of dirty diaper water was standing, carried it downstairs and used it to flush the toilet, then trudged slowly back upstairs. He resumed his college assignments by lamplight, wrapped in the blanket, his breath billowing cloud-like in the frigid air.

Lilo also got up and put Ingo back in his crib, first checking the electric heating pad placed under him to make sure it was working, but not too hot. This time he was awake, and she talked and sang to him as she worked. She set to work ripping up old sheets to use as diapers, roughly hand-hemming them, a task made clumsy by the old woolen gloves she was wearing to protect against the cold. Once finished, she folded them neatly and stacked them in a drawer filled with other diapers. By that time, Ingo was once again sleeping soundly. After checking him one last time, she went to where Rolf was sitting hunched over and deeply absorbed in his studies, put her arms around him from behind and kissed him on the cheek.

Smiling, she murmured in his ear, "We may be rich in many other ways, but I will go back to bed now and have dreams of a real sink and faucets with hot and cold running water."

Rolf interrupted his studies to smile up at her, kiss her hand and say, "We'll find a way to have that and more."

He did not tell her about the gruesome, repetitive nightmares he had been experiencing of late in which she was dead and he was viewing her body in a casket.

The walls facing the street glistened with ice as Lilo turned to go back to bed. Rolf usually continued his studies well into the early morning hours and Lilo often found him still slumped over his books and technical drawings when she got up in the morning.

The most exhausting task for Lilo was doing laundry—a backbreaking challenge in those times. In the basement of the house where they lived was a *Waschküche* (laundry room) equipped with an immense wood and coal burning stove, a huge kettle in which to heat water and boil the linens, and an assortment of washboards on which laundry could be scrubbed manually with a brush, as well as wooden tubs for rinsing. After scrubbing, rinsing and wringing out the sheets, towels and all other laundry by hand, the loads had to be carried up four flights of stairs to the attic for hanging in the winter and out to the courtyard in the summer. Each family in the building had three days assigned per month to do their laundry, but due to the fact that Lilo and Rolf had the only baby in the building, other tenants were considerate enough to allow them extra time to meet their washing needs.

Rolf and Lilo received only a single bushel of coal per month to burn in the stove in their apartment. One night in mid-winter during the blackout time, Ingo awakened, screaming furiously in his crib. Lilo rushed to pick him up and tried to hush him, but he would not stop crying. She checked his diaper, but it was not wet. Then she looked at his feet and found that something was wrong with one of his toes. She called for Rolf while working frantically to warm Ingo's feet. Rolf ran to the landlords' apartment, knocking a sharp staccato on their door. Frau Franz answered and hurried over to inspect Ingo's tiny toes. He was still wailing pathetically.

"He has a case of frostbite, but he will be all right," she stated reassuringly, and instructed them what to do.

A group of tenants from Rolf and Lilo's building had been making regular forays to the local railroad yard to steal coal from arriving coal transports. Lilo had resolutely refused to accompany them, but the day after Ingo's frozen-toe incident, while Rolf was away at the university, she felt desperate enough to join them. When a train pulled in, the men in the group jumped up onto the open coal cars and threw down chunks of coal while the women below hurriedly gathered it into bags. In the past they had always managed to make a successful getaway without being caught, but on that particular day, the police unexpectedly arrived, arrested them all and took them to the lockup area of the local jail, where they underwent interrogation.

A police officer asked the first defendant, "Where do you live?"

"Altstadtring 33."

The second defendant, "Altstadtring 33."

The third, fourth and fifth defendants, "Altstadtring 33."

"What! Is this a conspiracy?"

When Lilo was questioned, she stated that she had a seven-week-old baby at home who just the previous night had suffered from a case of frostbite. She was fined only twenty marks due to her extenuating circumstances. The others in the group were fined one hundred fifty marks each.

Lilo returned home to a very anxious Rolf, who was wondering what had become of her. When the landlords found out what happened, they immediately supplied Rolf and Lilo with an extra basket of coal and kindling. While Frau Franz crooned lovingly to Ingo, Herr Franz assured Rolf that he would make every effort to bring them extra coal and kindling on a regular basis from the factory where he worked as an accountant. They also further increased the provision of carrots and other vegetables. From that point on, the landlords were affectionately addressed as "*Onkel*" (Uncle) Franz and "*Tante*" (Aunt) Franz. By the time Ingo was four months old and starting to eat solid food, Rolf and Lilo began forfeiting their own carrot rations to mash up and feed to him instead.

All normal standards of what constituted edible food were overturned during the postwar years. With rations further reduced to 1,100 and then to a near-starvation level of only 900 calories per day for adults, both Rolf and Lilo became very thin and no opportunity for additional nutrition was ever turned down. Lilo inspected a small bag of flour received as a gift from a local farmer and noticed that it was crawling with maggots. Without hesitation, she put the flour through a sieve, discarded the maggots collected in it, then brought the flour to the local bakery to be baked into a loaf of bread. Due to the fact that Pomerania, the bread basket of Germany where most of the wheat was once grown, had by that time been given to Poland, flour was very scarce and all baked goods, including bread, rolls and cakes, were made with a bitter-tasting mixture of wheat flour and cornmeal.

On another occasion, a bagful of beans received through an acquaintance was found to have worms. Lilo spent hours cutting the worms out of the individual beans and then cooked them into a soup for their dinner.

"I don't know how you managed to make it so hearty and delicious," Rolf commented between appreciative spoonfuls.

Lilo only smiled at the compliment. She found her husband to be a very grateful and appreciative diner, seldom complaining about the ultra-simple and frequently unappetizing fare.

One day on the cleanup detail, Rolf and his fellow workers were shoveling cement from a railroad car into a truck. They soon were covered from head to toe by the choking gray dust. Towards the bottom of the cement shipment, Rolf spied something unusual.

"What's this?" he asked, stooping down to pluck a small object out of the dust and examining it closely.

He blew the cement dust off to see that it was an elbow macaroni. He and the others set to work picking a lot more elbow macaroni out of the shipment of cement as they shoveled. After dividing the macaroni up into equal portions, Rolf put his share into his cap and took it home. Later that evening, he and Lilo made a game out of blowing cement and sand out of each individual macaroni at the kitchen table. Next, they rinsed them all repeatedly. When they were done, Lilo cooked up what was, by postwar standards, a very special meal.

The extended family quickly evolved into a life-saving mutual support network. Rolf's mother, Maria, employed her exceptional skills to create exquisite embroidered, crocheted and knitted items to sell to American officers and servicemen in exchange for cigarettes. At the time there was a thriving black market in Germany in which cigarettes were the primary currency. Once Maria received the cigarettes for her work, she sent them on to Lilo and Rolf. In turn, Gertrud, who had since moved to Braunschweig in order to be closer to Lilo, Rolf and Ingo, sold the cigarettes to local farmers in exchange for bacon, butter, vegetables, bread, or any other available food items. In this way, the family managed to elevate survival to a well-choreographed team effort.

Eventually, Tante Franz also supplemented their diet with additional carrots and other vegetables that she obtained through her cleaning jobs at local farms, thereby enabling Rolf and Lilo to add even more vegetables to Ingo's diet and occasionally also to their own. By the time Ingo was two years old, the kindly landlady had earned the affectionate name Tante Franz Nudel (Aunt Franz Noodle) because she regularly gave Ingo long sticks of pasta to chew on while he was teething.

⋯⟡⋯

Restlessness overcame Gertrud yet again. She was determined to make one final trip back into the Soviet Occupied Zone, to visit her father and stepmother once more and to attempt to recover the remainder of the furniture, dishes and other household items from their former apartment in Havelberg that friends had retrieved and stored for them since the Russian occupation.

By that time the borders were officially closed and crossing them had become an illegal and highly dangerous endeavor. Rolf pointed out that if she were to be caught and arrested again, she would receive no fair trial under the Soviet system. But Gertrud's enterprising and adventurous spirit would not be deterred by such minor technicalities, and she adroitly overrode all of his objections.

Lilo told him, "My mother, as you must know by now, is a very stubborn and determined person. There is no stopping her once she gets an idea into her head."

None of them realized that it would be Gertrud's last opportunity to see her father and stepmother who would henceforth be trapped in the Soviet Occupied Zone. In the future, there would be no phone conversations with them, and even communication by mail, though possible, would be fraught with difficulty due to censorship and the fact that delivery to the intended destination would continue to be uncertain at best.

Gertrud returned from her expedition two weeks later, after arranging shipment via Lilo's former employer, the Silesian Steamship Company, of many of the items that had been in their possession before they fled Havelberg. They were reunited with a couch, three upholstered chairs, a wooden living room cabinet, and a table, as well as other household items, clothing and mementos. Lilo was most overjoyed to receive the urgently needed dishes. Additional items that Gertrud arranged to be shipped via truck in exchange for cash, cigarettes and knickknacks also arrived.

Nothing they owned was ever thrown away before it had outlived its usefulness. Everything was recycled. Even Lilo's bridal gown was put to good use once again when a friend from Havelberg arrived in Braunschweig to be married. Since no gown could be found for sale anywhere for her wedding day, Lilo offered hers. Then after the wedding, Lilo transformed the tulle skirt into a cover for Ingo's baby carriage, and was pleased how well it worked to keep the flies away from him during their daily strolls.

Even in those times, there were lighthearted moments as well. On one of those outings with Ingo, two little girls ran up to the carriage and requested to see the baby. Lilo responded by pulling aside the tulle cover. Ingo, whose soft baby hair tended to sprout upward rather than lying flat against his head, was awake and sitting up when they peered inside.

Lilo burst out laughing when upon seeing him, one of them screamed, "Eek! It's not a baby, it's a hedgehog!"

In April 1948, the Marshall Plan was put into effect by the US to provide four years of financial aid to rebuild the war-torn countries of Europe. For Rolf and Lilo, although life was still far from easy, it was settling into a manageable routine and they found much cause for gratitude. Soon, however, it would be changed forever by a turn of events that, while ultimately fortuitous, would once again part them from most of their treasured possessions. It would also require a courageous leap of blind faith into a radically different future.

Chapter 41

On the List for America

*I*n mid-December 1947, the streets were already covered with a dusting of snow. With Christmas just around the corner, Lilo stepped into a bookstore and began browsing. The shopkeeper strolled over and inquired whether she was looking for something in particular.

"Yes, something for my one-year-old son, something special that he might enjoy in the years to come."

He shuffled over to a shelf and pulled out a book, handing it to her. "I regret that it is used. There are few new copies available now after the war, but I am sure that will not matter to your little one. He will love this book, just as many children have for over half a century."

Lilo took the book. It was *Der Struwwelpeter*, the same book that she had sent seven years ago from Havelberg to her former boss's grandson, Peter, in Berlin and the same book that she had enjoyed as a child. Lilo hesitated a moment, then flipped open the front cover to look at the area where she had inscribed the greeting to little Peter seven years earlier. The surface of the paper lining was worn or rubbed away from that area, but there was no inscription there and perhaps never had been. Lilo closed the book and handed it to the shopkeeper with a smile.

"Yes, I agree that he will love this book."

One day a surprise package arrived for Rolf and Lilo from a place called Colorado, USA. Accompanying it was a letter explaining that their names had been supplied to a US charitable organization by Aunt Paula in an attempt to help them out. Rolf and Lilo eagerly opened the package, exclaiming with delight over each and every item enclosed—mainly towels, clothing and food items. Lilo tried on the dresses and found that they fit her perfectly, drawing admiring looks from Rolf who, in turn, clowned around in long underwear—the kind with a flap in the back—to the great merriment of Lilo. Ingo responded to their laughter by crowing and jumping up and down with delight.

They inspected the assorted food items with great interest, sounding out the unfamiliar English names, "Cris-co Veg-e-ta-ble Shor-ten-ing, Ka-ro Syr-up, Spam."

They soon determined that all of it was exquisitely delicious and that the USA must be a magical place of plenty if there was so much food left over to be given away.

Rolf occasionally received American technical magazines through his father and read them from cover to cover. Like seeds responding to a spring thaw, Rolf's engineering dreams for the future were beginning to revive. Most of the magazines included employment ads for beginning engineers in the US, offering an unbelievable starting salary of four to five hundred dollars per month, a rate of pay unheard of in postwar Germany, where even ill-paying positions were difficult to find. He allowed himself to dream.

Shortly another package arrived, this time from an American family by the name of Longfield, who lived in another unknown, faraway place called

Wakarusa, Indiana. Rolf and Lilo replied with a thank you letter and were gratified to receive a prompt reply asking what their most urgent needs were. They made out a list. Towels, underwear, baby items and food were their top priorities. After receiving the requested items in short order, Rolf and Lilo sent another letter to the Longfields dated May 1948. Rolf dictated the letter in English, offering occasional revisions and suggestions as Lilo typed:

Dear Mr. and Mrs. Longfield,

Thank you for your kindness in sending a second shipment of much-needed clothing, food and towels. We especially appreciate the baby clothes since our Ingo is now growing out of his clothes faster than we can keep him supplied.

In answer to your many concerned questions about the postwar conditions here in Germany, we can only say that the general standard of living is very poor with few comforts. Hunger, lack of adequate housing, and fuel shortages are our constant companions. Those of us who are able to receive help from kind friends such as you are very fortunate indeed.

In addition, the proximity of the Soviets is a constant threat that hangs over us like a gloomy shadow day and night. With the eastern part of Germany already under their control, there is widespread fear that they may eventually overrun all of Western Europe. We have one child now with hopes to have more, but the chances of a decent future for them here are remote since it will take decades to rebuild Germany. The thought of our children ever having to face the dangers and privations that we have endured is unthinkable. Moreover, I will probably not be allowed to use my aeronautical skills in Germany within my lifetime, and the results of my recent inquiries into salaries for engineering graduates in any field are not encouraging. It will be very difficult if not impossible to support a family on what I can earn here.

More and more frequently, we have been entertaining the possibility of immigrating to the United States. Since we are aware that sponsorship by someone in the US is required, we are wondering whether you might know someone who would be willing to sponsor us? If so, we would be eager to correspond with them and would appreciate if you could send us their address.

My father, Ernst, harbored dreams of immigrating to the USA ever since boyhood, when he used to sit for hours at a time on a hillside near his childhood home in Liepaja, Latvia, dreaming of faraway places. Barely discernible in the distance across farm fields and hills, glistening silver in the sunlight, he could see a sliver of the Baltic Sea across which ships frequently passed bound for distant ports. That view inspired his favorite daydream that he was captain of a ship setting sail for America. He still has that same dream today and is encouraging us in any way possible to make our way to the US in the hope that he will eventually be able to follow us.

In short order, the eagerly awaited reply arrived from the Longfields. Rolf ripped the envelope open with great anticipation:

Dear Rolf and Lilo,

It did not take much discussion between us to decide that we ourselves would be very happy to act as your sponsors for immigration.

"Lilo! Lilo! We are going to America!" Rolf called out excitedly.

Lilo came running from the other room to join him and they excitedly discussed their next step.

"We have to apply for immigration," Rolf stated in a determined tone. "Now that we have a sponsor, we can get on the list. So let's apply without delay."

Soon a letter arrived from the US Consulate in Munich. Rolf and Lilo were assigned number 20,840 on the list of emigrant hopefuls. In addition, they received a letter from Stanley Bittinger, the pastor at the Church of the Brethren in Wakarusa, Indiana where their sponsors resided:

Mrs. Longfield has shown me some of your letters and told me of your desire to come to the United States to live…The Church of the Brethren is a small church and I serve as minister only on Saturdays and Sundays. Wakarusa is a small, friendly town, but its people are not very rich. For this reason it will take time to gather enough funds to bring you to the United States, but with God's help, we shall bring it to pass.

"Processing is not likely to start soon and it looks as though money for our passage may not be available soon either," commented Rolf. "This may take years, so we will have to find ways to support ourselves here in the meantime."

With that thought in mind, he managed to secure a position working on a farm in Switzerland for the summer months. There he would be able to earn Swiss francs and purchase things currently unavailable in Germany, thereby helping to ensure the family's survival through lean times. Constantly at the back of Rolf's mind at that time were thoughts of America—the land of hopes, dreams, prosperity and the much-longed-for safety and freedom.

Chapter 42

I Look to the Hills

Rolf awoke in the pre-dawn stillness and hurriedly got dressed. Outside the building where he and the other farm workers were housed, he could see the ghostlike, snow-capped Alps glistening enticingly in the distance. The group of men headed for the fields where they cut grass, loaded the grass onto a horse-drawn wagon, drove the wagon back to the barn, fed the cows with the grass, milked the cows and then poured the milk into a twenty-gallon container. Finally, they took turns each day riding a bicycle to the local dairy with the heavy milk can sloshing precariously on their backs. After the milking and delivery routine, they were served breakfast consisting of *Müsli* (rolled oats with dried fruit and nuts), bread with butter, cheese and a delicious hot beverage that consisted of half coffee, half milk.

After breakfast they cut more grass for drying into hay, and carried the previously dried hay into the barn. Every so often they were put to work spreading manure. Rolf quickly found that this was not his favorite task. His muscles were often sore from all the hard work and he joked to his fellow workers that he was as ill-suited for the rigors of farm life as he had been for the military.

At midday, Rolf enjoyed eating his lunch outside in a spot where he could take in the tantalizing view of the mountains, a panorama that for him was infused with great meaning and deep longing. Those mountains came to symbolize his dreams for the future—a future free from oppression, hardship and violence, a future where his family would be safe, and a future where he would be free to pursue his passion for aeronautical engineering.

"Someday I want to see those mountains close up," he commented between mouthfuls of bread and cheese to a fellow worker sitting nearby.

When the farmer and his wife heard about Rolf's desire to go to the mountains, they generously arranged for him to take a Sunday bus tour to the Sustenpass with a travel group, but times were hard and the tour was cancelled due to poor ticket sales. For the time being, Rolf had to remain satisfied with his view of the Alps from afar on clear days.

A letter arrived from Lilo dated June 28, 1949:

Dearest Rolf,

Everyone is well, but otherwise the news I have to impart is not good. With the monetary reform here in Germany, the old Reichsmark has finally become nearly worthless. Every person is receiving forty new Deutsche Mark, but this is small consolation for the fact that our bank account of 2,590 Reichsmark has plunged to only 259 Deutsche Mark overnight. By this time, stores are better stocked again, but few people can afford to buy anything.

Also, I have tried several times to contact my former boss, Richard Mietke, and his family, who lived in Berlin before and during the war, but to no avail. No one knows anything of their whereabouts, but this must also mean that the house that he worked so hard to rebuild is no longer standing—not a good sign, I fear.

Our Ingo will probably follow in his father's footsteps and become an engineer. He is already saying "Atoo" in his baby lisp every time he sees an automobile, and just yesterday, I saw him point to a car and say, "Mama-eez." Do you think he meant Mercedes?

The farm work season over, Rolf received his meager pay of one hundred Swiss francs, forty francs of which he spent on new soles for his boots and the remainder on a set of tires for his bicycle and five pounds of butter to send home. His train trip to the border was paid for by the Swiss government, but he had no money left for the trip from the border back home to Braunschweig. He managed to board a train without a ticket, but was caught when the conductor came around to collect tickets. Upon arrival in Braunschweig, the conductor marched Rolf to the station office for identification and he was ordered to pay off the hundred-mark fare in ten monthly installments. This left Rolf with very little to show for the entire summer's work, except for the fact that he had managed to stay well fed during lean times—no small accomplishment under the circumstances.

Together once again, Lilo and Rolf managed to scrape by on income earned from magazine deliveries that Rolf made on his bicycle, typing assignments taken on by Lilo, and whatever help occasionally arrived from Rolf's parents and from Gertrud, who had once again started teaching piano and voice lessons. Several times a week, Rolf made the rounds on his bicycle with a cardboard box full of magazines attached to the back. He delivered new magazines, for which he collected the best commissions, to the few people who could afford them, then picked up the once-read magazines to distribute to a list of secondary customers. The magazines were collected two more times to distribute to the twice-read and three-times-read list of customers before their usefulness as reading material was finally exhausted.

In November 1949, Rolf received a one-thousand-mark student loan from a local bank, which enabled him to start his diploma project in automotive engineering—the design and assembly of a Formula I racing car using a racing engine that he had constructed during a previous project. The following year, he graduated with a degree in mechanical engineering to add to his previous degree in aeronautical engineering. However, jobs remained scarce in all branches of engineering and German citizens were still forbidden to work in the field of aeronautical engineering.

It was in 1949, that a democratic West German state, called the Federal Republic of Germany, was created from a combination of the American, British and French Zones of occupation. Around the same time, a rival nation was created by Stalin in the Soviet Zone, run by a Communist-dominated regime under the name German Democratic Republic. No one was misled. It was not a democracy and granted few freedoms to its citizens. Everyone in the Dutzmann family was uneasy about the new arrangement of a divided Germany with the eastern half under Soviet control. It meant not only that many of Lilo's family members including her father and grandparents were trapped behind Soviet lines, but also that Soviet Russia would continue to lurk at the very doorstep of West Germany.

Thanks in part to the fact that his father and sister were already employed at the Friesecke & Höpfner Company in Erlangen-Bruck, Bavaria, Rolf eventually also obtained a job there as a development engineer. He, Lilo and Ingo moved from Braunschweig one hundred ninety miles south to Erlangen-Bruck, with plans to stay with Rolf's parents and sister in their tiny, overcrowded crate house until they were able to find an apartment of their own. Due to the cramped quarters, they slept on folding beds in a small storage room. But what was intended as only a brief stay stretched out into a much longer one when their apartment search proved fruitless due to the severe housing crisis throughout Germany.

During the time that they were all living together, Ernst often waxed enthusiastic over their decision to pursue immigration to the United States, and commented that he too hoped to begin the application process soon.

Several of those conversations were conducted while sitting on the porch of the crate house. They occasionally broke off their discussion to laugh at the antics of Ingo, now three and a half, who romped in a nearby field clad in a pair of overalls to which Maria had sewn a fox tail. The little fox-child played a one-sided hide and seek, skipping merrily in and out of the rows of Maria's newly planted green beans, carrots, potatoes and lettuce, the bushy tail following him around like a faithful shadow.

Since Bavaria was still under American occupation, there was the daily rumble of US tanks and artillery practice in the distance. US soldiers had also dug foxholes nearby, where they regularly practiced maneuvers. Every now and then, US soldiers passed by in jeeps or on foot. It was not unusual for them to stop and talk to the little blonde boy who often played outside the crate house. Ingo liked the soldiers, who sometimes even gave him a chocolate bar or some other special treat.

One exceptionally warm summer day, Ingo was outside playing as usual while Maria sat on the porch trimming a bowl full of green beans that she planned to cook along with potatoes, onions and whatever small amount of meat was available into a soup for the family's dinner. Rolf, Ernst and Ruth were away at work and Lilo had gone to a local store on an errand, so Maria and Ingo were home alone. Maria looked up every now and then to check on Ingo as she continued with her work. The next time she glanced up, she did not see him, so putting the bowl down on the bench next to her, she stood up to see whether he had wandered to the far side of the vegetable garden closer to the road.

What she saw made her heart nearly stop in fright. On the far side of the vegetable garden, by that time grown quite tall, Maria saw two American soldiers. Standing about ten to fifteen feet away was tiny Ingo, smiling at them and waving, trusting that the men in uniform were friendly. But one of the soldiers had his pistol raised and was taking careful aim directly at the little boy, who now stood wide-eyed and immobilized, transfixed like a rabbit in a floodlight. As she broke into a run towards the scene, Maria could see the soldier's lips move as he pulled the trigger, but she could not hear what he was saying. In fact there was no sound at all and time seemed to stand still. Then there was yelling and the sound of scuffling. By the time Maria rounded the tall pole beans in the vegetable garden to scoop Ingo up, the second soldier had jumped the one with the pistol, confiscated the weapon, and was leading his companion away while looking back with an apologetic look.

"Verzeihen Sie uns, bitte!" ("Sorry, please excuse us!") he apologized in broken German with a heavy American accent.

When Maria asked Ingo what the soldier said to him, he replied, looking at her solemnly, "He said 'Bang!'"

In August 1950, Ernst's sisters Paula and Emily, along with their mother, Julia, immigrated to the USA by ship on a displaced persons quota and settled on 121st Street in New York City, a move that would prove to have far-reaching consequences for the rest of the family including Rolf and Lilo. Aunt Paula, with her boundless energy and resourcefulness, would become instrumental in paving the way for other family members to immigrate, as well as providing a safe haven for them upon arrival in a strange and bewildering new land. Rolf and Lilo remained in regular contact with her by mail while they waited for their own immigration plans to finalize.

Maria often sent Lilo to a local bakery to purchase rolls and cheese. The owners had a car, a nearly unheard of luxury in postwar Germany, which Lilo saw one day out front with the hood up. She went inside to order a chunk of the "cheese of the day." In those postwar times, people had become accustomed to limited food choices and were satisfied with whatever "mystery" cheese was readily available. When Lilo inquired about the car, the owner's wife told her that unfortunately it no longer ran and her husband had no idea how to repair it. Upon returning home, Lilo relayed that to Rolf. The next day he went to the bakery owners and offered to rebuild the engine, a worthwhile practice of the skills he had acquired at the university, but also a good deed that would yield unexpected rewards in the near future.

They were also industrious in other ways. With a neighbor's permission, Rolf and Ernst set to work digging a trench from the neighbor's garden that was supplied by a city water line to the crate house so that they finally had running water. They also constructed a peaked roof on the house, which created much-needed storage space under the eaves for most of Rolf and Lilo's possessions and also caused the house to be warmer in the winter and cooler in the summer.

During the long summer evenings Lilo enjoyed reading to Ingo from *Der Struwwelpeter*. His favorite story changed from month to month with the latest favorite being a little verse on the back cover entitled, *To the Children*. Lilo remembered it well from her own childhood—the verse that was surrounded by colorful illustrations of Christmas toys and treats poured down by angels at the top and scenes of well-behaved children at the bottom. Ingo always listened intently, sometimes smiling and other times with a serious expression as Lilo read:

When the children have been good,
That is, be it understood,
Good at mealtimes, good at play,
Good all night and good all day–
They shall have the pretty things
Merry Christmas always brings.
Naughty, romping girls and boys
Tear their clothes and make a noise,
Spoil their pinafores and frocks,
And deserve no Christmas box.
Such as these shall never look
At this pretty picture book.

One day after that reading he turned to Lilo and asked, "I must be one of the good children then?" But after some thought, he asked very solemnly, "Are there children who will never have a book, or any Christmas treats at all?"

After the story session, Lilo remarked to Rolf, "Our Ingo is developing a social conscience."

The occupation government finally allowed soaring and aeronautical clubs to be formed in Germany, and Rolf lost no time in joining a local aero club. Through a chance encounter at the club, Rolf and Lilo were able to obtain a two-room apartment consisting of a kitchen and one other room, but once again without running water. The closest bathroom and running water were two flights down.

The landlord allowed Rolf to construct a cinder block wall at the edge of an open area at the top of the stairs to create a third small room. It was while he was constructing the wall that Rolf and Lilo received an impromptu visit from a representative of the Brethren Service Center in Munich, who had been requested by the sponsors in Indiana to check them out. The representative was immediately impressed by the fact that Rolf, despite his two engineering degrees, was still willing to perform manual labor. He was also amused at the antics of Ingo, who spent hours at the front window, watching the cars passing by and exclaiming with delight over each one in his childlike lisp.

"Atoo, atoo! Opel! Volkswagen! More atoo!" When he said "Opel" it sounded more like *Opa*, the German term for "grandpa."

At three and a half years old, he was already familiar with most automobiles available in Germany.

In the spring of 1951, Rolf and Lilo finally received the eagerly awaited notice from the US Consulate in Munich that their quota number would soon be reached. Their sponsors in Wakarusa, Indiana, Jesse and Amanda Longfield, filled out and mailed the necessary papers. To Rolf and Lilo, it seemed that nothing now could possibly shatter their dream of immigration to the US.

Chapter 43

Last-Minute Surprises

*L*ilo was in the sixth month of her third pregnancy when they received another letter from Stanley Bittinger, the pastor at the Church of the Brethren in Wakarusa, Indiana. He assured them of his congregation's full support once they arrived in the States. In addition, he offered to lend them $500, his entire accumulated life's savings, for their ship fare to the US. Rolf and Lilo both felt tears rush to their eyes as they read and reread the letter, deeply touched by the sacrificial generosity of the offer. A future in the US seemed assured.

Everyone was stunned and dismayed, therefore, when they received a notice several weeks later stating that the Longfields' affidavit had been refused by the US Consulate. The Longfields' financial ability to support the family was considered inadequate should Rolf be unable to find employment. Typically only close relatives would go out on such a financial limb to sponsor immigrants. It was a demanding obligation that involved not only helping them to come to the States, but also assuming responsibility for them and all of their debts in the event that they should fall upon hard times after their arrival.

Suddenly Rolf and Lilo's hopes for the future were crashing down. To make matters worse, time was quickly running out: Lilo was already in the seventh month of pregnancy and would soon be unable to travel.

It was at that pivotal time that Rolf's work rebuilding the bakery owner's car engine paid off. After hearing of Rolf and Lilo's dilemma, the baker offered to lend them the car for the necessary trip to the consulate in Munich. Once there, armed with Pastor Bittinger's letter stating the full support, not only of the Longfields, but also of the entire Church of the Brethren congregation in Wakarusa, Indiana, and aided by additional negotiations conducted through the World Council of Churches, the affidavit was finally accepted, and Jesse and Amanda Longfield remained their official sponsors. Rolf and Lilo were jubilant, and wasted no time obtaining the required physical examinations and making final preparations.

Meanwhile, Rolf's sister Ruth, having been born in Latvia rather than Germany, qualified for immigration under the displaced persons quota and was able to book her passage via the *General Hershey*, a former troop transport vessel converted for peacetime use. She was slated to leave in mid-December 1951.

For Ernst, who also qualified under the displaced persons quota, the process was delayed only by his past service as an officer in the German Army. During the years of waiting, he contacted Wernher von Braun by mail to inquire about employment opportunities in the States, and received an encouraging reply:

Dear Mr. Dutzmann!

I was very happy to receive your friendly letter of August 11th. I want to tell you right up front that I am certain you will not regret your decision to come over to the USA…I have come to know and value you as an energetic man who does not hesitate to take a practical, hands-on approach to his work, and that is the most important deciding factor in this country."

Rolf and Lilo's visas arrived. Their tickets for the cross-Atlantic passage had already been received by the travel agency when they suddenly discovered, to their acute dismay, that pregnant women were only allowed on ships up to the sixth month. Their only remaining option was to fly, which presented a brand new dilemma: flying cost twice as much as travel by ship. After overcoming so many obstacles, could it be that the dream of immigration was yet again slipping out of their grasp?

"We could delay immigration until the baby is born and then wait another six months," said Rolf, thinking out loud, "but that will mean going through the whole visa and paperwork process again. Flying seems to be our only alternative, but how will we raise more than six hundred additional dollars for our flights?"

"Let's write some letters and see what can be done," replied Lilo, and they set about contacting their relatives, including Aunt Paula in New York City.

Within a very short time, a response arrived from Aunt Paula, who was seldom at a loss when faced with a challenge. She had already managed to scrape together $640 in loans from friends and relatives and had sent a check for their plane flights directly to Swissair. Along with Pastor Bittinger's loan, that sum was enough to cover the entire fare for Rolf, Lilo and Ingo.

Unfortunately, the strain of the previous weeks had taken their toll, and by this time, Lilo was not feeling well at all. Her doctor, who had previously given her the green light to travel, now ordered complete bed rest. He also recommended that she not even consider boarding a flight to the US until after the delivery. Aside from the necessity to start all over again with the visa and paperwork process if they were to delay the trip until after the baby was born, there were other considerations that motivated Rolf and Lilo to go forward with the immigration plan as scheduled. Rolf had already given notice at his place of employment that he would quit his job as of mid-December. Rolf and Lilo had also given up their apartment and were once again living temporarily in the tiny crate house with Ernst, Maria and Ruth. With the exception of four suitcases of clothing and personal items that they planned to take with them to America, they had also sold all of their furniture and other personal possessions. With the stage already set for their imminent departure, Rolf and Lilo steeled themselves for an all-out attempt to fly, come what may, on the scheduled date.

During the first week of December, Gertrud arrived for the farewell, bringing an early Christmas gift for Ingo, who was then almost five years old.

Ingo excitedly unwrapped the gift and proudly showed it to Lilo, "Look Mama, it is a little red suitcase, my very own! Now I am ready to go to New York City!"

"Well, open it, Ingolein. There might be something else for you inside."

Ingo opened it to find many little metal cars, all of the makes and models that he already recognized on the streets of Germany and many more that he would soon see on the busy avenues of New York City and in the tranquil country lanes of Wakarusa, Indiana.

Ernst Dutzmann at the
US POW camp in
Mourmelon, France, 1945

Rolf and Ingo (6 months), 1947

Lilo and Ingo, 1947

Ernst Dutzmann in his office at
Friesecke & Höpfner, 1947

Right: Rolf, Lilo and Ingo in
Erlangen-Bruck, Bavaria, 1949

Left:
Ingo
(age two),
1949

Ruth and Maria in front of the "crate house," Erlangen-Bruck, Bavaria, 1950

Ingo's bath time outside the "crate house," 1950

Ingo with the fox tail (age three), spring 1950

Right: December 18, 1951, day of departure for the US (Ingo's little suitcase is on top of the other luggage)

Right: Rolf and Lilo's passport, July 1951

From Dream to Reality

hen my parents and my brother, Ingo, finally took their leave of Germany, it was from a countryside thickly blanketed in fog. On December 18, 1951, with only four suitcases of personal possessions, half a lifetime of memories, and each other, they undertook a grueling, all-day journey. They crossed a desolate, rubble-strewn country, first by taxi, then by bus, by air and by train via Basel to Zürich, Switzerland. The next morning, on the brink of what should have been our odyssey to the New World, I unexpectedly emerged with a plaintive wail into the postwar Old World, disrupting the immigration plans yet again by my untimely arrival.

But the dream of America was only destined to be delayed, not abandoned. My mother and I enjoyed nine days of recuperation in a fine Swiss hospital after our ordeal. In between visits to the hospital, my father's dream to see the Alps close up was finally realized via bus tours that he took with my brother Ingo.

The final hurdle was overcome when the good people of Wakarusa, Indiana, along with my grandparents, Ernst and Maria, came through at the last minute with an additional sum of over three hundred dollars to cover all previously unanticipated expenses including hospital fees and the cost of one additional small passenger on the flight to the United States. When we boarded the plane eleven days later, on December 30, 1951, arriving just in time to ring in the New Year in a foreign land, my grandfather's lifelong dream of immigrating to America became a reality for his son.

When my parents left Germany for the US, they felt nearly boundless hope and optimism, tempered by a few lingering misgivings. Would we be accepted by the Americans, or would the country that had so recently been at war with Germany view us as "the enemy?" Would my father, as a veteran of the Luftwaffe, be considered a Nazi? Would my brother and I be harassed in school? Would my father be able to find work to support us? Could we find happiness in a new land with a very different language, lifestyle and culture? One by one, those worries dissipated like morning mist at the break of dawn.

Our family was first welcomed warmly by Aunt Paula and family in New York City. Already a week earlier they had received my father's sister, Ruth, who arrived via ship after a long and stormy passage. After a bewildering and somewhat intimidating week amidst the hustle and bustle of Manhattan, we traveled westward by train to a small, tranquil farming community in northern Indiana with a population of fewer than 1,600 people. In Wakarusa—a Potawatomi Indian word that means "knee deep in mud"—we were greeted with open arms by the townspeople and the Church of the Brethren. It was a tiny community with a huge heart that left us feeling more than "knee deep in gratitude." After sponsoring us with such great love and consideration, they also went to great lengths to make us feel comfortable and welcome, providing a house for us to live in (owned by the Weldys), as well as help with food, clothing, the English language and acclimating to a new and very different culture. Shortly after our arrival, a shower was held for our family in the fellowship hall of the Church of the Brethren. Furniture, appliances, bedding, towels, dishes, pots and pans, kitchen utensils—in short, everything we needed for a "real American" household—was gifted to us by the generous people there.

On January 11, 1952, just a few days after our arrival in Wakarusa, we celebrated my brother Ingo's fifth birthday, the first family birthday in the New World. An American-style birthday cake with candles was supplied by our sponsors, the Longfields, and the local paper sent a reporter to cover the story.

They ran a human-interest article featuring a photo of Ingo blowing out his candles and the rest of us looking on: I, with sleepy indifference from my mother's arms. The article also mentioned my father's technical qualifications and the fact that he was looking for his first job in the US. This led to an interview with C.G. Conn, Ltd. located in Elkhart, Indiana, the oldest continuous manufacturer of band instruments in America as well as the producer of the first all-electric organs and other innovative instruments. During the war, the company had been converted to the manufacture of precision instruments for defense purposes, but by 1952, they were back to designing and producing the musical instruments they had become famous for around the world. Due to the fact that our family had no car, the director of the electronics division conducted the first interview with my father at our house. The second interview, held at the plant, with my father driven there by a neighbor, resulted in the offer of a full time position in the electronics division. From birthday cake with five candles to full time job with an industry-leading firm—this seemed like a miracle to my parents, but confirmed what they had already anticipated: that in America, anything and everything was possible!

My grandfather, Ernst, finally realized his lifelong dream to be on a ship bound for America when he immigrated to the US with my grandmother, Maria, in 1952. They moved into the second floor of the Weldy house that we occupied and Ernst was immediately also offered a position with C.G. Conn.

In February 1953, my younger brother, Roland, was born in Elkhart, Indiana, the closest city to Wakarusa that had a hospital with a maternity ward.

That same year, my maternal grandmother, Gertrud, was sponsored for immigration to the US by Roy and Grace Summers and Edward and Liz Nusbaum of Wakarusa. She continued to teach piano and voice after her arrival. In 1964, at age sixty-eight she finally performed her first solo voice concert at the Ford Auditorium in Detroit, followed by another in Mt. Clemens, Michigan in 1966.

In 1953, both Rolf and Ernst secured positions with General Motors Saginaw Steering Gear Division in Saginaw, Michigan where they designed power steering units and test fixtures from 1953 to 1957. Our family regretfully said farewell to Wakarusa, but we never forgot the first years in the US and the place where our American Dream began. We returned to Wakarusa for visits, and my parents kept up correspondence with people there for several decades until the generation of Longfields, Summers, Nusbaums and others who originally helped us had passed away and there were no contacts left who still remembered the immigrant family from 1951.

Most of our family members became naturalized citizens in 1957, whereupon Rolf and Ernst were immediately hired as senior engineers for the Chrysler Corporation Missile and Space Division near Detroit, becoming instrumental in the early years of the US space program. Rolf worked on the Redstone and Jupiter missiles and was head of the team that designed and built the control systems for the Saturn I-B rocket, which enabled testing of key hardware for the Apollo spacecraft while in an earth orbit. The Saturn I-B technology was later successfully incorporated into all of the Apollo moon missions. Ernst continued working well past retirement age in the gyroscope department, designing and developing the components used in rocket guidance systems. From 1957 to 1984, Rolf was also the US correspondent reporting on all of the NASA missions for a German aerospace magazine, *Flug Revue* (*Flying Review*), which is still published today in German, English and French.

In 1957, my parents were able to purchase a home of their own with real sinks and hot and cold running water.

Ruth worked for nearly thirty years as a pathologist at Pontiac General Hospital in Pontiac, Michigan.

After working in university administration at Oakland University in Rochester, Michigan for seven years, Ingo received his pastoral education at Concordia Lutheran Seminary in St. Louis in the 1970s and has served as pastor at a number of locations including at the First Lutheran Church of Boston since 1997.

After Rolf's retirement in 1982, he and Lilo moved to New Hampshire where he volunteered tirelessly with hundreds of children in schools and summer camps around the Lakes Region to instill the same kind of enthusiasm for aerospace engineering that he himself had felt as a young person building model airplanes more than fifty years earlier in Latvia. He has been featured in many newspaper articles since 1982 and became somewhat of an area icon. Over the decades, he frequently appeared at local schools and summer camps wearing a rocket-printed tie secured with an airplane tie tack, to give presentations on a variety of topics, including the principles of flight, the Space Shuttle program, the International Space Station, the early years of the US space program and the Wright Brothers' early experimental flights, always armed with models that he assembled himself.

In 1985, Rolf organized one of the earliest NASA-supported Young Astronaut Chapters at the Alton Central School in Alton, New Hampshire, later designated as New Hampshire's pilot chapter. The curriculum that he taught in summer camps included the design, assembly and live launching of model rockets using standardized parts, and he also served as a consultant for groups of New Hampshire middle school and high school students who hoped to qualify for the annual National Model Rocketry Competition in Washington, D.C. Via his instruction of young people and his lectures at venues such as the Christa McAuliffe Planetarium in Concord, New Hampshire, Rolf worked to keep the dream of space flight alive and to encourage more students to enter engineering fields with a fully developed sense of high vision and enthusiasm.

Rolf and Lilo celebrated their sixty-seventh wedding anniversary in November, 2011, deeply thankful for their many years together and for their family that now includes seven grandchildren and two great-grandchildren. They never forgot the people and events that made possible their wartime survival and their immigration to the US. From their very first days in the States, they appreciated the place called America and never looked back with regret. It was only after Rolf's retirement in 1982 that they made their first trip back to the Old World to visit the place where, more than forty years earlier, their eventful life together began.

The book *Der Struwwelpeter* is still in the family collection today.

Front cover of the book
Der Struwwelpeter
by Dr. Heinrich Hoffman

Above and Left:
Ingo (age four),
in Zurich,
December 1951

Left: In New York City, January 1952
Back from Left: Ruth and Lilo
Front from left: Rolf, Rolf's grandmother Julia,
Aunt Paula with Ingo, Paula's husband, Alexander

Rolf and Ingo in Wakarusa, Indiana in front of the
house where the family lived for three months with
a car that Rolf purchased for $250, spring 1952

A reunion of Wernher von Braun (left) and Ernst (right), "the major with the
screwdriver," in Flint, Michigan, April 1957. Photo courtesy of *The Flint Journal*

The Dutzmann family, 1959:

Back, from left: Lilo, Rolf, Gertrud

Front, from left: Roland (age five), Ingo (age eleven), Marina, the author (age six)

Left: Ingo Dutzmann, Senior Pastor at the First Lutheran Church of Boston, 1998

Lilo and Rolf, 1990

Below and right: Rolf delivering a lecture on "The Age of Big Rockets" in Concord, NH at the Christa McAuliffe Planetarium, April 2008

Lilo and Rolf on Lilo's 90th birthday, March 2011

Rolf leading model rocketry with Kensington Summer Camp, August 2011

Dutzmann Family Album   289

Chapter 1

1   The Wikimedia Foundation, *Molotov–Ribbentrop Pact*, Wikipedia: the Free Encyclopedia, *Molotov–Ribbentrop Pact*, www.absoluteastronomy.com/topics/Molotov-Ribbentrop_Pact (Feb. 6, 2010).

Chapter 6

2   American Institute for Aeronautics and Astronautics, Inc., *History of Flight Timeline*, AIAA: the World's Forum for Aerospace Leadership, www.aiaa.org/content.cfm?pageid=260&period=1800s and www.aiaa.org/content.cfm?pageid=260&period=1900s (September 20, 2009).

Chapter 7

3   *Karlis Ulmanis*, Wikipedia: the Free Encyclopedia, http://en.wikipedia.org/wiki/Karlis_Ulmanis (Sept. 20, 2010).

Chapter 8

4   Philip Gavin, *The Triumph of Hitler: The Berlin Olympics*, The History Place: The Past into the Future, www.historyplace.com/worldwar2/triumph/tr-olympics.htm (June 26, 2010).

5   www.historyplace.com/worldwar2/ triumph/tr-olympics.htm.

6   *The Three Occupations of Latvia 1940-1991: Soviet and Nazi Take-Overs and their Consequences*, Occupation Museum Foundation, Riga, 2005, p. 28.

Chapter 10

7   Public Broadcasting Service (PBS), *Timeline: 1940*, Auschwitz: Inside the Nazi State, www.pbs.org/auschwitz/learning/timeline/1940.html (Oct. 7, 2010) and The American-Israeli Cooperative Enterprise (AICE), *The Lodz Ghetto*, Jewish Virtual Library, www.jewishvirtuallibrary.org/jsource/Holocaust/lodz.html (Oct. 7, 2010).

8 Yad Vashem, The Holocaust Martyrs' and Heroes' Remembrance Authority, *This Month in Holocaust History: December 1941*, www1.yadvashem.org/yv/ en/exhibitions/this_month/december/06.asp (Oct. 8, 2010).

9 *Free City of Danzig*, Wikipedia: the Free Encyclopedia, www.en.wikipedia. org/wiki/Free_City_of_Danzig (October 10, 2010).

Chapter 13

10 *Horst Wessel*, Wikipedia: the Free Encyclopedia, www.en.wikipedia.org/wiki/Horst_Wessel (October 21 1, 2010).

Chapter 14

11 *Kristallnacht*, Jewish Virtual Library, www.jewishvirtuallibrary.org/jsource/Holocaust/ kristallnacht.html (October 21, 2010).

Chapter 20

12 Volkhard Bode and Gerhard Kaiser, *Building Hitler's Missiles: Traces of History in Peenemünde*, Berlin, 2008, p. 38.

13 *Timeline: 1942*, Auschwitz: Inside the Nazi State, www.pbs.org/auschwitz/learning/timeline/1942.html (October 10, 2010).

14 *Joseph Stalin*, http://en.wikipedia.org/wiki/Joseph_Stalin (October 10, 2010).

Chapter 21

15 United States government, *Martin Niemöller: Biography*, United States Holocaust Memorial Museum, www.ushmm.org/wlc/en/article.php?ModuleId=10007391 (October 11, 2010).

Chapter 22

16 The New York Times Company, *Operation Gomorrah: Firebombing of Hamburg*, About.com, www.militaryhistory.about.com/od/aerial campaigns/p/gomorrah.htm (October 22, 2011).

Chapter 23

17 *Bombing of Berlin in World War II*, Wikipedia: the Free Encyclopedia, http://en.wikipedia.org/wiki/Bombing_ of_Berlin_in_World_War_II (October 22, 2011).

Chapter 26

18 *20 July Plot*, Wikipedia: the Free Encyclopedia, http://en.wikipedia.org/wiki/1944_Adolf_Hitler_assassination_attempt (October 23, 2010).

Chapter 27

19 Bode and Kaiser, p. 68.

20 Michael Brian Petersen, *Engineering Consent: Peenemünde, National Socialism and the V-2 Missile*, 1924-1945, 2005, p. 317-318.

21 Bode and Kaiser, p. 51.

22 André Sellier, *A History of the Dora Camp: The Story of the Nazi Slave Labor Camp that Secretly Manufactured V-2 Rockets*, Chicago, 2003, pp. 128-137.

23 Jens-Christian Wagner, *Konzentrationslager Mittelbau-Dora 1943-1945: Begleitband zur ständigen Ausstellung in der KZ-Gedenkstätte Mittelbau-Dora*, Göttingen, 2007, p. 47.

24 Testimony of Ernst Dutzmann, *The Essener Dora-Prozess*, Bundesarchiv Ludwigsburg, Zentrale Stelle der Landesjustizverwaltungen Ludwigsburg, IV 429 AR-Z 85/60, Bl. 1130-1131.

25 Sellier, p. 139.

26 Sellier, pp. 135 & 137.

27 Dutzmann, *The Essener Dora-Prozess*, Bl. 1131.

28 Petersen, p 344-45.

29 Sellier, p. 131.

30 Bode and Kaiser, p. 71.

31 Dutzmann, *Essener Dora-Prozess*, Bl. 1132.

32 Petersen, pp. 377-378.

33 Bode and Kaiser, p. 88.

Chapter 30

34 Online Highways, LLC, *Battle of the Bulge: The Ardennes Offensive—a Last-Ditch Effort*, U-S-History.com, www.u-s-history.com/pages/h1753.html (October 28, 2011).

35 *Bombing of Berlin in World War II*, Wikipedia: the Free Encyclopedia, http://en.wikipedia.org/wiki/Bombing_of_Berlin_in_World_War_II (October 28, 2011).

36 Massacre at Gardelegen, Jewish Virtual Library, www.jewishvirtuallibrary. org/jsource/Holocaust/Gardelegen.html, (November 14, 2011)

37 Wagner, p. 146.

38 *Army Historical Series*, The U.S. Army in the Occupation of Germany, 1944-46.

39 Bode and Kaiser, p. 107.

Chapter 34

40 David F. Krawczyk, *The Sinking of the M.S. Wilhelm Gustloff,* www.wilhelmgustloff.com/sinking.htm (October 30, 2011).

41 The POW camp at Bretzenheim where Rolf was held was one of the most poorly equipped Allied POW camps with one of the highest mortality rates. See the website http://en.wikipedia.org/wiki/Rheinwiesenlager (November 15, 2011).

A Word about Sources and Dialogue

This appendix will attempt to clarify, for those readers who are interested, the sources I used as the basis for writing *Flight of Remembrance*. It will also describe an instance where I filled in a gap in the story, as well as how the dialogue was created.

The most important source for this work was the carefully recorded 230-page family history that my parents wrote, copyrighted, printed, bound and gave as gifts to all of their children and grandchildren in 1993 with the title *Traces in History: A Family's Story*. Their version begins in the 1800s with much more ancestral background than I have supplied in this book. However, the bulk of it deals in considerable detail with their own childhoods and the World War II and postwar years, extending through our family's immigration to the US and wrapping up in the mid-1970s. Many of the historic dates and events appearing in this book's narrative were recorded in the family history and provided the backdrop against which the story plays out. For purposes of this book, however, I needed to access additional information. For a list of books and websites used as sources, please refer to the bibliography provided at the end of this book.

I would have liked to add much more about my grandfather Ernst's past, since his own personal story is so fascinating. I inserted sections about him throughout the story where appropriate, and I also included additional material relating to him and his work before, during and after the war in Appendix II in case some readers are interested.

Even though I followed my parents' family history faithfully, there were a few gaps where details were lacking or where actual knowledge of specific events did not tell the full story, so I carefully reconstructed a few scenes or partial scenes to fill those gaps. One example of this is the scene where my father returns to the bombed-out family home in Berlin and his subsequent reconsideration of the relationship with Lilo. Whereas that trip to the ruined family home is a fact supported by my father's photographs, neither of my parents could offer a concrete sense of what brought about my father's change of heart around that time. No doubt there were a number of reasons, not least of which might have been the attentions of his friend, Hans, towards Lilo and the sense of urgency created by the dire wartime conditions, accompanied by a poignant recognition of the transience of life and the realization that he himself, not his mother Maria, should determine his future and his choice of a life partner. In any event, after reading my version, both of my parents commented that "the sentiments and the mood of that time are well represented" by my version of the story. At the point in the story where my father arrives in Berge, the place where Lilo and Gertrud took temporary refuge from the nightly bombing of Berlin, the story once again rests firmly on the account recorded in the family history along with my parents' verbal recollections.

Flight of Remembrance includes a considerable amount of recreated dialogue. The original family history contains some dialogue, but it also contains many statements about what was said, which I translated into dialogue. An example of this is after the wedding, where my version of the story goes as follows:

"Before entering, they lingered at the front door of the building looking at the stars. Rolf kissed Lilo and pointed out a constellation in the sky.

" 'After we part again, just look for the Big Dipper in the night sky and know that I will be looking at it too from a place far, far away, praying for you.' "

The family history version simply mentions Lilo on Christmas Eve, about a month after the wedding:

"On Christmas Eve I walked outside the Dom and looked at the night sky to find the Big Dipper like I had done on many nights before. We had agreed to do this, each one in our part of the world, and, looking to the bright stars, to think of each other with a prayer in our hearts."

I also devised some dialogue based on how my parents, grandparents and other characters might actually have spoken. My grandfather had two favorite comments: "Better to swim in a barrel of water than in a barrel of mud" and "Auch dass Pech noch!" which loosely translates as, "And this misfortune too (in addition to all the rest)!" Both are actual statements that he used throughout his life, so I inserted them (or versions thereof) in a few key places in the book.

In other cases, I included dialogue based on actual reminiscences in the family history and used as much of my parents' own wording as available. An important source of information, in addition to their family history, were my parents' verbal recollections which I painstakingly took down on countless legal pads and on my laptop over the course of about six years. My mother, especially, is a master at remembering verbatim poetry, songs and anecdotes. The gem in Chapter 10 about Ludwig Schlott's argument that sewer gas should be used as fuel in the war effort, for example, was recalled spontaneously by my mother and corroborated by my father, when I requested more info about Ludwig a few years ago. My mother was horrified at first that I would include such a comically vulgar scene, but later agreed that it was simply too hilarious to leave out.

The dialogue in Chapter 20, during the awkward first meeting of Lilo with Rolf's parents where Lilo declined another piece of cheesecake and Ernst delivered a humorous response, was likewise recounted by my parents during a question-and-answer session that I had with them a few years ago, at which time I took many pages of notes. My mother recounted in detail the flirtatious talk and behavior of Rolf's friend, Vera, and my father filled me in on additional information regarding his mother's reservations about Lilo, enabling me to construct some of the dialogue between Rolf and Maria. My brother Ingo related the incident in Chapter 42 about the soldier pointing a revolver at him, pulling the trigger and saying "Bang!"

Most of the dialogue was created via one of the methods above. In addition, at each stage I solicited my parents' guidance to make sure I did not stray from the facts. I sought to supply dialogue that would not only be in keeping with the personalities of my family members, but that would also maintain the essence of the wartime and postwar years.

The indented areas in italics are letters that my parents wrote to each other. My mother saved all of the letters from my father that reached her during the wartime and postwar years. Unfortunately, few of the letters that my mother wrote to my father still exist. The ones written by her during the war, which my father attempted to send home from the front towards the war's end, never reached their destination—a huge loss! Therefore, the letters from Lilo that I include in the book are constructed from facts, thoughts and reminiscences that my mother recorded in the family history or related to me verbally in interviews, and that might be difficult or awkward to introduce into the story some other way. My parents were communicating by mail all throughout that time period with the exception of most of the first year of their marriage, during which time my father was at the front and then in a prisoner-of-war camp, and my mother was fleeing the advancing Red Army. Therefore, it would have been untrue to the story to fail to include letters from my mother to my father. During the period of lost contact, neither knew whether the other had survived. My father wrote and mailed a number of letters to my mother during that time, none of which reached their destination. My mother wrote none to my father during that time because she had no idea where he was or how to address them.

How much did my parents and others in the family know about the existence of concentration camps and the crimes against humanity committed there? Based on their own testimony, they had no concrete knowledge of those during the war, even though the warning signs existed. Hitler and other Nazi leaders had talked about resolving the "Jewish Question" as well as dealing harshly with other non-Aryan groups, and they had imposed numerous restrictions on them. For my father and his family, however, who were living in Latvia at the time of Hitler's rise to power, the events in Germany throughout the 1930s were only known via rumors.

During the war, both of my parents have memories of people vanishing, but they did not know where they were taken or whether they had simply fled voluntarily. With many arrests carried out suddenly and arbitrarily in the middle of the night when most people were asleep, it was not so obvious what was happening. Besides, many people, my parents included, were forced to flee their own homes on numerous occasions, so sudden disappearance was not an unusual phenomenon. Disappearance and/or mass transport of large groups of people was also not equated with extermination because the death camps were only established late in the war—from 1942 on—and all of them were outside of Germany proper in Poland. It was only after the war ended that my parents and many other people found out the gruesome truth via newspapers and the previously forbidden radio broadcasts from the BBC, Radio Moscow, and the Voice of America. (See more info on this topic in connection with Ernst Dutzmann's work at Peenemünde and Mittelwerk in Appendix II.)

Finally, I must make mention of the synchronicities in Chapters 36 through 38. These include the slip of paper with the words *Rolf lebt!* (Rolf lives!) on it that was retrieved by my grandmother during her second heroic trek back into the Soviet Occupied Zone to visit her father and stepmother, the letter written by my father that he was determined to give to "the first woman I see," and his risky escape from the prisoner-of-war camp, aided by my mother. All of those events actually happened as told in this book and are also explicitly recorded in the family history. None of them would have come to pass had it not been for my grandmother's second solo journey into a part of Germany that had, by that time, been officially closed to the West by the Soviets. As the reader can see in the photo section of this book, the faded slip of paper with the words *Rolf lebt!* still exists with the scribbled notes by Johann Kanter in the right margin. For over sixty five years, my mother has preserved that slip of paper, along with the letter "to the first woman I see," and other wartime letters and memorabilia from my father. All are now kept in a secure place and are still, to this day, tied with a faded pink ribbon.

A Word about Ernst Dutzmann

My grandfather Ernst's story is so riveting that I considered at first whether I should make him the main protagonist and my parents the secondary ones. I decided against this for three reasons: 1) because my grandfather is no longer alive to corroborate facts and I would have had to reconstruct too much of his story in view of the small amount of information at my disposal, 2) because my parents are both still alive to provide feedback, to answer questions and to help preserve accuracy in the story, and 3) because my parents' love story provides the most positive component of the family's World War II story that serves to lift it from just another wartime survival narrative to a universal story of love, hope and optimism.

Ernst Dutzmann was born into a Baltic German family in Latvia on March 13, 1895. At that time, Latvia was not independent, but formed a part of the vast Czarist Russian Empire. As a young boy, Ernst used to sit for hours at a time on a hillside of his family's farm and dream of faraway places. Barely discernible in the distance across farm fields and hills, he could see a glistening sliver of the Baltic Sea across which ships frequently passed bound for distant ports. That view inspired his favorite daydream that he was captain of a ship setting sail for America. Nearly fifty years later, that dream would finally materialize.

From a young age, Ernst excelled in science and engineering courses, developing a profound interest in electrical engineering, astronomy and chemistry. After graduating from a German engineering college at Mitweida, Ernst promptly enlisted in the Czarist Army. Shortly after that, when World War I broke out, he was sent to officer's training school in Vilna, Lithuania and then to the front. In his long military career, he served as an officer under three different regimes: the Czarist Russian regime during World War I, the independent Latvian Republic between the two World Wars, and, although he was not a Nazi himself and never joined the Nazi Party or the SS, he was drafted into the Wehrmacht of the Nazi German regime during World War II.

Ernst was twice taken prisoner of war. In August 1915, when he was a twenty-year-old Czarist Russian officer, German troops surrounded his unit near Sauliai, Lithuania and took Ernst prisoner. In 1945, as a Wehrmacht (German Army) major, he was taken by US troops. In each case the country that took him prisoner ended up becoming his home, at least temporarily. After spending only a short time in the German prisoner of war camp during World War I, his Baltic German ancestry enabled him to continue to work as a civilian in German industry for several years. Around that time, he would have preferred to immigrate to America, but his native Latvian citizenship rendered unlikely the possibility of obtaining a sponsor, and without sponsorship, immigration to America was not possible. Instead he lived and worked in Germany for several more years, but once Latvia achieved its hard-won independence, he returned. When he left Germany for Latvia in 1921, it was with his new wife, Maria, a woman he had met in the Rhineland, and their two-year-old son, Rolf.

Ernst served in the Latvian Army from 1921 to 1939, first as a second lieutenant, and from 1935 on, with the rank of captain. During that time, he worked at the artillery laboratory in Kara Osta, just north of Liepaja on the Baltic coast. In response to a tragic accident in 1930, where three workers were killed while boiling old shells in a kettle to melt out the charge, Ernst distinguished himself by designing an automatic assembly machine that was capable of filling percussion primer casings with powder and sealing them shut remotely, thereby removing workers from some of the most dangerous tasks and greatly improving safety conditions at the plant. Other inventions and improvements followed including a new fuse for artillery shells and a device to measure initial shell velocity.

In addition to his inventions for the artillery laboratory, Ernst also built custom radios which he sold to well-to-do Latvians in the Liepaja area, since at that time, radios were not commercially available in Latvia. He also tinkered with a multitude of other peace-time projects and inventions including a machine for a local jeweler to automate the manufacture of gold chains, an aircraft-propeller-driven speedboat, a handmade kayak and a custom-finished motorboat that the family used for outings on the nearby Lake of Liepaja and the Bartava River.

But then, as recounted in this book, Ernst and his family repatriated to Germany in 1939 just prior to the Soviet takeover of Latvia. By October of 1939, the Soviets were poised on the doorstep of the Baltic States. Ernst was the officer in charge of evacuation of the artillery laboratory in Kara Osta, one of the first army bases slated for occupation by the Soviets. His job was to ensure that nothing but an empty shell would remain once the Soviets arrived in the area. For an officer of Ernst's status in the Latvian military, who had previously served in the Czarist Russian military and who held outspoken anti-Communist views, the threat of execution or exile to Siberia loomed as a distinct risk, not only for himself, but for his family as well. Staying in Latvia would have also exposed his extended family, to heightened risk by association. He decided to accept the best option open to him as a Latvian of Baltic German descent—repatriation to Germany, a country already steeped in Nazism and embroiled in World War II. Of course, at that time, no one knew what the Nazi regime would bring to pass in Europe, and no one knew that the war that had just started would prove to be the most brutal of all time. As for the fate of Latvia, not even Ernst could have known that the tiny nation, along with its neighbors, Estonia and Lithuania, was already doomed to destruction, although he may have guessed at some of the turmoil to come. Within three short years, the independent Latvian nation would cease to exist, and by the end of the war, one-third of its prewar population would disappear—casualties of the war itself, executions, deportations, the Holocaust and grim conditions in prisoner-of-war, refugee and prison camps.

Once repatriated to Germany, Ernst and family found themselves at the whim of Hitler and the Nazi regime. They received no advance notice of where they would be resettled or what Ernst's employment would be. They were sent for a short time to the posh Baltic seaside resort of Seebad Bansin while awaiting further orders, then were transferred by train to the Warthegau, a portion of Poland occupied by Germany, first to the city of Posen and then to Litzmannstadt (Lodz), with dismal accommodations in both places.

Most of Ernst's prior work in Latvia had to do with "things that went bang" (Rolf's tongue-in-cheek reference to his father's early work). It was inevitable that he would once again be assigned to work in some branch of the armaments industry and/or the military, and that his engineering skills, once recognized, would be exploited to advance the German war effort. Ernst was over-qualified for the existing jobs in the Litzmannstadt area and was subsequently sent to Berlin, where he was put in charge of the layout and equipping of a new production facility for large-caliber aircraft bombs at the Rheinmetall Borsig plant. In 1942, he was drafted into the Wehrmacht (German Army) and transferred to an artillery proving ground in Bourges, France, where his invention in Latvia for measuring the initial velocity of artillery shells was once again successfully employed.

Finally, in 1943, Ernst was ordered to Peenemünde, where he trained under Wernher von Braun for the position of chief inspector of V-2 rockets, a technology then still in its infancy. Beginning with his assignment to Peenemünde, his survival as well as that of his family became a high priority for the Third Reich, a regime that treated its ground troops with callous indifference but valued its scientists and engineers. In August 1943, he was promoted to major, and came to be referred to by von Braun as *der Major mit dem Schraubenzieher* (the major with the screwdriver) due to his practical, hands-on approach to engineering. He was present at Peenemünde when it was bombed by the Allies later that month, an attack that he narrowly escaped with his life.

After the devastating air raid at Peenemünde, Ernst was transferred to Raderach near the Bodensee (Lake Constance) where a large, elaborate facility was being built to test V-2 rocket engines. It was not long, however, before Ernst and the other Raderach engineers picked up a Swiss newspaper and saw the headline, "What is going on in Raderach?" The article reported mysterious fires and ominous thundering sounds on the German side of the Bodensee. It was clear to those in charge that testing at the site could no longer continue, since that kind of publicity was sure to be followed by Allied air raids.

The Raderach facility was hastily abandoned and a highly classified facility called Mittelwerk was established deep in the Harz Mountains. In February 1944, Ernst was sent there to oversee the inspection process for V-2 rocket production. He was in charge of over two hundred former Peenemünde scientists, design engineers and technicians, most of whom were by that time conscripted to the military. His department was charged with quality control at inspection sites spaced along the assembly line as well as at the main inspection site between the two largest underground tunnels (Bode and Kaiser, p. 68). In his work, he dealt primarily with army and civilian engineers and technicians as well as with Wernher von Braun, who recognized how critical the inspection process was to the project's overall success, and therefore remained closely involved in all decision making regarding its functions.

By the spring of 1943, concentration camp inmates and political prisoners were deployed to carry out much of the production at Peenemünde, a protocol established by the SS and rationalized on the basis of the extreme wartime labor shortages in Germany. At Mittelwerk, the construction of the tunnels and then the manufacturing inside them was carried out under grueling conditions by thousands of prisoners shipped to the site from all over Germany as well as from surrounding occupied countries and other countries still at war with Germany. By the time Ernst arrived in February of 1944, the living conditions, while still harsh for those inmates working on construction Kommandos (units), had improved dramatically for those working on production inside the tunnels. There were only three inmates employed in Ernst's department, with one of whom, a Czech by the name of Jiri Beneš, Ernst came to be on especially cordial terms (Sellier, p. 137). Due to the highly technical nature of their work, these prisoners were treated better than most. Every V-2 rocket produced at Mittelwerk had to pass Ernst's inspection—a total of almost six thousand rockets in the time period from February 1944 through March 1945 (Bode & Kaiser, p. 74)—and he was also actively engaged in setting up and constantly revising the complex protocols under which the inspections were carried out.

When the Allies advanced nearly to the gates of the Mittelwerk installation in early April 1945, Ernst and the other officers and civilian engineers were ordered to evacuate the plant and to proceed eastward on foot. No transportation was available anymore, not even for officers. Ernst followed orders to proceed eastward, moving slowly and deliberately, preferring to be captured by US or British rather than Soviet troops. He was taken prisoner of war by American troops less than a week later. Ernst spent more than a year in an American POW camp in Mourmelon, France, where his skills were employed to refurbish used military trucks. After his release, he obtained a job for Friesecke & Höpfner, a US Army vehicle repair plant in Erlangen-Bruck, Bavaria.

Ernst's dream of immigration to the US was encouraged by letters from Wernher von Braun after the war. In 1952, with his wife, Maria, he finally immigrated to the US, the country that had so recently taken him prisoner of war. Ah yes, the winds of fortune blow in mysterious ways! He of all people would have recognized and pondered the irony of the postwar relocation, but since he passed away in 1977, it is no longer possible to ask him for additional insights or reflections about his life's story.

From 1952 to late 1953, both Ernst and Rolf worked for the electronics division of C.G. Conn, Ltd. in Elkhart, Indiana, a company known worldwide for its manufacture of superior-quality musical instruments, followed by positions at General Motors Steering Gear Division in Saginaw, Michigan designing power steering units and test fixtures.

In the spring of 1957, a reunion between Ernst and Wernher von Braun was arranged by the local press when von Braun visited Flint, Michigan (see photo on page 273, courtesy of *The Flint Journal*).

As soon as they became naturalized citizens in August 1957, Ernst and Rolf were hired as senior engineers for the Chrysler Corporation Missile and Space Division near Detroit, where they were instrumental in the early years of the US space program. Ernst continued working well past retirement age in the gyroscope department, designing and developing the components used in rocket guidance systems.

Throughout the 1950s and 1960s, Ernst built telescopes, radios, televisions, oscilloscopes and other devices in a large, well-equipped workshop in his basement, which also included a darkroom for photo developing. In keeping with one of his lifelong passions—astronomy—he built a powerful telescope in the mid-1950s that, for many decades, towered over fifteen feet high in the backyard. He even permitted his grandchildren (the author included) to help grind the discs that became the telescope's lenses. Every so often, he would spend hours carefully aiming the telescope at a planet or at the moon according to complex calculations, and then would call friends and family over on the next clear night to view such wonders of the solar system as the craters of the moon, the rings of Saturn and the remnants of ancient seas on the planet Mars.

Even though Ernst kept an old-fashioned rifle and a pistol in the house, they were always under lock and key. Other than occasional target practice, he had no interest in pursuits involving firearms.

Ernst retired in 1968, followed in 1969 by his participation in the *Essener Dora-Prozess*, the trial of three SS officers who were suspected to have committed crimes against concentration camp inmates at Mittelwerk. The trial took place in the years 1967-1970, partly in Germany, and partly in the US in order to accommodate Wernher von Braun, Ernst and others who were unable or unwilling to travel to Germany to testify. The three officers being tried were Ernst Sander, a Gestapo officer; Helmut Bischoff, security chief of the Mittelbau region; and Erwin Busta, the dreaded SS guard, "Pferdekopf" (Horsehead), mentioned later in this appendix and in Chapter 27 of the narrative. (This information was obtained from *Mittelbau: Aftermath and Trials*, from the Holocaust Encyclopedia section of the United States Holocaust Memorial Museum website at www.ushmm.org/wlc/en/article.php?ModuleId=10007321).

Ernst Dutzmann passed away in 1977 at age eighty two. There is much about his highly classified wartime service in Germany that will unfortunately remain unknown unless additional sources of information become available.

My older brother, Ingo, who appears as the little boy in the prologue and also in the last few chapters of the book, began interviewing his grandfather and taping his life story in the late 1960s when Ernst was approaching his mid-seventies. He found his grandfather to be a candid and willing subject, with a wide-ranging intellect that did not shy away from life's deeper questions. Unfortunately, not only are the tapes that my brother made of my grandfather's verbal recollections no longer to be found, but the material on them covered mainly Ernst's early years and did not extend as far as the World War II era.

Ernst always exhibited a refreshing streak of bold, unconventional thinking and a strong sense of military-style self-discipline along with a sparkling sense of humor. He was a soft touch with his family, but ruled himself with an iron will. When he found out in the mid-1950s that the chest pain he was experiencing was angina pectoris, he researched what was to be done about it. Instead of the standard recommendations of a restricted, sedentary lifestyle and medication, he opted for an active lifestyle, weight loss, Vitamin E therapy, and a strict diet for life. As a result, he enjoyed more than twenty additional active, healthy years, working part-time for Chrysler Missile and Space Division until age seventy-two and retaining the ability to do pushups well beyond that.

I was fortunate to have considerable information about my grandfather's early and later life from my father's portion of the family history. However, due to the highly classified nature of Ernst's work on the V-2 rocket at Peenemünde and Mittelwerk during World War II and the fact that he spoke little about it even after the war, there was a gaping hole in the story that I could not fill, requiring information that was unlikely to be provided by anyone still living.

Then one day in October 2009, I hit the mother lode. Using GoodSearch, Google, and other web search engines, I entered my grandfather's name, Ernst Dutzmann, and clicked "search." The result was numerous references to books both in English and German with information about his work at Peenemünde and Mittelwerk. In addition, I also unearthed a lot of photographs and general information about the developmental work at Peenemünde and the inspection process in the underground tunnels at Mittelwerk via books and articles. On the basis of these and the limited information available in the family history, I was able to construct the portion of Chapter 27 that describes his employment at Mittelwerk, as well as adding a few more details to the other sections that deal with his time at Peenemünde, Raderach and Mittelwerk. As a result, those parts of the book have numerous footnotes to support the statements made. I am convinced that more information exists that I have not yet managed to unearth, much of it residing in German archives that may not be accessible via the Internet. I would appreciate hearing from anyone who can offer additional sources of information. For that purpose, please see the copyright page for publisher website and author contact information.

The one thing that is very clear about Ernst is that he was ardently opposed to Communism throughout his life. To stay in Latvia rather than repatriating to Germany in 1939 would have resulted in almost certain death for him, either immediately or upon being exiled to Siberia. Many people around him were aware of his outspoken anti-Communist attitudes and activities and would have relished the opportunity to turn him in. As a result, Ernst considered the offer of repatriation to Germany to be the family's most viable option, especially as his wife, Maria, and son, Rolf, had both been born in Germany. It was a decision that he also hoped would improve the chances of survival for the entire family, including those remaining behind in Latvia.

How much did Ernst know about the Nazi regime in 1939? According to my father, he and Ernst knew only what they had heard and read via the limited radio reports and newspaper articles then available in Latvia. The family knew that Germany had started a war, but at the time, no one knew that it would prove to be the most devastating and brutal war of all time, nor that it would entail heinous industrial-scale crimes against humanity. They also had none of the inside information and experiences of people who had already been living in Germany throughout the 1930s. In 1938-1939, deportation of Jews and other groups considered to be "enemies of the Reich" had already begun, but Hitler's genocidal intentions were not yet common knowledge. By that time, however, he was already recognized as a fanatic by people on both sides of my family. They viewed fanaticism with distrust then, just as my parents still do today. I think the most telling fact about my grandfather's stance on Nazi ideology is that he never joined the Nazi Party nor the SS, and he advised Rolf to refuse as well, especially since he knew that his son preferred to continue his studies in aeronautical engineering rather than being sent to the front or becoming involved in political extremism. Their refusal to join the Nazi Party and the SS proved to be fortuitous to their welfare and survival at the war's end.

In writing *Flight of Remembrance*, I recognized the necessity to walk a fine line in my depiction of Ernst—neither whitewashing his role during the war, nor taking an apologetic stance—so I attempted to adhere to what is known. I surmise, however, that there may have been considerable ambivalence on his part towards the work he carried out. From piecing together the existing information and statements by him, along with my father's recollections of him and my own from the postwar years, the main reasons for his compliance were most likely a combination of the following: a determination to keep himself and his family alive; his strong anti-Communist sentiments; his professional goals, which included furthering the emerging rocket technology; and his strong sense of duty as a military officer.

Ernst considered Germany to be the only nation in Europe powerful enough to combat the Soviet threat. The Soviets were regarded, not only by my grandfather, but by many Europeans at the time, with a sense of morbid dread that was further exacerbated by Nazi anti-Communist, political propaganda. In view of the facts that are known today, there is no doubt that the Stalin regime was at least as merciless, bloodthirsty and treacherous as the Hitler regime. An important thing of which to be aware is that the Communist threat came not only from the Soviet Union, but also from within Germany, Latvia and all other European countries, where Communist ideals had infiltrated and gained at least a marginal following. Ernst and family, when faced with a choice between Communism and Fascism, chose what they considered to be the lesser of the two evils.

As documented in the family history written by my parents, Ernst had a strong military sense of duty and responsibility, a code of honor drilled into him by decades of military service in the countries that he served. During the war, his military assignments, particularly at Peenemünde and Mittelwerk, posed stimulating technical challenges, though under difficult and extreme circumstances. The challenging conditions he encountered included living in a veritable secret society away from home and family under extreme rules of security and secrecy. He was not able to speak to anyone, not even family members, about his work; he had to memorize and use complex sequences of letter and number codes in place of ordinary descriptive words to camouflage technical terms at all times; and it was expected that all of his communications to and from family members and friends would be censored (Petersen, *Engineering Consent*, pp 106-136). There were many informers in both installations, with severe punishment meted out for treason and sabotage. The death sentence was carried out more than twenty times at Peenemünde alone (Bode and Kaiser, *Building Hitler's Missiles*, p. 30), and although most of the condemned were inmates, the threat of execution was very real for military personnel as well. His work also subjected him to the constant menace of bombing attacks, especially after the August 1943 attack on Peenemünde where he nearly lost his life. Allied intelligence was keenly intent on pinpointing and destroying all German weapons installations.

On the positive side, Ernst must have been well compensated for his work and must have gained a considerable amount of technical satisfaction from it. That kind of work, performed on the cutting edge of rocket science and technology, would have been personally challenging and motivating to him. For many of the army and civilian engineers, including Ernst, the importance and caliber of the work itself may have greatly outweighed considerations of ideology, national defense or lack of allegiance to the Nazi regime. Technical work of that magnitude, significance and complexity was rare, and only a large, well-developed, industrialized nation could provide the massive amounts of funding and resources required for such an undertaking (Petersen, *Engineering Consent*, p. 59).

Moreover, Ernst must have received some comfort from knowing that he would be unlikely to be sent to the front and that his wife and daughter would be moved out of harm's way to safer areas of Germany by the regime as necessary. Since V-2 rocket technology was intended to eliminate the need for airplane crews, it was also hoped that the lives of German pilots would be spared. The possibility that one of those saved lives might eventually prove to be that of his own son, Rolf, after his induction into the Luftwaffe, would certainly not have failed to occur to Ernst.

No one knows for certain how the photo of Ernst at Mittelwerk as well as a New Year's card and a set of six hand-illustrated birthday cards managed to make it out of the installation intact and into the family collection. The work there was so highly classified and security generally so tight that it is unlikely that anything of that nature would have been allowed to leave the premises under normal circumstances. The photo is the only known surviving image of Ernst at work taken inside either of the top-secret installations. The man leaning over him is most likely one of the inspectors who worked under him. As for the cards, one of them was given to Ernst on his forty-ninth birthday in 1944, one on New Year's Day, 1945, and five on his fiftieth birthday on March 13, 1945. All but one of the cards have multiple original signatures from coworkers. One of them is signed by twenty-seven different civilian and military staff people. The exquisite illustrations on three of them depict Ernst's lifelong passion for astronomy and another, his interest in radio technology. The photo and the cards were discovered only after his death amidst a collection of family photos and personal effects.

When Ernst realized that evacuation was imminent towards the end of the war, he may have carried them out as mentioned in Chapter 30 of the narrative, since by early April of 1945, a state of general chaos and reduced security had probably set in at Mittelwerk. During the next seven years, the items moved from place to place in Germany, then to the US in 1952. In September 2011, the photo and all seven cards finally returned to their place of origin when the Dutzmann family donated them to the Mittelbau-Dora Concentration Camp Memorial in Nordhausen—the site of the former Mittelwerk, and therefore, a fitting final resting place. (View the donated items at www.kirschstonebooks.com.)

The V-2 rocket was much more dangerous than the V-1 due to its lightning-fast speed. At 5,500 kilometers per hour (over 3,400 miles per hour), it could travel from launch sites in Holland to central London in just five minutes and twenty seconds, rendering the British all but defenseless against a weapon that had the capability of dropping out of the sky almost soundlessly and without warning. However, both the V-1 and V-2 were relatively imprecise. The deviation from the intended target of up to seventeen kilometers resulted in a poor hit ratio, with many of the rockets exploding in residential areas rather than in the military and industrial complexes at which they were aimed (Bode & Kaiser, p. 88). A total of 3,225 V-2 rockets were deployed during World War II, with 1,610 hitting Antwerp, 1,359 hitting London and the remainder dropping on other targets. Being perfected so late in the war effort and with only minor navigational modifications possible in the initial stage of flight which rendered them imprecise, those secret weapons were unable to turn the tide of the war in the favor of Nazi Germany (Bode & Kaiser, p. 91). The A-10, an even larger two-stage missile, conceived as the world's first intercontinental ballistic missile, remained on the drawing board throughout the war (Petersen, *Engineering Consent*, p. 155).

Wernher von Braun and Ernst were quite well acquainted on a professional level. Ernst trained directly under him for the job of chief inspector while at Peenemünde, and then went on to work in that capacity at Mittelwerk from February 1944 to April 1945. During that time, von Braun continued to be actively involved with the department and must have communicated with Ernst frequently and directly. That he actually called my grandfather *der Major mit dem Schraubenzieher* (the major with the screwdriver), as mentioned in the story, was related by my grandfather himself after the war and is also mentioned in the 1957 *Flint Journal* newspaper article covering the reunion of Ernst with von Braun in Flint, Michigan.

One of the most troubling aspects regarding the work that Ernst carried out during the war was that thousands of concentration camp inmates and political prisoners were exploited as forced laborers at Peenemünde and Mittelwerk under grueling conditions, with the most notorious camp being the Mittelbau-Dora camp directly outside the Mittelwerk installation in Kohnstein Mountain where the V-1 and V-2 rockets were mass-produced. This is something that was not widely known until the 1960s and which I only became aware of shortly before submitting the manuscript for the first round of editing. Until then, I was under the naive impression that Ernst and the other engineers worked under ivory tower technical conditions, shielded not only from the grim reality of the front, but also from any direct involvement with the criminal brutality of concentration camps.

I have so many questions that can no longer be answered by my grandfather directly. When did he find out that concentration camp inmates would be used as forced laborers? By the time he found out, was it too late to back out or was backing out never even an option, unless he was willing to face imprisonment or death, and possibly bring misfortune on his family as well? Was he ever sickened, depressed or angry about the inhumane treatment of inmates or did he consider the forced labor to be an unfortunate, but unavoidable consequence of war?

I find it difficult to imagine that Ernst's personal sense of integrity would have allowed him to condone the forced labor, and yet his participation in V-2 development and mass production, in and of itself, lent unspoken support to the inhumane conditions that were visited upon thousands of workers. At best, there may have been a decision on his part to keep all objections to himself for fear of harsh reprisal. Whereas there is no evidence to suggest that he was aware of the mass exterminations carried out in death camps, he most certainly knew more than he was able or willing to speak out against. Even my father cannot provide any insight on this topic because the highly classified nature of Ernst's work during the war involved a code of silence that was not broken even after the war's end. What my grandfather saw and experienced then may have included situations that he did not wish to relive. Whatever the reasons, he did not convey very much about his wartime experiences even to his son.

In researching the V-2 rocket program, it struck me as odd that Rolf did not become employed in it as well, especially since Ernst was already engaged in it. The documented severe labor shortage in Germany late in the war, especially of technically skilled workers, along with Rolf's already established aeronautical engineering expertise, would almost certainly have rendered him a valuable asset to the workforce at Mittelwerk or Peenemünde. The answer may be that Ernst himself saw to it that his son would not become involved when Rolf requested of his father to be transferred to Mittelwerk around October of 1944 due to the increasingly dangerous military assignments he was receiving in Slovakia. On the other hand, it may have been the fact that he was serving in the Luftwaffe that kept him from being assigned to the V-1 and V-2 rocket programs which were under the auspices of the German army and staffed primarily by army and civilian engineers. Either way, it was fortunate for Rolf that he was spared any involvement with the brutal forced labor conditions imposed on thousands of concentration camp inmates.

Whereas my grandfather had to have been aware of many of the gruesome concentration camp circumstances during the war due to his military service at Peenemünde and Mittelwerk, he was not involved in the set-up and management of the camps and did not spend any time in them. Also, most of the prisoners at Mittelbau-Dora were not imprisoned for religious, ethnic, racial or cultural reasons. The two exceptions to this were the Hungarian Jews who experienced deportation late in the war and several hundred Gypsies of German origin who arrived from Auschwitz via Buchenwald in 1944 (Sellier, *A History of the Dora Camp*, pp. 119-121). Rather, most of the prisoners were Soviets, Poles, Czechs, French, Belgians, Dutch, Italians (after the Italian armistice with the Allies) and Yugoslavians who were mostly captured resistance fighters or partisans (as in the case of the Czechs in particular), political prisoners, prisoners of war, or simply civilian workers from occupied countries who had suffered the misfortune of being rounded up and pressed into service on the spot. Some unfortunates from Alsace-Lorraine were university professors and students. German common criminals and political prisoners made up the remainder of the inmates in both camps, with common criminals comprising the bulk of German nationals in both the Peenemünde and Mittelbau-Dora camps (Sellier, pp. 108-119).

The fact that many of the inmates were political prisoners or criminals may have made their deplorable circumstances somewhat easier to rationalize. It is also a fact that their treatment at both Peenemünde and Mittelwerk was based almost entirely on their technical capability irrespective of ethnic, racial or cultural factors. The skilled workers received preferential treatment and the unskilled laborers were assigned to the more exhausting details (Petersen, *Engineering Consent*, p. 330). With the exception of twelve women kept in a bordello at the Mittelbau-Dora camp, there were no women and few children detained in either of the camps directly associated with the two top-secret installations. From 1943 on, some 14- to 15-year-old boys were in the Dora camp, and from 1944 on, a few Hungarian Jewish boys 10 years old and younger were relocated from Auschwitz to work there. Other women and children were taken instead to sub-camps in the area.

In Petersen's *Engineering Consent*, page 334, he discusses that the conditions for prisoners, as originally established by the SS, improved considerably once excavation of the main tunnels had been completed and underground production commenced:

> "One of the principle [*sic*] reasons for this was that technical considerations forced the SS to defer to the authority of civilian engineers and administrators. Though the SS did indeed set up the framework in which the factory functioned, civilian engineers were fundamentally entrusted with production. Ernst Dutzmann, the former head of the Army Acceptance Office [Heeresabnahmestelle—responsible for testing and delivering finished missiles and other materials to the missile battalions], stated that 'I did not see prisoners who were employed in assembly get mistreated by SS guards while they worked. The German expert employees were their direct supervisors during work.' Another civilian engineer remarked that 'I myself only saw a few SS men in the underground factory. They were occasionally in the long tunnels. I never saw SS men in the side tunnels (where sub-assemblies were put together).' On the shop floor, civilians could, within their areas of expertise, exert authority even over SS men. Some were even able to keep the vicious 'Pferdekopf' [nickname of SS guard] in check. The conversion from construction to mass production enhanced the authority of the civilian missile specialists in the factory while weakening the power of the SS."

Many engineers at Peenemünde were either totally unaware of the existence of a labor or concentration camp at Peenemünde, in denial about it, or simply unwilling to divulge their knowledge of the camp's existence in their postwar accounts. According to Bode and Kaiser, page 52:

> "Even today, former Peenemünde engineers claim that they never knew anything about the existence of a concentration camp in their Army Research Centre over all the years."

Knowledge of the existence of the Mittelbau-Dora camp at Mittelwerk, however, must have been unavoidable, given the thousands of forced laborers working there from 1943 until the end of the war. How much did Ernst know about the treatment of the Mittelbau-Dora inmates at Mittelwerk? Some light is shed on Ernst's personal knowledge of conditions in the camp by his answers to questions posed to him in Detroit in 1969 during the *Essener Dora-Prozess* (Dora trial in Essen) mentioned earlier in this appendix.

The following quote is taken from the testimony of Ernst Dutzmann during the *Essener Dora-Prozess*, Bundesarchiv (Federal Archives) Ludwigsburg, Zentrale Stelle der Landesjustizverwaltungen (Central Office of the State Justice) Ludwigsburg, IV 429 AR-Z 85/60, Bl. 1130, and presented here both in the original German and in English translation:

"Ich weiß wohl, das die Häftlinge, die eingesetzt waren, den Stollen weiter voranzutreiben, unter sehr schweren Bedingungen arbeiten mussten und bei dieser Arbeit zum Teil zusammenbrachen. In diesem Teil des Stollens hatte ich nichts zu tun. Als ich das erste Mal in das Werk kam, sah ich jedoch, dass tote Häftlinge auf einem Schubkarren aus dem Stollen herausgefahren wurden."

"I was aware that the inmates who were ordered to complete the tunnels, were forced to work under very harsh conditions and that many collapsed and died during that work. I did not have responsibility for that part of the tunnels. But as I entered the plant for the first time, I saw dead inmates being transported out of the tunnels in wheelbarrows."

Below are quotes from books and other documents where Ernst is mentioned, as well as general quotes about the work at the two top-secret installations. The first quote is a brief summary of Ernst's work at Peenemünde and Mittelwerk, taken from page 68 of Bode and Kaiser:

"Ernst Dutzmann, previously Technical Manager of a test stand in Raderach near Friedrichshafen, had been trained to inspect long-range rockets in Peenemünde. As of February, 1944, he was then made Department Manager for army inspection of the A4 in the Mittelwerk, with the rank of a major. He was in charge of the main inspection site between Tunnels A and B and all inspection sites on the assembly line. A total of over 200 Peenemünde scientists, design engineers and technicians, mainly now conscripted to the military, worked in the inspection department."

The second quotation is taken from Sellier, page 139:

"The prisoners who were assigned to secretarial work or to relatively delicate operations such as checking gyroscopes were put in barracks inside the tunnel along with their Meister and often with engineers. Their relations were usually acceptable and sometimes became cordial. That was the case for Ribault, Baillon, Jean-Paul Renard, and Bailly. It was also the case for the Czech Benès with Major Dutzmann of the Wehrmacht."

Gyroscopes are used for guidance systems in rockets and missiles. After obtaining his US citizenship in 1957, Ernst's work at the Chrysler Corporation Missile and Space Division near Detroit was in the experimental gyroscope department, so it is not unreasonable to assume that he was also closely involved with gyroscope inspection at Mittelwerk.

Ernst seems to have been one of the officers who kept the impulses of some of the more sadistic SS and civilian engineers under control, as he reported in the following statement during the *Essener Dora-Prozess* (Bl 1130-1131):

"Einer (der deutschen Fachleute), ein Mitarbeiter meiner Dienststelle, soll—wie ich gehört habe—die Häftlinge schlecht behandelt haben. Ich kann mich an seinen Namen nicht erinnern. Er soll an den Häftlingen nicht vorbeigegangen sein, ohne ihnen einen Fußtritt zu versetzen. Ich habe ihn zu mir gerufen und ihm gesagt, dass ich ihn von der Dienststelle entfernen lassen würde, wenn ich noch einmal von solchen Vorfällen hören würde. Das ist dann nicht mehr vorgekommen."

"One (of the German civilian engineers), a worker in my department, was reported to me as having mistreated the inmates. I cannot remember his name. He reportedly never passed by the inmates without giving them a kick. I called him into my office and told him that I would have him removed from the department if I heard of another such incident. No such incidents occurred again after that."

The inspection work in Ernst's department was of such a highly sensitive and complex technical nature that abusive conduct toward the inmates would have been far too disruptive and, from the beginning, was not to be tolerated. (Dutzmann, *Essener Dora-Prozess*, Bl. 1133):

"Das Sicherheitspersonal (also SS, SD, Werkschutz) wusste, dass die Montage in unserer Abteilung eminent wichtig war, dass Störungen in jedem Fall vermieden werden mussten. Die Häftlinge, die hier arbeiteten, sollen eine bessere Verpflegungsration erhalten haben als die übrigen Häftlinge."

"The Security Personnel (in other words, the SS, SD, Plant Security) knew that the work performed in our department was absolutely essential, and that disruptions, by all means, had to be prevented. The inmates who worked there were supposed to have been provided with better rations than the other inmates."

There was certainly a unique set of circumstances at both Peenemünde and Mittelwerk that led to a tacit consent to terrible working and living conditions for prisoners that might otherwise not have been tolerated by civilian and military technical personnel. As stated by Michael Brian Petersen on page two of his book *Missiles for the Fatherland: Peenemünde, National Socialism, and the V-2 Missile* (Cambridge University Press, Cambridge, New York, Melbourne, Madrid, Cape Town, Singapore, São Paulo, Delhi, 2009):

"There was a unique and complex interaction of professional ambition, internal cultural dynamics, military pressure, and political coercion which coalesced in the texture of life at the facility. The interaction of these forces made the rapid development of the V-2 possible, but also contributed to an environment in which stunning brutality could be committed against concentration camp prisoners who manufactured the missile."

Had Ernst or others objected more vehemently to the treatment of prisoners at Mittelwerk, they would most likely have ended up in a striped uniform in their midst as mentioned by Bode and Kaiser, p. 74:

"When the German skilled worker Alfred Backhaus was drafted into Mittelwerk and defended a prisoner maltreated by engineers in Hall 11 at the beginning of 1944, he was denounced and ended up in the prisoners' troop himself."

Ernst seems to have felt compelled to adopt an attitude of non-involvement in affairs that were not specifically part of his job, probably out of an instinctive sense of self-preservation. The following quote from Ernst during the *Essener Dora-Prozess* implies that, even as he had not come to know the defendants in the trial, he may also have refrained from familiarizing himself with and raising objections to the conditions at Mittelwerk, even if he personally disapproved of them (Bl. 1131):

"Ich kann über Straftaten, die den Angeklagten vorgeworfen werden, nichts aussagen. Es klingt heute vielleicht merkwürdig, dass ich mich an die Namen der Angeklagten (Busta, Sander, Bischoff) nicht erinnern kann. Es war damals mein Prinzip, mich von allem, was mich nicht anging, herauszuhalten."

"I cannot testify regarding crimes with which the defendants are charged. It may sound odd today, that I do not remember the names of the defendants (Busta, Sander, Bischoff). It was my practice in those days to refrain from involvement in anything that was not explicitly designated as my concern."

As much as what has been said by and about Ernst, I consider significant what has not been stated about him. He was never described as sadistic, bigoted, inhumane or fanatic. No major interrogations of him were ever carried out, nothing adverse was ever even suggested about him, and he was never accused, much less convicted of any crimes. With his Slavic appearance, he certainly did not fit the ideal Aryan profile, and with the numerous friendships that the Dutzmann family maintained with Jewish people both before and after the war, he could never be labeled as anti-Semitic. Yet, due to the fact that Ernst took most of his World War II memories silently to the grave, there is a lot of conjecture about the circumstances surrounding his work during the war, and I regret that so many questions regarding his role and experiences at Peenemünde and Mittelwerk remain unanswered.

The Mittelbau-Dora
Concentration Camp Memorial
www.dora.de

ittelbau-Dora is a prototypical example of forced labor by concentration camp inmates, and thus of a new camp type within the National Socialist concentration camp system—a type not represented by other concentration camp memorials. Between 1943 and 1945, some 60,000 persons from nearly all the countries of Europe, above all the Soviet Union, Poland and France, were deported to the Harz Mountains as concentration camp

Above: View into transverse chamber 45 of the tunnel of the former Mittelwerk. Inmates were housed here until June 1944; later V-1 flying bombs were produced here. (Photo: Claus Bach, Mittelbau-Dora Concentration Camp Memorial)

Left: Memorial sculpture by the artist Jürgen von Woyski, in front of the former crematorium of the Mittelbau-Dora concentration camp, erected 1964 (Photo: Jens-Christian Wagner, Mittelbau-Dora Concentration Camp Memorial)

inmates to perform forced labor for the German armament industry. One in three of them died.

Today Mittelbau-Dora is a European place of remembrance. By making the Mittelbau-Dora Concentration Camp Memorial an integral part of its memorial conception in 1999, the German federal government acknowledged the special national and international importance of this site. After decades of neglect, the memorial has meanwhile been thoroughly restructured in accordance with its historical significance. The core of the new concept was the construction of a new Mittelbau-Dora museum, which was inaugurated in 2005 on the sixtieth anniversary of the camp's liberation. Since September 2006 it has housed a permanent exhibition on the camp history which presents Mittelbau-Dora as a paradigm of forced labor by concentration camp inmates.

KZ Gedenkstätte Mittelbau-Dora
Kohnsteinweg 20
D-99734 Nordhausen

Tel.: +49 (0)3631 49 58 0
Email: info@dora.de

www.dora.de

All photos and text provided courtesy of the Mittelbau-Dora Concentration Camp Memorial.

Former inmates and their families during a commemoration ceremony in front of the former crematorium of the Mittelbau-Dora concentration camp, September 2006 (Photo: Daniel Gaede, Mittelbau-Dora Concentration Camp Memorial)

Museum building of the Mittelbau-Dora Concentration Camp Memorial (Photo: Claus Bach, Mittelbau-Dora Concentration Camp Memorial)

View of the exhibition in the museum of the Mittelbau-Dora Concentration Camp Memorial (Photo: Claus Bach, Mittelbau-Dora Concentration Camp Memorial)

Bibliography

The list below is not intended to be comprehensive on the subject of World War II and only includes the resources that were accessed to write this book.

Books:

Bode, Volkhard and Kaiser, Gerhard, *Building Hitler's Missiles: Traces of History in Peenemünde*, Berlin, Christoph Links Verlag–LinksDruck GmbH, 2008.

Essener Dora-Prozess, Bundesarchiv Ludwigsburg, Zentrale Stelle der Landesjustizverwaltungen Ludwigsburg IV 429 AR-Z 85/60.

Le Maner, Yves and Sellier, André, *Bilder aus Dora: Zwangsarbeit im Raketentunnel, 1943-1945*, Berlin, Westkreuz-Verlag GmbH, 2001.

Neufeld, Michael J., *The Rocket and the Reich: Peenemünde and the Coming of the Ballistic Missile Era*, Cambridge, MA, Harvard University Press, 1995.

Neufeld, Michael J., *Von Braun: Dreamer of Space, Engineer of War*, New York, Vintage Books, 2008.

Petersen, Michael Brian, *Engineering Consent: Peenemünde, National Socialism and the V-2 Missile, 1924-1945*, Dissertation submitted to the Faculty of the Graduate School of the University of Maryland, College Park, 2005.

Petersen, Michael B., *Missiles for the Fatherland: Peenemünde, National Socialism, and the V-2 Missile*, (Cambridge Centennial of Flight Series), New York, Cambridge University Press, 2009.

Sellier, André, *A History of the Dora Camp: The Story of the Nazi Slave Labor Camp that Secretly Manufactured V-2 Rockets*, Chicago, Ivan R. Dee, 2003.

The Three Occupations of Latvia 1940-1991: Soviet and Nazi Take-Overs and their Consequences, ed. by staff members of the Museum of the Occupation of Latvia: Valters Nollendorfs, Ojars Celle, Gundega Michele, Uldis Neiburgs, Dagnija Stasko, Occupation Museum Foundation, Riga, 2005.

Wagner, Jens-Christian, *Konzentrationslager Mittelbau-Dora 1943-1945: Begleitband zur ständigen Ausstellung in der KZ-Gedenkstätte Mittelbau-Dora*, Göttingen, Wallstein Verlag, 2007.

Wagner, Jens-Christian, *Lern- und Dokumentationszentrum Mittelbau-Dora: Die Neukonzeption der KZ-Gedenkstätte Mittelbau-Dora*, Weimar, Buch- und Kunstdruckerei Kessler GmbH, 2003.

Wagner, Jens-Christian, *Produktion des Todes: das KZ Mittelbau-Dora*, Göttingen, Wallstein Verlag, 2001.

Websites:

www.aiaa.org

www.absoluteastronomy.com/topics/Operation_Paperclip

www.absoluteastronomy.com/topics/Wernher_von_Braun

http://www.crwflags.com/fotw/flags/lv%5Eair.html (referenced for Latvian National Guard cross)

www.dora.de

www.encyclopedia2.thefreedictionary.com

www.en.wikipedia.org/wiki/Bombing_of_Berlin_in_World_War_II

www.en.wikipedia.org/wiki/Karlis_Ulmanis

www.history.howstuffworks.com/world-war-ii

www.historyplace.com/worldwar2/riseofhitler/success.htm

www.historyplace.com/worldwar2/timeline/ww2time.htm

www.jewishvirtuallibrary.org/jsource/Holocaust/killedtable.html

http://www.omf.lv/index.php?option=com_content&task=view&id=36&Itemid=43&lang=english

www.onwar.com/chrono/index.htm

www.pbs.org/auschwitz/learning/timeline/1940.html

www.remember.org/nordhausen

www.theverylongview.com

www.u-s-history.com/pages/h1753.html

www.ushmm.org/wlc/en/article.php?ModuleId=10007321 & www.ushmm.org/wlc/en/article.php?ModuleId=10007319 (the Holocaust Encyclopedia section of the United States Holocaust Memorial Museum website)

www.wilhelmgustloff.com

www.yadvashem.org

A

A10 rocket, 311
A4 rocket, 132, 146-47, 315. *See also* V-2 rocket
Advanced Flight Technical School (Höhere Fliegertechnische Schule), 128-29, 133
aeronautical engineering, 3, 22, 37, 39, 54-55, 57, 125, 128, 163, 251, 268, 269, 308
Africa Corps, 128
air raids, 106, 109-10, 123, 132, 136-38, 146, 150-51, 157, 160, 162, 165, 184, 243, 302
    first daytime air raid, Berlin, 162-63
Aizsargs paramilitary group, Latvia, 46-49, 68
Akaflieg (Akademische Fliegergruppe), 53-56, 73 (photo), 123
Allied troops, 198, 200, 201, 213, 216, 222
America, Americans, 17, 33, 132, 177, 193, 201, 208, 210, 214, 224, 252, 262-63, 265-66, 281-83, 299-300. *See also* US
American magazines
    Model Airplane News, 14, 32, 40
    Modern Mechanics, 14, 46-47
Army Acceptance Office (Heeresabnahmestelle), 168, 314
army engineers, 169-70
artillery laboratory, Latvia, 8, 11, 13, 15, 34, 36, 42, 45, 47, 300-01. *See also* Latvian Artillery Laboratory
Aryan, 25, 43, 172, 297, 318
Auschwitz Concentration Camp, 132, 204, 313, 314
Axis powers, xviii, 125, 147, 319

B

Baltic Sea, 3-4, 6, 8, 17, 23, 27, 29-31, 52, 104, 132, 145-46, 220, 265, 299
Baltic States, xiii, xvii-iii, 5, 14
Barbarossa (Red Beard), invasion of Soviet Union by Germany, 123
basketball, 22, 41-42, 45, 56, 73 (photo)
Battle of Berlin, 147
Battle of the Bulge, 193
Bavaria, 205, 270, 279-80, 304
BBC, 132, 298
Benneckenstein, Germany, xxv (map), 183, 198, 202, 207, 209-10, 215, 219, 221, 223, 225, 228-33, 235

Berge, Germany, xxv (map), 151, 160, 162, 165, 295
Berlin, Germany, xxv (map), 42-44, 54, 58-61, 74, 83, 99, 103-04, 124-25, 127-29, 135-40, 144-45, 151-53, 159-60, 162-65, 187 (photo), 194-95, 292-93
    employment bureau, 152, 164-65
Bingen, Germany, xxv (map), 242-43
Bischoff, Helmut, 305, 318
Bodensee (Lake Constance), xxv (map), 157-58, 302
Boelke Kaserne sub-camp, 200
bomb furlough, 159
bombing, xviii, 148, 154
    of British cities, 132
    of German cities, xix, 132, 143, 144, 150-52, 158, 160, 162, 195, 228, 295, 291. *See also* individual cities
    of Peenemünde, 146, 309
    of Warsaw, 49
    of Nordhausen, 198
borders, 57, 173, 193, 230-31, 234, 243-44, 260, 269
Braunschweig, Germany, xxv (map), 249-50, 259, 261, 269-70
    Technical University of, 249
Bretzenheim, Germany, xxv (map), 223-4, 233, 235-6, 241, 245, 252
Busta, Erwin, 170, 305, 318. *See also* "Pferdekopf"

C

C-Rations, 221, 223, 225
camps, 24, 43, 132-33, 197, 200, 206, 216, 221-26, 231-32, 234, 236-38, 240, 242, 311-18, 320-21. *See also* death camps, concentration camps, POW camps
Catholic church, xiv, 38-39, 131, 179
Cecilienschule, Berlin, 92-94
Chrysler Corporation Missile and Space Division, 284, 304, 316
Churchill, Prime Minister Winston, 230
communist/anti-communist, xiii, 11, 36, 40, 52, 89, 92, 220, 270, 301, 307-8
concentration camp, 47, 96, 132-33, 158, 168-69, 183, 197, 200, 212, 216, 297-98, 303, 305, 311-18, 320-21. *See also* death camp and specific camp names

concentration camp, cont'd.
    inmates, 168-69, 183, 197-98, 200, 204, 253,
        303, 305, 309, 311-18, 320-21
    inmate tattoos, 206
Conn, C. G., Ltd., ix, 283
Czarist Russian
    army, 141, 300
    Empire, 299
    officer(s), 5 (Ernst), 7
    regime, 5, 300-01

D

Dancing lessons (*Tanzstunde*)
    Lilo, 95
    Rolf, 45
Danzig (Gdansk), Poland, xxv (map), 54, 60, 62,
        73 (photos), 112, 123, 126, 218, 291
    Technical University of, 54, 73, 75 (photos)
Daugava River, Latvia, 3-4
death camp, 132-33, 206, 216, 298, 312. *See also*
        concentration camp and specific camp names
Depression, Great, 36, 80
displaced persons quota, 272, 276
Drachenberge, East Prussia, xxv (map), 58, 75
Dutzmann, Alfons, 10-13, 220
Dutzmann, Ernst
    anti-Communism, 20, 36, 307
    artillery laboratory, 8, 13, 36, 45
    astronomy, interest in, 30, 246, 299, 305, 310
    attitude at home, 8
    attitude toward Germany, 17, 308
    death of, 305
    employment in US, 283-84, 304, 316
    family in Latvia, 10
    immigration to US, 276, 283, 304
    inventions and hobbies, 29-30, 34, 37, 53, 252,
        301, 305
    the Major with the Screwdriver (*der Major mit
        dem Schraubenzieher*), 146, 287 (photo),
        302, 311
    military service, 5, 22, 45, 300, 302-04
    photographs of, 63, 65-66, 70, 73-74, 185-86,
        279, 287
    in pre-war England, 48
    repatriation to Germany, 301-02
    refusal to join Nazi Party or SS, 300, 307
    rocket guidance system design and development,
        284, 304
    testimony in war trials, 292, 305, 315-18

V-2 rocket chief inspector, 172, 303, 316
    at Mittelwerk, 168, 198-200, 303-04
    at Peenemünde, 146-47, 157, 302, 306,
        308-09, 311, 315-16
    at Raderach, 157-58, 302, 307, 315
von Braun and, 146-47, 276, 287, 302, 304, 311
World War I prisoner of war, 6, 300
WWII prisoner of war, 252, 279 (photo), 300,
    304
Dutzmann, Ingo, xxi-ii, 253, 255-61, 263-64, 268,
        270-73, 277-78, 305
    photographs of, 279-80, 286-88
Dutzmann, Lilo (Liselotte Wassull) xix, xxii, 61-62,
        79-119, 124-27, 129-32, 137-42, 144-45,
        148-52, 159-63, 174-84, 193-96, 201-11,
        228-45, 249-65, 268-77, 295-97
    and Berlin air raids, 109-10, 137-38
    and Berlin, first air raid drill, 105-06
    birth of daughter, 281
    birth of son, Ingo, 253
    birth of son, Roland, 283
    childhood, 79-95, 113, 207-08
    courtship, 61, 94, 119. *See also* Dutzmann, Rolf
        and Lilo, courtship
    early graduation from school, 95
    employment offer, 151-52
    engagement to Rolf, 172
    father Walter, 95, 188 (photo)
    first awareness of changes under Nazi regime,
        92-93
    first job, 96
    first meeting with Rolf's family, 129-30
    flight. *See* flights (escapes)
    grandparents, 87-88, 180-81, 203, 205, 233-35,
        260
    great aunts, 103-05, 136
    immigration to America, xxi-iii, 265, 270, 272,
        274-77, 280 (photo), 281-82
    Jewish friends, 93-94
    leg and hip problems, 85-88, 113, 207-08
    letters from Rolf, 109, 140-42, 145, 174, 198,
        202, 210-11, 238-39, 297-98
    letters to Rolf, 109, 135, 159, 165, 193-94, 268,
        297
    first meeting with Rolf, 61
    miscarriage, 250
    parents' divorce, 90-91
    photographs of, 115-19, 186, 188-90, 279-80
        287-89

Dutzmann, Lilo (Liselotte Wassull), cont'd.
    postwar hardships, 251, 255, 257-59
    pregnancy, 249, 252, 275, 277
    Reich ID (*Kennkarte*), 118 (photos)
    religious upbringing, 83, 139, 179
    rescue of Rolf from POW camp, 232, 235-43
    reunion with Rolf, 161, 239
    Silesian Steamship Company, 151-52, 165, 195,
        260
    visa, 276
    voice lessons, 107, 125
    wartime employer, 97, 111, 138
    wedding, 172-82, 188-190 (photos)
Dutzmann, Maria, xix, 6-12, 38, 63-68, 70-71,
        123-27, 129-31, 140-41, 158-59, 179-80,
        183-86, 210-11, 219, 228-29, 270-72, 281-83,
        309, 310
    photographs of, 63-68, 70-71, 73-74, 185-86,
        189-90, 280
Dutzmann, Paula, 7, 10-03, 39, 124, 220, 231, 263,
        272, 277, 282
    photographs of, 64, 66, 287
Dutzmann, Rolf,
    aeronautical engineering, xvii, 3-4, 54-55, 57, 75
        (photos), 125, 128, 163, 251, 268-269,284,
        308, 312
    aircraft mechanic training, 128
    at artillery laboratory, Latvia, 36-37, 47
    athletic pursuits, 41-42, 56
    aviation pursuits, 32-35, 40, 44, 46-47, 49, 273
    birth in Germany, 6
    courtship of Lilo, 60-62, 109-10, 112-14, 126,
        129, 142, 145, 161-63, 172
    discrimination against, 21, 25-28, 46, 126
    draft notice, 125-27
    flight training, 57-58, 75 (photo), 126, 153-54,
        185 (photo)
    as instructor, 128-29
    honeymoon, 183
    immigration to America, xxi-xxiii, 265, 270,
        272, 274, 276-78, 281-82
    letters from Lilo, 109, 135, 159, 165, 193-94,
        268, 297
    letters to Lilo, 109, 140-42, 145, 174, 198, 202,
        210-11, 238-39, 297, 210-11
    military service, 127, 133-35, 140, 143-44,
        152-53, 156-57, 166-67, 196-98, 212-18, 312
    model plane building. *See* model airplanes and
        gliders

navigator training, 153-56, 185 (photo)
Olympics, attendance at. *See* Olympiad, Games
        of the XI
photographs of, 63-73, 119, 185-86, 188-90,
        245, 279-80, 287-89
postwar employment, 249-50, 267-70
postwar studies, 251, 254, 256, 269
prisoner of war, 220-26, 231-42
postwar life, 250-51, 253, 255-59, 261, 263-64,
        269, 272-73
refusal to join Nazi Party or SS, 21, 307-08
religious upbringing, 38-39
repatriation to Germany, 14-19
retired life, 284-85
school years, 25, 27-29, 39-41, 45-46, 48, 54, 125
US employment, 283-84, 304
wedding, 172-82, 188-190 (photos)
Dutzmann, Ruth, 7-12, 15-16, 23, 30-31, 34-35,
        38-39, 54, 71, 74, 140-41, 158-59, 209-11,
        219, 221, 228-29
    photographs of, 63-67, 70-71, 74, 186, 189-90,
        280, 287
Dutzmann family, xii-xiii, xvi-xix, xxv (travels of,
        on map), 7, 9-10, 19-21, 24, 34, 51, 53-54,
        123, 270, 294, 297, 299, 301-02, 318
    photographs of, 63, 66, 70, 287, 288

E

Eastern Front, 125, 131-32, 135, 140, 151, 155-58,
        198
East Prussia, xxv (map), 49, 57, 75, 99, 154
engineering
    aeronautical, 22, 37, 39, 54-55, 75 (photos), 125,
        128, 163, 251, 269, 308, 312
    aerospace, 284
    automotive, 251, 269
    Ernst's approach to, 302
    mechanical, 48, 251, 269
engineers, 15, 33, 169-70, 268, 302, 311, 314-317
    civilian, 146-47, 168-70, 302-04, 309, 314, 316
Erlangen-Bruck, Germany, xxv (map), 270, 279-80
        (photos), 304, 310
escapes. *See* flights (escapes)
Essener Dora-Prozess, 292-93, 305, 315-18, 323
Estonia, xxv (map), 4-5, 45, 301
Evangelical Church of the Hohenzollerndam,
        Berlin, 139

F

famine in Ukraine (Holodomor), 133
Federal Republic of Germany, 269
Final Solution, 133
Finland, invasion of, 20
flights (escapes)
    from Benneckenstein to escape the Soviet Zone (Lilo, Gertrud, Ruth and Maria), 228-29
    from Berlin to Havelberg to escape the bombing (Lilo and Gertrud), 164-65
    from the front (Rolf), xxv (map), 214-18
    from Havelberg to Benneckenstein to escape the Soviet troops (Lilo and Gertrud), xxv (map), 201-210
    from Latvia, in advance of the Soviet takeover (Ernst, Maria, Rolf, Ruth), xxv (map), 14-18
    from Peenemünde bombing (Ernst), 146
    from postwar Germany to the US, 281-83
    from POW camp (Rolf), 241-43, 298
Flug Revue (*Flying Review*), 284
Friesecke & Höpfner (US Army vehicle repair plant), 252, 270, 279 (photo), 304
fuel shortage, 56-57, 156, 164
Führer, 50, 54, 93, 104-05, 126, 212, *See also* Hitler, Adolf

G

Gardelegen, 197
German Aircraft Development Center (Deutsche Versuchsanstalt für Luftfahrt), 57
German-Soviet Non-Aggression Treaty, 5, 57. *See also* Molotov-Ribbentrop Pact
Germany, German, xiii-iv, xvi-iii, xxv (map), 5-6, 10-11, 14-17, 19-33, 36, 42-43, 44, 46, 49-51, 80-81, 89-90, 132-33, 167-70, 212, 249-52, 264, 300-03, 307-09. *See also* entries by city name
    ancestry, 26-28, 42
    army, 19, 71, 124, 175, 205, 214, 276, 300, 302. *See also* Wehrmacht
    retreat, 170, 213-14
    borders, xxv (map), 57, 173, 193
    cities, xix, 132, 143, 158, 215
        destruction of, 132, 143, 158
    citizens, 249, 253, 269. *See also* people
    democratic government, 36, 80
    descent, xvii, 5-6, 14, 25, 301,

economy, 80, 92
    magazines and newspapers
        The Berlin Illustrated (*Berliner Illustrierte*), 124, 186 (photo of Rolf reading)
        Flug Revue (*Flying Review*), 284
        The Green Post (*Die Grüne Post*), 32, 47
        The Week (*Die Woche*), 47
    occupation forces (in Latvia), 31, 131, 220
    people, 89, 91, 132, 220, 250. *See also* citizens
    postwar, 244, 250, 258, 263, 272, 294
    prisoner-of-war camp, 141, 144
    rearmament, 44, 89
    resistance movement, 166
    soldiers, 44, 123-24, 170, 193, 201, 203, 214, 219, 300
    unemployment, 80-81, 83
    war effort, 125, 129, 132, 302
German Democratic Republic, 270
gliders. *See also* model airplanes and gliders
    flight training, 57-58, 75 (photo), 126, 153-154
    full-size, construction and testing of, 47, 68 (photo)
    models, construction and testing, 32-35, 39-40, 46-47, 53, 67 (photos)
Göppingen, xxv (map), 157-59
Great Britain, 5, 48, 195
Great Purge, the, under Stalin, 133
Great War, the, 141. *See also* World War I
Gypsies, 52, 313

H

Hamburg, firebombing of (Operation Gomorrah), 143, 291
hammer and sickle, Soviet, 5
Harz Mountains, 158-59, 198, 208-09, 217, 221, 225, 303
Havelberg, Germany, xxv (map), 87-88, 95, 152, 163-66, 173, 183, 188 (photo), 190 (photo), 194, 196, 202-03, 205-06, 210, 220, 225-26, 233-35, 244, 260, 262
    train station, 175, 177
Havelberger Dom Cathedral, 166, 179, 181, 188-90 (photos)
Henke, Madame Frieda (Omi Henke), 99, 101, 107, 165
high school
    Rolf, 39, 41-42, 45-48
    Lilo, 86, 88-89, 92-95

Himmler, Heinrich, 132

Hitler, Adolf, 5, 18, 30, 36, 43-44, 50, 57-58, 88-90, 92-93, 163, 166-167, 172, 206, 224, 292, 297, 301. *See also* Führer

   assassination attempt (Operation Valkyrie), 166

   suicide of, 206, 224

Hitler Youth Movement, 93

Hoffman, Heinrich, Dr., xvi

Holocaust, xix, 45, 96, 301, 305, 321, 290-93

Holodomor (genocidal famine in Soviet Union), 133

Horst Wessell Song, Die Fahne Hoch (Raise High the Flag), 89

I

Indiana, ix, xi, 264-65, 273-76, 278, 281, 283, 287 (photo), 304

immigration to the US, xii, xiii, 270, 274, 283, 285, 294, 300, 304

invasion

   of Finland by Soviet Union, 20

   of Latvia by Germany, 123-24

   of Poland by Germany, 5, 19

   of Poland by Soviet Union, 20

   of Soviet Union by Germany, 57-58, 123

Iron Curtain, 230

J

Jews, xix, 6, 29, 44, 51-53, 60, 93-94, 96, 124, 133, 201, 204, 291, 297, 313, 318

   and concentration camps, 96, 204, 313, 314

   deportation of, 307, 313-14

   destruction of property of, 96

   discrimination against, 25, 29, 93-94

   extermination of, xix, 52-53, 96, 124, 133, 201, 204

   Hungarian, 313-314

   Kristallnacht and, 96

   relocation to Poland (rumors of), 60

Jüterbog, Germany, xxv (map), 128, 135, 143-44

K

Kara Osta, Latvia, xxv (map), 6-7, 35, 38, 40-41, 49, 300-01

Kohnstein Mountain, site of Mittelwerk, 168, 311

Kommandantur, 210, 220, 244

Krefeld, Germany, x, xxv (map), 65, 229-32, 243, 249, 310

Kristallnacht, 96, 291

L

Lake Constance. *See* Bodensee

Latvia, Latvian, xiii, xvii, xx, xxiii, xxv (map), 3, 5-7, 9-12, 14-17, 19, 21-22, 25-31, 33, 34, 37-45, 47-49, 52-53, 56, 59-60, 63-71 (photos), 81, 123-24, 131, 133, 218-20, 265, 276, 284, 297, 299-302, 307-08, 323-24. *See also* entries by city name

   Baltic Germans, 6, 11, 14, 27, 46, 299-301

   citizens, 50, 123-24

   government, 45, 47-48

   heritage, 5-6, 11, 27

   language, 6-7, 11-12 27-28, 39

   military, 5, 7-8, 300-01

   military families, 7

   Model Airplane Club, 40

   National Guard, xxiii, 46-47, 67, 323

   Soviet takeover of, 14, 40, 47, 301

Latvian Artillery Laboratory, 8-9, 11, 13, 15, 34, 36, 42, 45, 47-48, 52, 70 (photo), 300-01

League of German Girls (Bund Deutscher Mädel, BDM), 93

League of Nations, expulsion of Soviet Union, 20

Liepaja, Latvia, xxv (map), 4, 6-7, 9, 16, 30-31, 39, 52, 66 (photo), 68-69 (photos), 123, 220, 265, 300-01

Leipzig, Germany, xxv (map), 128

Lindbergh, Charles, 33

Lithuania, xxv (map), 5, 30, 45, 218, 301

Litzmannstadt, Poland, xxv (map), 51, 54, 301

   ghetto, 52-53

Lodz, Poland. See Litzmannstadt, Poland

London, 171-72, 310

Luftmine (type of bomb), 136

Luftwaffe, 21, 123, 126-27, 142, 153, 157, 186 (photo), 193, 212, 216, 282, 309, 312

   Navigator School, 185 (photo)

Lutheran, 38, 131, 179, 288 (photo, Ingo as pastor)

M

Malatzky, Slovakia, xxv (map), 175, 196, 245 (photo)

Marshall Plan, 250, 261
Mein Kampf, 30-31
Meissen figurine, 104-5
Messerschmitt fighters, 143
Michigan, 283-84, 304, 311
missiles, 171, 284, 314, 315, 317. *See also* V-2
    rocket, *and* V-1 rocket
Mittelbau-Dora concentration camp, 168-69, 197,
    200, 311, 314, 320-21
Mittelbau-Dora Concentration Camp Memorial,
    320-21
Mittelwerk, xxv (map), 168, 171, 183, 186 (photo),
    198-200, 246 (photo), 298, 303-18, 320
    and concentration camp inmates, 168-71, 183,
        199, 303, 311-18, 320-21
    underground tunnels, 168-69, 303, 314-15, 320
model airplanes and gliders, xx, 14, 16, 32-36,
    39-40, 42, 46-47, 53, 67 (photos), 284-285
Molotov-Ribbentrop Pact, 5, 291
Morgenrot (song), 28
Munich, xxv (map), 111, 265, 273-74, 276

N

National Socialist Flying Corps (NSFK), 21-3,
    26, 126
Nazi Party, xiv, 19, 21, 30, 83, 89, 92, 96, 300,
    307-08, 317, 320
Nazi regime, xviii, 18, 22, 43, 47, 50-51, 54, 92,
    94, 132, 139, 147, 158, 163, 170, 184, 193,
    197, 300-01, 307, 309. *See also* Third Reich
Nazi war crimes, 197-98
New Hampshire, 284-85
New York City, 272, 277-78, 282
Niemöller, Pastor Martin, 139, 291
Nordhausen, xxv (map), 168, 175, 199, 200, 221,
    321
Nuremberg Laws, 94

O

Olympiad, Games of the XI (1936 Olympics),
    42-44, 56, 69 (photo)
Olympic Stadium Cafe, Berlin, 60, 62
Operation Valkyrie, 166

P

Pact, Molotov-Ribbentrop, 5, 291
partisans, 312-13

Polish, 51
    Slovakian, 174-75
passport photo (Rolf's and Lilo's), 280
Patton, General George S., 173, 212
Pearl Harbor, 125
Peenemünde, xxv (map), 132, 146-47, 157, 168,
    171, 298, 302-03, 306, 308-09, 311-17, 323
    bombing of, 146
    first successful V-2 launch and, 132
    Mittelwerk and, 306, 308, 311, 313-15 317
"Pferdekopf," 170, 305, 314. *See also* Busta,
    Erwin
Poland, xviii, xxv (map), 5, 19-20, 24, 49, 57-58,
    60, 73 (photo), 98-99, 104, 132-33, 185
    (photo), 201, 258, 298, 319. *See also* entries
    by city name
    German-occupied, 16, 24, 26, 51, 98, 153, 302
    Polish front, 23
    Polish partisans, 51
Posen, Poland, xxv (map), 24-25, 52, 73 (photos),
    98-99, 302
postcards, 60, 238-39
postwar period
    after World War I, 5-6, 300
    after World War II, ix, x, xv, xx, 44, 244, 249-78,
        279-80 (photos), 281-84, 294, 297, 304, 308,
        314
POW camps, 221-226, 231-34, 236-42, 244, 252,
    279 (Ernst photo), 304
    prisoners, xviii, 40, 132, 169-71, 183, 207, 214,
        217, 220, 223, 226, 232, 236, 242, 297,
        300-01, 303-04, 311-17
    guards, 223, 226, 236-37, 242
prisoners of war, 203, 217, 219, 221-27, 232, 236-39,
    241-42, 252, 303. *See also* POW camps
    German, 223-24, 226
propaganda
    Nazi, 47, 89, 96, 132, 167, 201, 220, 308
    Russian, 12
purge, 133, 167

Q

Quaker American Friends Service Committee
    postwar feeding of children, 31, 81

R

Raderach, Germany, xxv (map), 157-58, 302-03,
    307, 315

Radio Moscow, 132, 298

rationing, 60, 111, 130, 132, 172, 206, 222, 250, 252, 254-55, 258

ersatz coffee, 20, 130, 136, 161, 204

rearmament, 44, 89

Red Army, 155, 205, 297

refugees, 151, 202-06, 215, 220

Reich Labor Service (Reichsarbeitsdienst), 92

Reich, Third, 57, 92, 166, 170, 199, 201, 214, 302. *See also* Nazi regime

repatriation, 10-11, 14, 20, 301, 307

Rheinmetall Borsig, 54, 302

Rommel, General Erwin, 128

Russia, Russian, 5, 8, 10, 12, 22, 30, 57, 99, 125, 131, 133, 201-03, 205, 207, 228. *See also* Czarist Russian, Soviet Union, Soviet

Russian Revolution, 5

S

Salaspils, Latvia, xxv (map), 8, 13-14, 16

Sander, Ernst, 305

Saturn I-B rocket technology, 284

school, 27, 39-42, 45, 81, 83, 89, 91, 93-95, 98, 202, 282, 284

secret weapon, 132, 147, 167, 170, 197, 311

Security Enforcement (Sicherheitsdienst, SD), 21, 317

Seebad Bansin, Germany, xxv (map), 19-20, 23, 72 (photos), 214, 302

Siegfried Line, Germany, 193

Silesia, Poland, 195

Silesian Steamship Company, 151-52, 165, 195, 260

Skede, Latvia, the dunes at, site of Jewish mass-murder, 49, 52

Slovakia, xxv (map), 174-75, 196

Soviet Union, Soviet, 5, 10-11, 17, 20-21, 31, 40, 50-51, 58, 123, 195-96, 198, 199, 201, 222, 301, 308. *See also* Russia, Russian

dissidents, 123

driven out of Latvia, 123

invasion of by Germany, ("Barbarossa," "Red Beard"), 123

occupation forces, 49, 51, 131

prisoners, 169, 313

regime, 9, 14, 57, 319

takeover of Latvia, 7, 10-11, 14, 17, 301, 323

troops, 10-11, 14, 123, 156, 184, 195-96, 199, 202-05, 220, 304

victory at Stalingrad, 133

zone of occupation, 225, 226, 228, 229-31, 234-35, 244

Spanish Civil War, 45

SS, 19, 21-23, 89, 96, 169-70, 195, 197, 207, 221, 244, 300, 303, 305, 307, 308, 314, 316-17

guards, 169-70, 183, 314

tattoos, blood type, 221

Stalin, Joseph, xiii, xviii, 21, 31, 57, 133, 270, 291, 308

Stalingrad, 132-33

Star of David, 60

The Stars and Stripes (US newspaper), 224-25

Storm Troopers (Sturmabteilung), 89

Struwwelpeter, Der (*Shock-Headed Peter*), xvi, xxii, 82, 112, 194, 262, 272, 285, 286 (photo)

Swinemünde, xxv (map), 19, 71 (photos)

Switzerland, 266, 281

T

Teutonic Order, in Latvia, 14

Thorn airbase, Poland, xxv (map), 153-54, 166, 185 (photo)

training

aircraft mechanic, Rolf, 127

basic, Rolf, 127

for V-2 rocket inspection, Ernst, 147, 302

glider (soaring), Rolf, 57-58, 123, 126, 153-54

navigator, Rolf, 153-54, 156, 215

officer's, Ernst, 300

officer's, Rolf, 133-35, 300

pilot, Rolf, 22, 46-47, 56, 154

specialized, Rolf, 127-28, 131

voice (singing), Gertrud, 98-101

Trassenheide Labor Camp (at Peenemünde), 146, 314

Treaty

German-Soviet Non-Aggression, 5, 57

of Versailles, 44, 54, 89, 94

U

Udet, Ernst, World War I ace, 33

Ukraine, 133

Ulmanis, Karlis, 40, 321

University of Latvia, 3, 25, 48

US, xix, 33, 205, 261, 263-65, 275-77, 272, 277, 280, 282-85, 294, 304-05, 310. *See also* America, Americans

Index   331

US, cont'd.
   Consulate, 265, 274-75
   occupation forces, 219
   Olympic team, 43
soldiers (army, troops, forces), 173, 184, 199-200,
      204, 212, 217, 220, 223-24, 252, 270-71, 300
   space program, 284-85, 304

V

V-1 rocket (flying bomb), 170, 310, 312, 320
V-2 rocket, 146, 157-58, 168, 170-72, 179, 183,
      186 (photo), 197, 198, 213-14, 302-03,
      306, 309-12, 317. *See also* A4 rocket *and*
      Dutzmann, Ernst, V-2 rocket chief inspector
   first strike on London, 172
   first successful launch, 132
   inspection process, 168, 170-71, 303, 306
   inspection sites, 168, 171, 303, 316
   production, 168, 170, 172, 214, 312, 314
Valkyrie, Operation, 166
Voice of America, 132, 298
von Braun, Wernher, 146-47, 168, 200, 276, 287
      (photo), 302-05, 311, 322
von Stauffenberg, Colonel Claus, Schenk Graf, 166
von Wedel family, 19-21, 23, 25, 72 (photos of von
      Wedel home)

W

Wakarusa, Indiana, ix, xi, 264-65, 274-76, 278,
      281-84, 287 (photo)
   Church of the Brethren, 265, 275-76, 282
Wannsee Conference, 133
Warsaw, 49-50
Warthegau, Poland, 16, 24, 302
Wassull, Gertrud, xix, xxv (map of escapes and
      journeys), 80-83, 85-87, 90-92, 94, 96,
      98-104, 106, 110, 137-39, 144, 148-52,
      160-65, 172, 174-77, 180, 195-96, 201-11,
      220, 226, 228-32, 234-38, 240, 242-44,
      259-61, 269, 277, 283, 295
   photographs of, 115-16, 119, 189, 288

Wassull, Liselotte. *See* Dutzmann, Lilo
Wassull, Walter, 80-81, 82, 85-86, 90-91, 94-95,
      115 (photos), 175-76, 179, 181, 188-90
      (photos)
wedding of Rolf and Lilo
   accommodations for guests, 176
   attire, Lilo's, 176-77, 181
   civil ceremony, 181
   church (cathedral) ceremony, 181-82
   food for reception, 176, 182
   photographs, 188-90
   Polterabend, German tradition, 180-81
   reception site, 176
Wehrmacht, 124, 135, 166, 185-86 (photos, Ernst
      in uniform), 300, 302, 316
Wessel, Horst, 89, 291
Wiegandsthal, xxv (map), 145, 157
Wilhelm Gustloff, the sinking of, 220, 324
Wilmersdorf, Berlin, 61, 91-92, 94
World War I, xiii, xviii, 5-6, 10, 28, 31, 33, 54,
      80-81, 87, 89, 94, 99, 102, 108, 139, 300.
      See also the Great War
World War II death rates, xviii-xix

Z

zones of occupation
   American (US), 225, 269
   British, 225, 243, 244, 269
   French, 225, 236, 243, 269
   Soviet, 225, 226, 228, 229-31, 234-35, 244, 298
Zoppot, in German-occupied Poland, xxv (map),
      112-114, 119 (photo), 144-45, 160
Zurich, Switzerland, xxv (map), 281

Made in the USA
Middletown, DE
13 April 2017